THOMSON
COURSE TECHNOLOGY
Professional ■ Technical ■ Reference

AF888027

GAME CHARACTER DESIGN COMPLETE

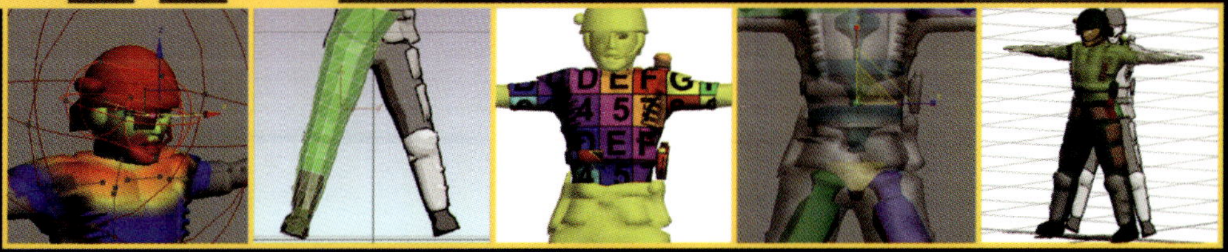

Using 3ds Max® 8 and Adobe® Photoshop® CS2

David Franson
Eric Thomas

© 2007 Thomson Course Technology, a division of Thomson Learning Inc. All rights reserved. No part of this book may be reproduced or transmitted in any form or by any means, electronic or mechanical, including photocopying, recording, or by any information storage or retrieval system without written permission from Thomson Course Technology PTR, except for the inclusion of brief quotations in a review.

The Thomson Course Technology PTR logo and related trade dress are trademarks of Thomson Course Technology, a division of Thomson Learning Inc., and may not be used without written permission.

Photoshop is a registered trademark of Adobe Systems Incorporated. 3ds Max is a registered trademark of Autodesk, Inc.

All other trademarks are the property of their respective owners.

Important: Thomson Course Technology PTR cannot provide software support. Please contact the appropriate software manufacturer's technical support line or Web site for assistance.

Thomson Course Technology PTR and the authors have attempted throughout this book to distinguish proprietary trademarks from descriptive terms by following the capitalization style used by the manufacturer.

Information contained in this book has been obtained by Thomson Course Technology PTR from sources believed to be reliable. However, because of the possibility of human or mechanical error by our sources, Thomson Course Technology PTR, or others, the Publisher does not guarantee the accuracy, adequacy, or completeness of any information and is not responsible for any errors or omissions or the results obtained from use of such information. Readers should be particularly aware of the fact that the Internet is an ever-changing entity. Some facts may have changed since this book went to press.

Educational facilities, companies, and organizations interested in multiple copies or licensing of this book should contact the Publisher for quantity discount information. Training manuals, CD-ROMs, and portions of this book are also available individually or can be tailored for specific needs.

ISBN-10: 1-59863-270-1

ISBN-13: 978-1-59863-270-5

Library of Congress Catalog Card Number: 2006923480

Printed in the United States of America

07 08 09 10 11 BU 10 9 8 7 6 5 4 3 2 1

Publisher and General Manager, Thomson Course Technology PTR:
Stacy L. Hiquet

Associate Director of Marketing:
Sarah O'Donnell

Manager of Editorial Services:
Heather Talbot

Marketing Manager:
Heather Hurley

Senior Acquisitions Editor:
Emi Smith

Marketing Coordinator:
Meg Dunkerly

Project/Copy Editor:
Karen A. Gill

Technical Reviewer:
Les Pardew

PTR Editorial Services Coordinator:
Elizabeth Furbish

Interior Layout Tech:
Bill Hartman

Cover Designer:
Mike Tanamachi

CD-ROM Producer:
Brandon Penticuff

Indexer:
Larry Sweazy

Proofreader:
Sara Gullion

THOMSON
COURSE TECHNOLOGY
Professional ■ Technical ■ Reference

Thomson Course Technology PTR, a division of Thomson Learning Inc.
25 Thomson Place ■ Boston, MA 02210 ■ http://www.courseptr.com

Sleep is overrated.
A nightly activity that by me is hated.
It disrupts my busy life,
And fills my nights full of strife.
I'd rather stay awake and keep on working,
Instead of feeling like my deadlines I'm shirking.
If I didn't sleep, I wouldn't need a bed,
And I'd have another room in my house instead.
Wearing pajamas is such a fashion bore,
And changing into them is always such a chore.
If I could stay awake, I'd get so much done,
And maybe even have time to have some fun.
So tonight, I'll start my life with no sleep,
It shouldn't be a schedule too hard to keep.
It will really make my life one of ease,
If I could just get away from all these ZZZs.
So before I start, I'll just lie down for a second,
And start my plan after a couple days of sleep, I reckon.

This book is dedicated to Michelle, who understands what it means to lack sleep.

Acknowledgments

There are so many people to acknowledge on this project that I guess I'd better just jump in and get started. First, I'd have to say thanks to Ridley Scott and the design team who worked on the *Alien* films. These movies are just plain awesome and inspiring for artists and character designers. Thanks also to the numerous design teams behind the recent slew of cool games like *Unreal*, *DOOM*, *Halo*, *Half-Life*, *Splinter Cell*, and numerous other games that make working in the game industry so much fun. You guys rock, and I salute you.

I'd also like to thank all the people who work for Autodesk and Adobe for creating such cool tools. 3ds Max and Photoshop are not only professional-level tools, but they also make the creative process easy and fun. Keep up the good work. The groups behind the various game engines are also awesome.

Thanks also to the excellent staff at Thomson. Emi Smith and Karen Gill have offered a huge amount of help and have made this book possible when it seemed to be on the verge of disappearing completely. You two are the greatest! Thanks also to the rest of the behind-the-scenes team at Thomson, including those who worked on the CD and the cover, and those who laid out, proofread, and indexed. The end result looks great!

Big thanks to David who spearheaded this project, outlined and wrote most of the chapters, and added his enthusiastic and expert experience to the book. David got so busy doing cool stuff that he didn't have time to finish this book, but the book carries his spirit throughout.

Finally, thanks to my family for their love and support. It is hard to work around computer book authors at times, but your patience makes it all worth it.

—*Eric Thomas*

About the Authors

David Franson has been a professional in the field of networking, programming, and 2D and 3D computer graphics since 1990. In 2000, he resigned his position as information technology director of one of the largest entertainment law firms in New York City to pursue a full-time career in game development. He is the author of *2D Artwork and 3D Modeling for Game Artists*, *The Dark Side of Game Texturing*, and the full-page article "How Video Games Are Made," which appeared in 45 newspapers worldwide. He has also produced digital artwork for 3D video games, film, and television.

Eric Thomas is a longtime 3ds Max user extending all the way back to DOS days. During his years with the program, he's seen a number of changes and a dramatic shift in how the software is used. Eric has used Max to create a variety of projects from movies and games. He is currently working as the creative director for Side Pictures Inc., a firm specializing in 3d games and visualization tools.

Contents

Introduction

DOOM 3. Half-Life 2. Movies like *Resident Evil* and *Alien.* Take characters from those games and movies, merge them, and you'll get a totally cool game character. The 3D game characters in my mind are almost always dark, sinister, or have some killer attitude deserving of any cool video game shelved on today's software market. Standing next to these vicious creatures of the night is a bad-ass hero with a futuristic weapon that puts evil in its place. Imagine some being that if physically present would scare the living hell out of the player and the uber-cool soldier for the being to fight against. Welcome to my world of game character design complete.

My intentions with this book are to demonstrate all steps and aspects of modeling, texturing, and animating a heroic game character. What I will show you will be how to model in Autodesk 3ds Max 8 from sketch references, texture in Adobe Photoshop CS2 (version 9), and then rig bones and animate a character in 3ds Max 8.

This is both a technical and a creative art book. You can't have just one skill in 3D game art design nowadays, so I'll saturate you with all the necessary tools and skills to get you to know how to hand over a finished character model for any 3D video game development company using only the aforementioned software tools and a hardcore, geared-up, creative brain.

What You Need to Know

I'm not much of a Macintosh person, although game content creation is possible with that platform. However, for this book, you need to have a solid, working knowledge of Microsoft Windows and the ability to manipulate and handle files. You'll be creating and juggling files all over the place, so keep that in mind when creating your game characters.

Also, I don't assume you have decent artistic ability, especially when it comes to computer graphics. I will walk you through step by step with the design process—the most difficult being the texturing and animating of the character. But don't fret. Most of my techniques involve simple mesh modeling techniques (like working with clay), use of some general Photoshop tools and filters, and lots of experimentation.

Finally, I won't be introducing 3ds Max or Photoshop as I would to a beginner. This is an intermediate-level book where I assume you've poked around with 2D and 3D graphics programs and aren't wholly unfamiliar with what's going on. My tutorials are stepwise, and simply following them verbatim will produce the results you're looking for. A beginning graphics arts student with the acumen to figure out software packages in general can easily cut through this book. I also understand that these programs are expensive and that demos are always limited by either the inability to save work or by a 30-day trial period, but this is software that a majority of game artists *must* know to work for a game development house. The cheap stuff, such as freeware and the like, simply won't do. It isn't powerful enough to get the job done for the big games. The other competing titles like Maya and SOFTIMAGE are also popular and are just as or more expensive, but knowing how to do character design work in 3ds Max will easily get your foot in the door with the latter.

Note

You can use many of this book's modeling and texturing tutorials with previous versions of 3ds Max (5, 6, and 7) and Photoshop (6, 7, and 8).

What You Need to Have

The type of computer that you need to create these killer characters is the same type of machine that you use to play these types of games. Just like with first-person shooter games, the faster the computer and the more memory you have, the better. To get the most from this book, here is a list of the minimum system you need:

- Intel Pentium III or later processor or AMD running at 500MHz minimum (Dual Intel Xeon or dual AMD Athalon or Opteron [32 bit] system recommended).
- Primary operating systems: Windows XP Professional (SP1), Windows 2000 (SP4), or Windows XP Home (SP1).
- 512MB of RAM (1GB or higher recommended).
- Graphics card supporting 1024×768 16-bit color with 64MB RAM. (OpenGL and Direct3D hardware acceleration supported; 3D graphics accelerator 1280×1024 32-bit color with 256MB RAM preferred.)
- CD-ROM drive.

- Optional: sound card and speakers; cabling for TCP/IP-compliant network; 3D hardware graphics acceleration; video input and output devices; joystick; 3-button mouse.
- A graphics tablet (optional), which greatly helps with texturing.
- Internet Explorer 6.

Also, having a digitizing tablet like a Wacom is helpful. Mine is a 4×6, and it's great for texturing. It lets you sketch as if you're drawing on paper and ideally incorporates itself with Photoshop. The Wacoms are pressure sensitive, so the harder you press on the tablet, the thicker the brush lines are.

Finally, please check out the Web sites in Appendix B, "Related Web Sites and Links." I didn't figure out everything in this book on my own! I spent years perusing Web sites and learning techniques and info to create this stuff. If you want a job in this industry, do this type of homework. In the end, you'll have a remarkable portfolio.

How This Book Is Organized

As a game character development book, what you hold in your hands follows the general visual art workflow pattern of most game development companies. In Chapter 1, "3D Game Character Design Basics," we'll go step by step through the general character creation process, which includes 2D and 3D computer art concepts, file and image formatting, and some art history. Then in Chapter 2, "Preparing to Model: Configuring 3ds Max and Referencing Sketch Art," we'll start off with character sketches and setting up the 3ds Max 8 environment in preparation for modeling the book's character. Just about every 3D design is referenced by sketches, so we'll use them to develop a 3D character model.

The meat of the book will be Chapters 3 through 6, using the primary software tools to create the character's foundation—that is, the 3D mesh and skin textures. These chapters are as follows:

- Chapter 3: "Box Modeling in 3ds Max 8"
- Chapter 4: "Mesh Optimization in 3ds Max"
- Chapter 5: "UV Mapping the Character in 3ds Max"
- Chapter 6: "Skin Texturing with Photoshop CS2"

Then I introduce rigging and animation using 3ds Max's Biped feature in Chapters 7 and 8:

- Chapter 7: "Rigging a Character with Biped in 3ds Max"
- Chapter 8: "Character Animation in 3ds Max"

This book also has two appendixes. Appendix A, "3ds Max 8 and Photoshop CS2 Keyboard Shortcuts," is a perfect reference for making your modeling and texturing work go quickly, and Appendix B, "Related Web Sites and Links," is a great listing of sites that you should visit often to keep up to date with your visual art techniques or for general information in this field.

What's on the CD-ROM

The CD in the back of this book contains the following:

- Autodesk 3ds Max 8 demo
- Adobe Photoshop CS2 (version 9) demo for Windows
- All chapter tutorial files
- Royalty-free texture images (that is, pictures of things I took for your personal texturing use)

Crack Your Knuckles!

Let's get started! Whether you're new to this field or even somewhat experienced, I highly recommend reading Chapter 1 before you begin because it contains vital information you should know to get things done right. Other than that, grab your coffee, Red Bull, or other favorite beverage, and let's kick it into high gear!

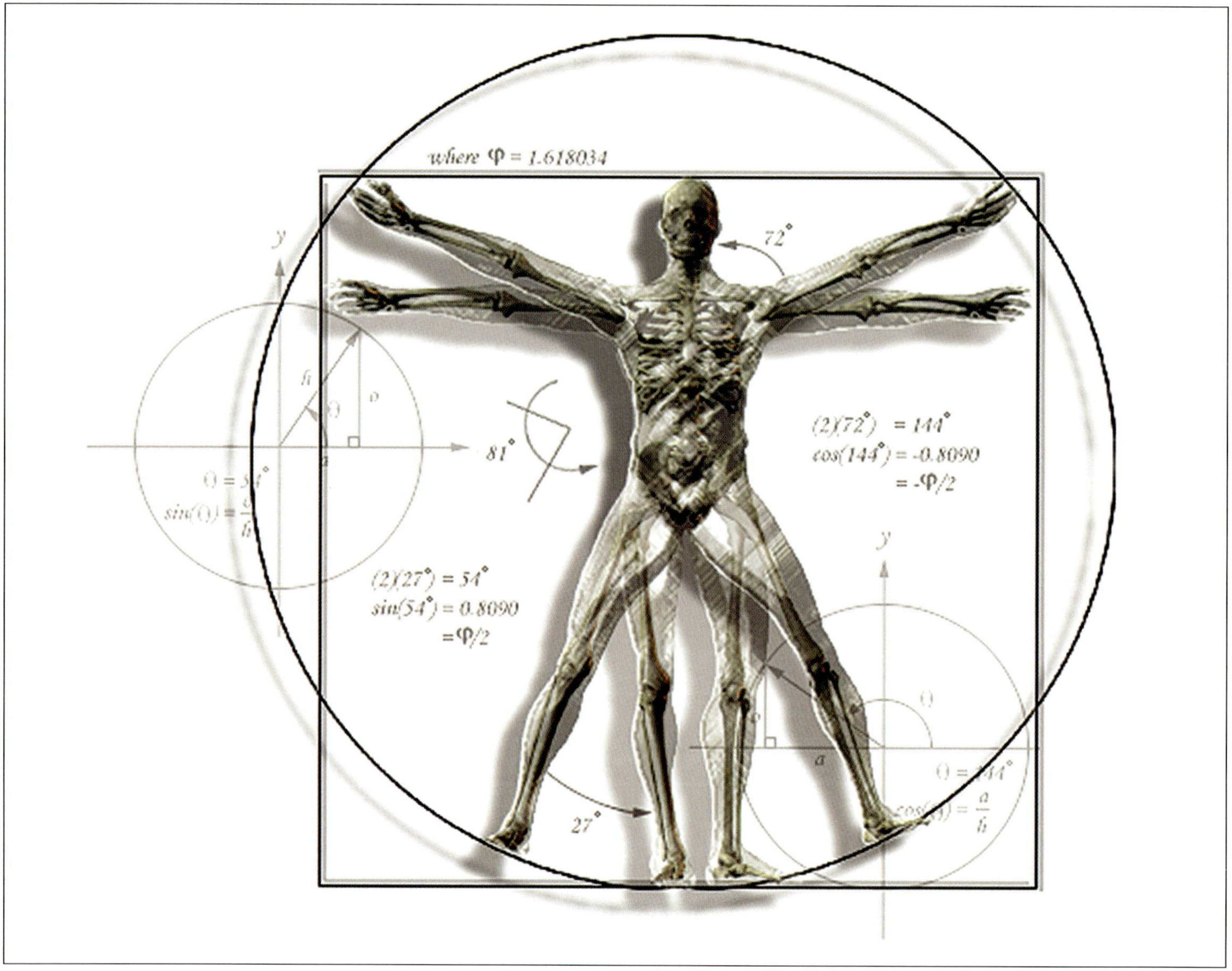

Where the spirit does not work with the hand there is no art.
—*Leonardo da Vinci*

Chapter 1

3D Game Character Design Basics

The video game development community has come a long way since its general inception in the late 1970s. That's particularly true of character design and texturing. The intention of this book is to completely focus on modeling a cool game character that is endowed with a texture, optimized, rigged with what is called a *skeleton*, animated, and then exported to a few popular game engines. This is quite a process, but don't be discouraged. The entire character creation sequence is straightforward and logical, and I'm sure you'll be content with your end results.

Here's the workflow for creating a cool character. Notice how this corresponds to the book's chapters. This chapter describes the process involved in completing each of these steps.

- Learning the process for creating a character
- Conceptualizing a character and its model type
- Generating sketch art in preparation for modeling
- Modeling a character in 3ds Max 8
- Mapping the UV texture coordinates, in preparation for texturing a character in Photoshop CS2
- Creating textures and relief maps in Photoshop
- Applying a biped skeletal rig to your character mesh to prepare it for animation
- Creating animation sequences in Max that will be called by a game engine during gameplay

Creating a video game character is a somewhat complicated process but is fairly straightforward and linear. This process applies to most available 2D and 3D digital art programs for both video games and film. There are several differences between a character that is built for a video game and a character that is built for film, but as game consoles become more and more powerful, these differences are fading. Currently, a big difference is that film characters have a much higher polygon count, and the game characters need to be specially rigged and exported for specific game engine requirements. This section takes a closer look at the workflow we will follow throughout this book. Figure 1.1 shows an abridged diagram for creating a game character.

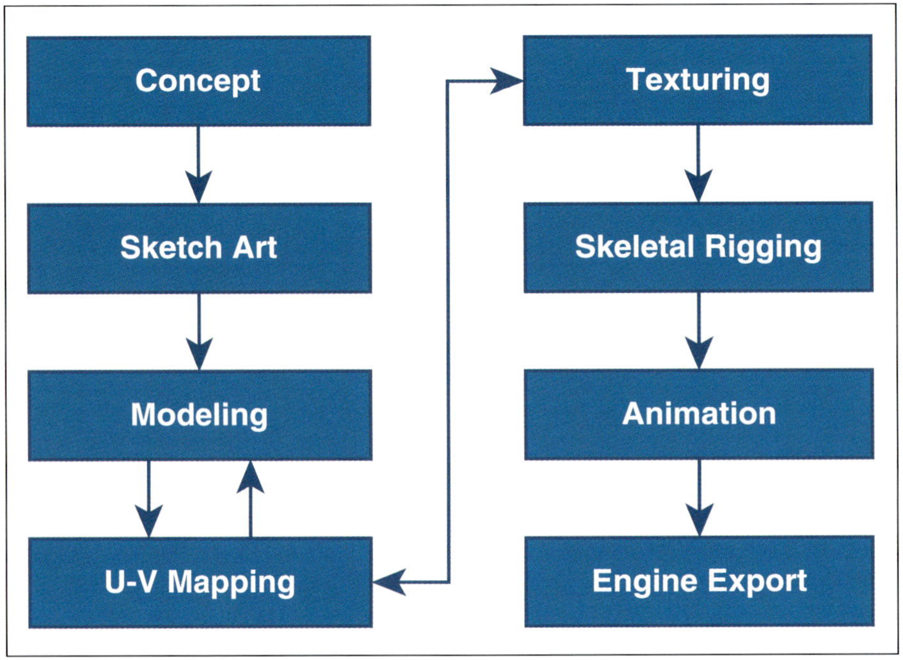

Figure 1.1 The game character creation process.

This workflow pattern hasn't changed much over the years, except in the character's constituent resolutions. That is, the polygon counts for the character model's mesh have dramatically increased, the texture maps are larger and more detailed, and animation sequences are greater in number and more complex. These key points of a character will continue to increase in parallel with developing computer technology. The faster the computer, the more able it will be to handle more complex game objects.

From Figure 1.1, I will break down this general process into detailed components.

Character Concept

Whether you are working for a game development company or by yourself, you should always implement a character through a general concept of what it will be. For instance, consider the game environment. Is this a first-person-shooter (FPS) game, third-person, role-playing game (RPG), strategy, or what? Is the character to be a human player or an AI (artificially intelligent) opponent? What is the character's background? Is it humanoid or multilegged with a tail? What type of weapons or objects will it wield? These considerations are vital to successfully developing a quality character because they provide a heads-up preview of modeling and animation techniques that you need to implement, give the character attributes that the player will understand and utilize, and provide documentation details during publishing.

Game Styles

The style of game dictates nearly all the components of a character model. One of the most common game styles that use the type of character that we are creating is FPS, meaning that the player views and controls the gameplay through the eyes of the player's character. If you have difficulty discerning between the terms *first*, *second*, and *third* in terms of gameplay, here's how it works. In first person, you, the player, are actually "in the game" as if you have taken over the main character's digital body in the computer world. Examples of first-person games are *DOOM*, *Half-Life*, and *Call of Duty*. When playing these games, you walk through the game world seeing only what you would see if you were there—your arms and hands holding a weapon, and your feet (see Figure 1.2). This doesn't mean that's all that is present in the game. The game engine is aware of the full character's position in the scene, but most of the body is not displayed to you, the player. Other players that might be present will see your full body (as in any multiplayer FPS game).

Figure 1.2 An FPS-style game. The character's 3D model is fully present but only partially visible to the player through his character's eyes. *Half-Life 2*. © 2006 Valve Corporation. All Rights Reserved.

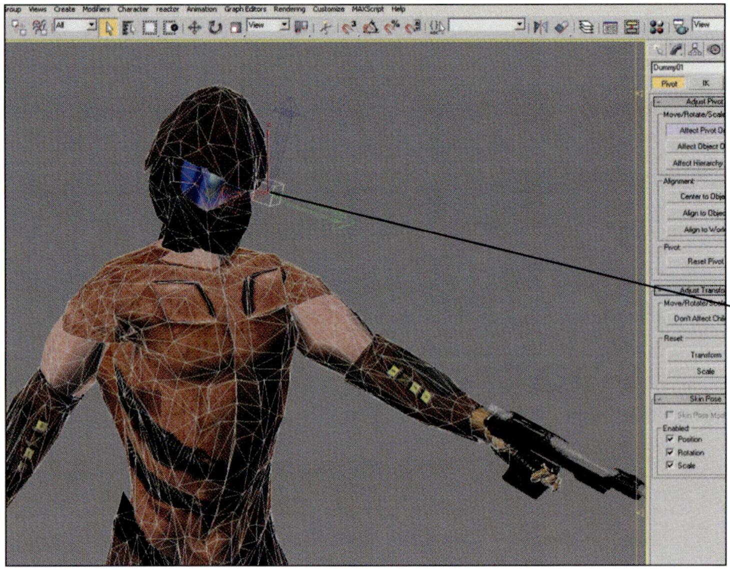

Figure 1.3 A camera dummy object being placed and attached on a character model. The camera represents the second person in a video game.

Ever wonder why we skip from first-person-shooter to third? Although it's not really used, the term *second person* refers to the actual camera object that the game uses to display images to the player onscreen. The camera is an invisible dummy object, usually represented by a simple small box model you create. This object is technically part of a character mesh, attached to a point on the character's body, usually located between the character's eyes. The orientation of the object (that is, its X-, Y-, and Z-axes) is aligned in a specific direction, usually with the Y- or Z-axis pointing forward to the game world. The camera object's name, location, and orientation are specified by the game programmers, who use these objects in the programming code to properly display the game to the player. Figure 1.3 shows what the camera object looks like when developing a character model.

Dummy objects are used for other things like weapon placement and character attachment points (such as where the player's hands and feet go when he's hopping onto a vehicle). I will explain more about this in Chapter 7, "Rigging a Character with Biped in 3ds Max."

A third-person-style game is similar to first-person in that you are still controlling the main character but you see the world through the eyes of an *orbital*, or *positional camera*. Not only can you see your player character in full detail, but you can position your world view around the character and in almost all directions (see Figure 1.4). The reason that this style is labeled third person is that you are no longer "in the game world" but viewing the world from outside of your player character. Examples of games like this are *Tomb Raider*, *Hitman*, and *Splinter Cell*. The camera object floats behind the player character, and both move together through the game world but also independently of one another.

Some games allow you to switch between first- and third-person perspectives, but both styles have the same character model specifications. The polygon count, textures, and animations are the highest quality of any

Figure 1.4 A third-person perspective game. The camera object displays the entire player character and is linked to it yet independently mobile. *Splinter Cell*. © 2005 Ubisoft Entertainment. All Rights Reserved.

other model in the game because the player constantly views them.

Lastly, there are what I consider fourth-person-style games. Technically, these are still third person, but instead of controlling one player character, you control many, as in the *Age of Empires* series, *Diabolo*, and even *Call of Duty* and *Brothers in Arms* (when controlling multiple characters at once). I want to single out *Age of Empires* and that respective style because the character models are small and usually viewed from afar (see Figure 1.5). This is a strategy game, but having the characters so small means that the polygon count and texture maps are also small. This is important because it means you shouldn't spend too much time creating a complex game character—the polygon count is low, and there is only a handful of animations.

Taking into consideration the style of game for which you are creating a character is important so that you know how detailed your character will be. A first- or third-person game character, as the player model, has relatively high polygon counts for the mesh, detailed textures, and dozens of animation sequences. Computer AI characters also have high quality and most likely incorporate many facial expressions and lip-syncing animations.

Character Type

This book describes how to develop a first-person game character in detail. Creating monsters and enemies is fun but not as detailed, because opposing characters either don't wield weapons

Figure 1.5 Another version of a third-person style game, although I refer to it as fourth person. The player still views the world via a positional camera but controls more than one character. *Age of Empires II.* © 2001 Microsoft Corporation. All Rights Reserved.

or drive vehicles, or they have only one weapon. In conceiving of a character type, know beforehand some of the character's attributes. If a character is human or humanoid, the process of adding a skeleton to a 3D mesh will be easy because most 3D programs like 3ds Max 8 have a default skeleton that takes on a humanoid form. If your character is to be, say, a six-legged monster with two tails and a goofy long ponytail, you'll have to manipulate a humanoid skeleton to fit and drive the character mesh.

The weapon models that a player character uses also drive its polygon count and animations. Different weapons require different postures and attachment locations and sometimes force you to increase the polygon count on the model at joint areas so that the model flexes more naturally. Multiple dummy objects are also needed so that the game engine knows where on a character a weapon should be attached or what limbs of the character should attach to certain points on a vehicle or other object.

A background story for the character in question is important because it dictates many attributes such as how the character looks, moves, and sounds throughout the game. The background story also provides a history for your character and is usually documented in reference material printed while and after the game is published. In Chapter 2, "Preparing to Model: Configuring 3ds Max and Referencing Sketch Art," I develop a character concept and background story in conjunction with some sketch art to be used for creating characters throughout this book.

Sketch Art

Generally, a sketch artist in a game company spends his time drawing game characters on paper for the 2D/3D artists to use as a visual reference during character creation. As a character artist, you don't normally spawn your models and animations on your own—you work closely with the concept/sketch artists and programmers and create models via their ideas and recommendations. In the next chapter, I show you how to use sketch art images on 3D modeling planes so that you can use them as a reference for modeling a character.

Modeling

Modeling is the most complex task when creating a game character and is the heart of this book. I'll show you how to model (and animate) a character from scratch using 3ds Max 8, but the techniques are similar with other popular 3D modeling programs. 3ds Max is an extremely versatile and widely used graphics tool for games, television, and film, but because of this, it carries with it a significant price tag (approximately $3,500). This is typical of higher-end graphics software. I've heard complaints from readers about my election to write about software that's unaffordable; my response is that nearly all game development companies use these packages, and as an artist, you must be an intermediate to advanced user of at least one of them. Table 1.1 lists a number of popular modeling packages, their prices, and Web sites.

The CD-ROM that accompanies this book contains the demo version of 3ds Max 8. You'll be able to follow every example in this book using it, if you don't already own Max. Note that the demo works for only 30 days, though.

Note

If you're looking for some freeware and shareware 3D tools to play around with, check out Blender 3D at http://www.blender3d.org and MilkShape 3D at http://www.swissquake.ch/chumbalum-soft. Note that they have limited ability for creating game content. In fact, I can't think of a single published game developer who uses them. The higher-end stuff is far more powerful, with Max, Maya, and SoftImage as the frontrunners for game modeling, animation, and special effects.

Table 1.1 3D Modeling Programs Used in the Game Industry

Program	Version	Company	Price	Web Site
3ds Max	8	Autodesk	$3,500	http://www.autodesk.com
Maya	7	Autodesk	$2,000–$6,000	http://www.autodesk.com
SoftImage|XSI	5.0	Avid Technology	$2,000	http://www.softimage.com/home/
LightWave 3D	8	Newtek	$800	http://www.newtek.com
ZBrush	2	Pixologic	$489	http://pixologic.com/home/home.shtml
gameSpace	1.6	Caligari	$300	http://www.caligari.com

Modeling Techniques

You can employ many modeling techniques to create characters, such as spline, subdivision surface, NURBS, and box modeling. We'll be using the box modeling technique to physically shape the character—that is, creating a rough 3D model by tracing perspective character sketches on reference planes, in combination with some subdivision surfacing. The model will initially be boxy in shape, but after applying a smoothing modifier in 3ds Max and increasing the polygon count in critical areas, the character will come into focus nicely. Box modeling is a more precise, less detailed way of modeling that is perfect for game characters. It allows you to rapidly develop a character that is shaped just like the sketch art and has a lower polygon count than other modeling techniques. As of 2006, the average 3D video game's characters have around 5,000–7,000 faces that comprise the 3D mesh. This will be our target count because any higher count would slow down the computer during gameplay. However, as computer speeds increase, this number will also increase. Movie characters can contain upward of 100,000 faces per model, but that is currently not feasible to render in real-time gaming.

Note

A *polygon* is a 3D structure consisting of three or more points called *vertices* that are connected in 3D space with lines called *edges*. The smallest polygon is simply a triangle serving as the basic unit of measurement for a 3D model. Several polygons together complete a mesh object that can be deformed and animated, as you will see in later chapters. A target polygon count refers to the target face count of a model.

Repairing, Adjusting, and Optimizing

When you are finished modeling a character, you must fix and finalize it so that it can be properly UV mapped for the texturing process, properly animated without invalid mesh deformations, and work properly in a game without producing game engine errors. On first pass, you will analyze the character mesh for holes—that is, places on the model where faces are not connected with other edges. This will cause render problems within the game engine and in some cases will cause the engine to bail out completely from gameplay. Fixing these holes is a matter of creating new edges to link the faces. 3ds Max has STL Check and Patch Holes modifiers that help automate repair of your mesh.

Another step in the character creation process is UV mapping—preparing your model for texturing. Before UV mapping, it is good practice to model your character with mapping in mind to make the UV unwrapping process easier, as I will explain in Chapter 5, "UV Mapping the Character in 3ds Max." Here we'll dissect the mesh into body parts and lay them out flat so that we can texture them in Photoshop. Having the polygons of the mesh nice and even at the seams of the model will make the UV mapping process easy. You'll also check your mesh for crossed vertices. When two vertices are crossed, their edges that link them to other vertices overlap one another. This means that if a texture were wrapped around the character mesh, the crossed areas would distort the texture. Repairing crossed vertices is a matter of moving them to their proper positions in 3D space.

Lastly, optimizing the mesh helps reduce the overall face count of the model. We'll do so by welding together superfluous vertices and deleting any stray ones. Also, certain areas of the mesh need to have their polygon counts increased somewhat to allow for smoother deformations, such as bending limbs. These areas are the knees, elbows, biceps, shoulders, neck, and particularly the face (for smooth lip-syncing movements).

3D Modeling File Types

Table 1.2 lists the file types and their extensions used by the programs shown in Table 1.1. Some of these files represent an entire 3D scene in a program, some are proprietary to the particular software, and others are universal between programs. This is a handy list because you might need to import or export files among several programs.

3ds Max is capable of importing from and exporting to several of these file formats; other formats require free plug-ins available on the Internet. (See Appendix B, "Related Web Sites and Links," to find links to these plug-ins.)

UV Unwrapping and Mapping

This next phase in character development involves preparing your model to be textured. As I briefly explained earlier, a model consists of a large number of points called vertices, and these points are connected via edges to make up a mesh object. Every vertex in 3D space has an X, Y, and Z

Table 1.2 3D Modeling File Types Used by Popular Modeling Software

Program	Type	File Extension	Notes
3ds Max	Scene file	MAX	
3ds Max	Mesh file	3DS	
3ds Max	AutoCAD drawing file	DXF	
Maya	Binary model file	MB	Used with *DOOM 3*
Maya	ASCII scene file	MA	
SoftImage	Scene file	SCN	
SoftImage	Image file	SI	
gameSpace	Scene file	SCN	
gameSpace	Object file	COB	Same for trueSpace
WaveFront	Object file	OBJ	
LightWave 3D	Object file	LWO	
LightWave 3D	Scene file	LWS	
ZBrush	ZTool native file	ZTL	
Blender 3D	Image file	BLEND	
(universal)	Stereo lithography image file	STL	Used for error checking
(universal)	Microsoft Direct3D object file	X	

coordinate that defines its location in that space. When a mesh is created in a modeling program, a duplicate set of invisible vertices is also created, called *texture coordinates,* or *UVs*. By default, these vertices occupy the same space as the mesh vertices and are used to define how the texture bitmap wraps onto the model.

The letters *u* and *v* (and sometimes *w*) are initially the same coordinate values of the X, Y, and Z coordinates of a 3D model. After you've finished creating your character model, it is your job in 3ds Max to create a UV texture map so that you can use a program like Photoshop to paint a texture using this map as a reference. A texture map is two-dimensional; the X coordinate is horizontal and the Y coordinate is vertical, just like in planar geometry. In Max, UV mapping involves taking apart the texture coordinates and projecting them flat on a texture map plane. This is analogous to cutting a t-shirt at the seams and laying the pieces flat on a square surface.

During the UV process, a model's texture coordinates have been separated at "seams" and laid flat on a UV workspace. When the points here are no longer in 3D space, they do not have a third dimension, or W value—hence the term *UV*. From here, you can copy this map to Photoshop, paint it, and use the image in Max to texture your model. At this point, when *any* texture map is applied to your model, it is wrapped around the model according to the new UV layout. Also note that the model's vertices are unaffected by the UV coordinate manipulation process.

UV mapping is somewhat complex because you must take time to properly cut apart the UV vertices at hidden areas called seams. For instance, if you cut the front of a t-shirt up the middle, the texture will display a visible seam right up the middle because this is the start and end point around which the texture is wrapped. It is ideal to instead cut the vertices along the *sides* of the model so that the seams are not quite visible to the player.

Sometimes vertices might be crossed or the geometry might be invalid, causing kinks or errors in the UV map. It is also common practice to create a *checkerboard* map, to make it easier to view these errors.

Notice from Figure 1.1 at the beginning of this chapter that the UV mapping process bounces back and forth between modeling and texturing. You'll be doing this as you preview your texture and make model adjustments to finalize your character.

Texturing

Later in this book, I will be showing you how to use the UV map you've created for your character model to paint a 2D bitmap, or texture. This map is a square image file that displays colors and faux detail to your model as your game engine renders it in real-time. Until recently, texturing was a fairly simple process of painting images onto a UV map in Photoshop and using a program like 3ds Max to apply the texture to a model. With increased game quality, characters and other objects now have multiple texture attributes and layers aside from just a texture map. Such attributes can be grouped to form a *shader*, such as specularity, glossiness, ambient and diffuse colors, reflection, self-illumination, and transparency. A model's overall texture could contain layers of texture maps and shaders, bump maps, and normal maps. The combination of several of these properties makes your character appear much more lifelike and assists in speeding up rendering, because the game engine is now rendering texture maps to create a faux finish instead of having to render an extremely high polygon count model. In Chapter 6, "Skin Texturing with Photoshop CS2," I will show you how to create a high-quality, multiple-attribute texture that is suitable for a modern video game.

Shaders

A shader is a predefined set of lighting and rendering parameters, created by programmers or by you, that tells both modeling and game software how to render a texture map. A map rendered by itself can be dull or flat without some specific attribute or shader applied to it. For instance, in Figure 1.6, the sphere on the left is rendered

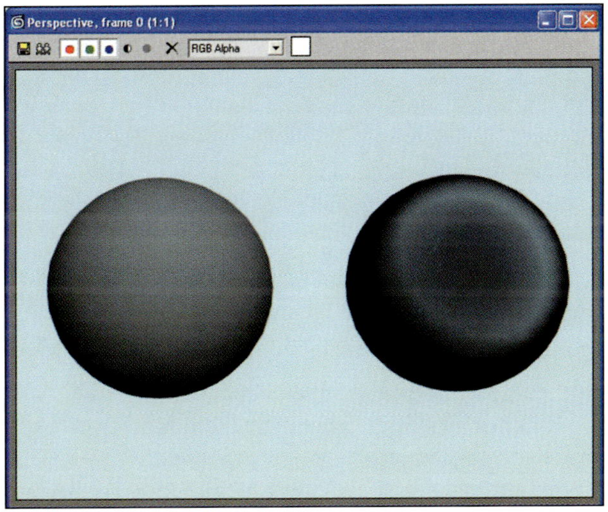

Figure 1.6 A sphere with a basic texture map rendered in 3ds Max. The sphere on the left has no other texture attributes, while the sphere on the right has metal shader attributes.

with a simple diffuse texture map with general ambient lighting. The sphere on the right has the same map, with a metal shader applied. This shader contains rendering specifications like specularity and glossiness, making the object appear to be metal.

Some video games like *DOOM 3* take advantage of shaders and other texture attributes to create spectacular game imagery without sacrificing processing speed. In general, game programmers and the software development kits (SDKs) they create will provide documentation as to what types of textures and shaders you should apply to your models.

Bump Maps

A bump map isn't really a texture but is used in conjunction with one to simulate 3D surfaces on a 3D object. This generally reduces the polygon count of an object; instead of meshing out, say, a bumpy dinosaur skin by creating a 20,000-polygon model, you can use a bump map and a 2,000 polygon-count model to simulate this detail. The bump map is a grayscale map that the game or modeling engine uses to provide artificial relief on the existing texture (see Figure 1.7). The engine interprets the varying shades of gray, with white being the highest and black being the lowest.

There's also a disadvantage to using bump maps. For the relief, or visual depth, on the rendered model, the light source always seems to come from one direction—usually above. An advanced technique to providing a much better relief that changes with lighting direction (and makes the model appear extremely detailed) is using normal maps.

Note

Although people often use the words *bump map* and *displacement map* interchangeably, a displacement map is more appropriately a term for a texture map that creates the relief for a terrain. A game engine can use a displacement map, which is similar to a grayscale bump map, to create a height map for the terrain in a game. The engine translates the shades of gray on the map to build a surface accordingly. The more white on the map, the higher the terrain's surface; the more black on the map, the flatter the surface.

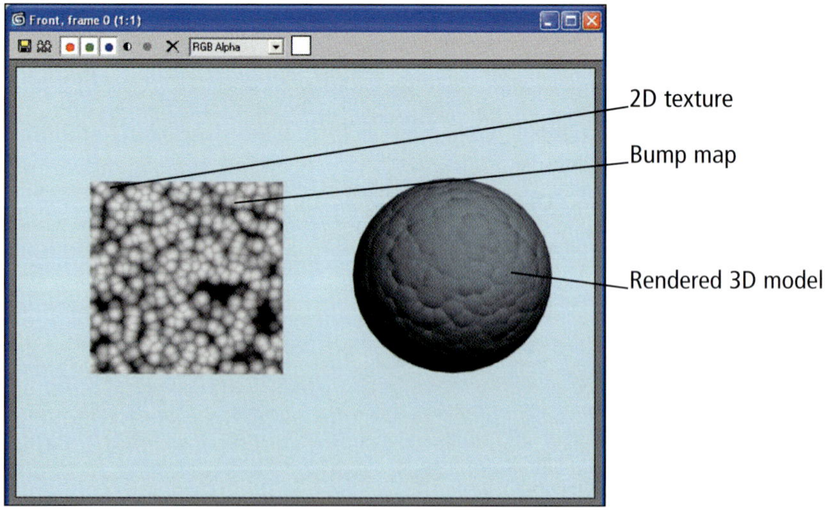

Figure 1.7 A bump map gives the model the illusion of a 3D texture during render time.

Normal Maps

A *normal map* refers to a color-coded bump map that the game engine can use to dynamically render faux 3D surfaces on a model from any direction. Unlike a grayscale bump map, whose relief is only applied to the model on a per-vertex basis, a normal map provides relief on a per-pixel basis, using the colors in the map to create artificial normals on the object's faces. First let me explain what an object's surface normals are and how an object reflects light in a program.

Every face, or triangle, on a 3D model has an invisible attribute called a *normal*, which is a vector pointing away from and perpendicular to the face. This vector is a line that the rendering software uses to determine how the light in the scene should reflect from the face. In essence, the greater the angle that the normal is from the direction that the light source is pointing at the model, the darker the face appears in the scene. Conversely, face normals that point closer to the direction of the light source appear lighter.

Until recently, modeling and game software rendered each face of a model, based on the face's normal, by creating a lighting gradient and shading the face appropriately by interpolating the adjacent normals of the vertices that made up the model's mesh. This is known as *per-vertex shading*, or *Gouraud* ("goo-row") shading. Although it provided some lighting realism, it wasn't a smooth rendering technique. With the advent of newer DirectX shading technology and video cards that could handle it, per-pixel shading came of age. This meant that faces on a model could be lit on a per-pixel basis according to a normal map.

A *normal map* is a texture map that a rendering program uses to generate individual pixel normals for the faces on an otherwise low resolution (low polygon count) model. The normal map is a red-, green-, and blue-shaded image that dictates how the faces of a model should be lit. The program looks at the colors on the map and interprets them as a height map, where individual pixels on the map represent vectors. The red, green, and blue values of the normal map are respectively interpolated as X-, Y-, and Z-coordinate values for individual normals. The software then illuminates the faces of a model according to the values of these normals.

This process might seem complex, but it really isn't. In Chapter 6, I will show you how to create normal maps and apply and render them in real-time.

Texture Map File Types

I'm going to wrap up this section with some of the primary image formats you'll be using when saving your work. Each file format offers different techniques of saving image information, content, and compression. Your general file-format options are these:

- PSD
- BMP
- JPG
- PNG
- TGA
- TIF

The format in which you save your texture map depends on the game engine you're using. See Table 1.3 later in this chapter for a list of different engines and their respective texture specifications.

PSD

The default image format in Photoshop is PSD. When you create an image, all the components of the image such as layers, styles, channels, and paths are stored in the PSD file. Always save your original work in this format first, and then save it in another format. If you don't save your image as a PSD but need to go back to make a modification, you'll simply open a flattened image without the original layers.

BMP

This is the Windows Bitmap file, based on an 8-bit (256) color palette. Typically, you'll create an image in 24-bit color mode; when you save it as a BMP file, the colors in the image are palletized to 8-bit. The original *Half-Life* engine uses this format. The BMP format has been updated from its original format to handle 24-bit images in addition to 8-bit.

JPG (JPEG)

This is the Joint Photographic Experts Group file format, invented primarily for optimizing file sizes for things like the World Wide Web. It offers decent quality with high compression.

PCX

ZSOFT developed this popular format as a proprietary format for its PC Paintbrush program back in the DOS days. PCX has a better compression ratio than BMP but retains the same image quality. The *Unreal* and *Unreal Tournament* engines use this format.

PNG

The Portable Network Graphics format is one of the best ways to preserve image data and have compression at the same time. I'm not sure why PNGs aren't used more often; this graphics format has lossless, high compression with the capability of storing alpha (transparency) information. This format was designed to replace the popular GIF format and be seamlessly portable between computer systems. Garage Games' Torque engine uses the PNG format.

TGA

The Targa format, developed originally for the TrueVision video board, is used often when saving animation frames in 3D programs due to the high-quality image content-to-compression ratio. TGAs also store layers and transparency channels, and they're used within the Quake engine for images requiring transparency information.

TIF (TIFF)

The Tagged Image File Format is another high-quality image format that allows for storage of layers and transparency, just as with PSD files. The downside is its compression. TIF files are high quality, but they're usually huge.

Skeletal Rigging

This is the final stage of character model creation, where you'll install a "bones" system in your character so that you can articulate and animate its mesh. The skeleton is much like a real skeleton in that it contains bonelike objects connected at joints that when moved cause the surrounding mesh to move with them. These bone objects are invisible during render time.

3ds Max 8 has an integrated set of features called biped that is used to implement a humanoid skeleton into your model. You can adjust this skeleton in many ways to suit all forms of a character, from humanoid to animal. By default, the skeleton mimics the way a human body can move in real-time by using preprogrammed inverse kinematics (IK). A biped skeleton (more commonly known as a *rig*) moves naturally using IK. For instance, if you pull on the hand object of the rig, the skeleton's forearm and upper arm move with it naturally, as if you were to grab and pull on the hand of a person.

Rigging a character involves properly sizing and adjusting a rig to fit the dimensions of your character's mesh. After you've aligned and shaped the bones of the rig properly, you attach the mesh to the rig through a skin modifier in 3ds Max. This modifier enables the mesh to move, or deform, along with the movements of the rig's bones. You then make adjustments to both the mesh and the rig so that your character animates without bizarre bends or kinks. See Chapter 7.

Animating

At this stage in character development, your model is complete with a mesh, some textures, a skeletal rig, and dummy nodes. What is left is to create individual animation sequences that a game engine will call depending on the player's actions in a game. If you've played some popular 3D games (and I hope you have), you've seen dozens of these sequences, nearly all of which are created manually by an animator or by motion capture. The rest of the animations might be rag-doll effects generated by software such as the Havok physics engine. A typical player character in an FPS can have 50–100 animation sequences.

Also contained within 3ds Max is a fairly powerful animation tool that allows you to key-frame your rig with user-defined footstep patterns in combination with natural physics effects. Key framing is a process whereby you define start and end positions of a basic motion for your character. Then Max fills in the in-between animation frames. For instance, instead of having to create every frame of movement to make a character crouch and stand up, you make two postures (standing and squatting), tell Max the total number of frames, and let it create the rest of the frames. The two postures you create are called *key frames*, and the process of filling in the frames that Max performs is called *tweening*.

Max also allows you to import MoCap (motion capture) files that drive your rig and the 3D mesh surrounding it. MoCap is a much better alternative to creating animation sequences because it involves capturing the actual motions of a human actor in a studio and porting them to your character rig. This is an expensive process because it requires a large studio with special image-tracking cameras positioned in three axes. An alternative could be purchasing pre-made MoCap files, but I will show you how to manually create some animations for your character in Chapter 8, "Character Animation in 3ds Max."

Some games like *Half-Life 2* incorporate a purchased physics engine, such as Havok, to provide realistic, dynamic character behavior instead of using predefined animations. For instance, if an opponent is killed and falls from a ledge onto other objects, you can see the aforementioned rag-doll effect—the character tumbles like a rag doll, with arms and legs flopping around as they react to being struck. These are animations that the game engine provides on its own instead of calling premade sequences.

You save as files each of the animation sequences you create and name them according to whatever programmers want to call them, such as player_walk or player_jump. Then, when a user presses a certain key or button or uses the joystick in a certain way, the game calls up a particular animation sequence related to that action. After you create all of the animation files, you can package them along with the character mesh, textures, and skeleton and export them from Max to a proprietary game file format using special Max plug-ins that are designed for that game.

Game Engine Exporting

When you're finished creating characters and animations, the final step is to port them to a game. Whether you're working in-house for a game company or creating a character for a published game, you need to encode your work and pack it into one or several files designed for the game engine in question. Many pre-existing games also come with SDKs that contain documentation and plug-ins for use with Max, Maya, and other software packages so that you can export your character properly.

Engine File Types

Many of the popular FPS-style games you might have played are based on a handful of available game engines. An *engine* is the complex million lines of code written by well-known developers like id Software. Typically, a game company purchases a game engine and modifies it to make its own game, but the file types and formats remain consistent with the engine. Table 1.3 lists a number of popular game engines and some helpful file information and extensions.

Summary

Creating a game character is an involved process with several distinct steps in its workflow. In Chapter 1, I have broken down the basic steps involved in creating modern 3D, first-person-shooter (FPS)-style game characters, from concept, modeling, texturing, animating, and exporting them in preparation for popular video games. This chapter should give you a clear heads up for what to expect when creating your character. In the remaining chapters, I will thoroughly elaborate on each of these key points for creating a quality modern game character. It will be a wild ride, so hold on and dive in.

Table 1.3 Typical Game Engine File Specifications

Game Engine	Texture File	Model File	Animation Engine	Games Using This
DOOM 3	TGA	MD5MESH	MD5ANIM	*DOOM 3, Quake 4*
Quake 3: Team Arena	JPG/TGA	MD3	MD3	*Return to Castle Wolfenstein, Metal of Honor, Call of Duty 2*
Goldsource *Quake*	BMP	MDL	MDL	*Half-Life, Counter Strike, Day of Defeat*
Valve's Source	TGA/VMT/ VTF	MDL	MDL	*Half-Life 2, Vampire: Bloodlines*
Unreal	PCX/UTX	USX	UKX	*Unreal, Unreal Tournament, Deus Ex*
Unreal Engine 2.5 (Warfare)	PCX	PSK	PSA	*Unreal 2, Unreal Tournament 4, Splinter Cell (1, 2, 3)*
Torque	PNG, JPG	DTS	DTS	*Tribes 2, Realm Wars*

Anatomy is destiny.
—*Sigmund Freud*

Chapter 2

Preparing to Model: Configuring 3ds Max and Referencing Sketch Art

Before modeling this book's character, I want to walk you through changing some of the default settings in Max and then present some orthogonal sketches of the character that I will show you how to create throughout the book. I'm going to assume that you've just installed 3ds Max 8 (either the full version or the demo on the CD-ROM) but that you are somewhat familiar with the Max environment. Please note that this is *not* a beginner tutorial on the usage of 3ds Max 8; I will, however, be straightforward in telling you what to do in every tutorial. Also note that if you need additional information or assistance on any subject, you can click on Max's User Reference in the Help section.

Adjusting the hardware and software settings in Windows and Max is important because much of the graphics work depends on having these proper configurations. I strongly urge you to read this chapter for details on creating the proper modeling environment before you begin your work. Having quality sketch art to follow when modeling is also important because it allows you to properly and accurately model your character. In this chapter, I will review

- Installing the latest version of DirectX 9 to take advantage of Direct3D shaders in Max and video games
- Having the proper video card that can handle DirectX functions
- Setting your Windows graphics environment to display your graphics at the highest resolution
- Configuring the Max environment in preparation for modeling your game character
- Applying orthogonal sketch art to 2D planes in Max so that you can use them as a reference when modeling

Hardware and Software Considerations

The graphics capabilities of 3ds Max are somewhat limited by your computer's hardware and software. You need to configure your system properly so that it can display high-quality 3D graphics and shaders and you can view your work in real-time as you would in an actual video game. As you might know, most video games require or prompt you to load DirectX 9c (as of the spring of 2006—soon to be DirectX 10) before they can run properly because DirectX graphics commands drive the game's engine. Such commands also drive 3ds Max when the DirectX video mode is enabled in Max. But for DirectX to do its job, it needs to run on the proper hardware, dictated by your computer's video card. Here I will expose you to some of the hardware and related software drivers that you should have in your computer.

Note

> The latest version of DirectX, 9c, is located on this book's CD-ROM. It is advisable that you install it on your system before installing 3ds Max 8 and other video games.

Choosing a Proper Video Card

You need to have a video card that supports Direct3D, the portion of DirectX that is dedicated to creating 3D graphics. Not all cards support the latest version of Direct3D, so look at the manufacturer's specifications when selecting one. NVIDIA, which I highly recommend, is the most popular 3D video chip manufacturer. I have a GeForce 5900 PCX; NVIDIA recommends a minimum of a GeForce 2 card. Another popular chip manufacturer is ATI, producer of the Radeon cards that also support DirectX 9.0c. You also need a card that supports the latest version of Direct3D if you want to real-time render your character model's textures using 3ds Max's DirectX .fx shaders. (See Chapter 6, "Skin Texturing with Photoshop CS2," for details using Max shaders.)

Graphics Software and Drivers

When you first install Max 8, it asks you in which video mode you want the program to run. With an NVIDIA GeForce 2 or greater video card installed, you should choose Direct3D. Then click on the Advanced button, make sure DirectX 9.0 is selected, and click OK (see Figure 2.1). This enables software rendering

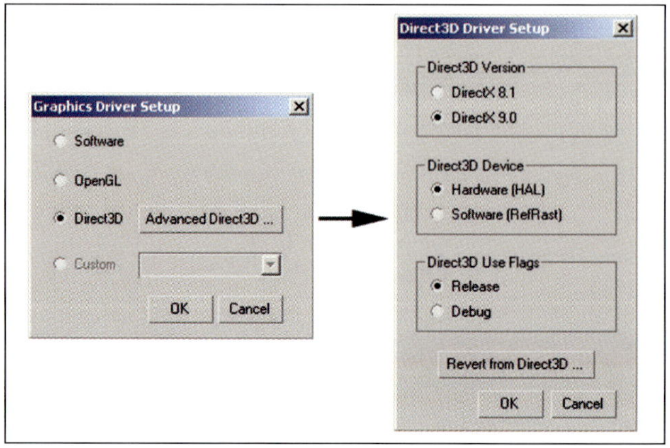

Figure 2.1 Be sure to configure 3ds Max's graphics driver to Direct3D before proceeding so that you can render your character models with real-time shading, simulating the end results in a video game.

by Max using DirectX, thereby simulating the real-time rendering environment produced with modern 3D video games.

If your video card doesn't support DirectX 9, this option is unavailable, but you can still texture and real-time render your character models. (The render quality isn't that good, however.) If you've already installed Max and need to change to the proper Direct3D driver setup, in Max just choose Customize, Preferences, Viewports, and in the Configure Driver section, click Choose Driver to select Direct3D. Be aware that you'll need to restart Max before you use the selected driver.

After you install and configure Max, it is also advisable that you download and install the latest Max 8 service pack (SP1) from http://www.autodesk.com. This patches any bugs found after the final release of Max. Also, some video cards don't render or display graphics properly in Max or other video games unless you have the most recent video card drivers installed in Windows. You can download these from your card's manufacturer. (See Appendix B, "Related Web Sites and Links," for more hardware sources.)

Monitors and Settings

A final note on properly displaying your graphics work is to have a large monitor and high-quality video mode settings in Windows. A decent monitor should be at least 17 inches diagonally, which is standard nowadays and fairly inexpensive. Since 1997, I've had a 21-inch monitor (a mere $1,100 back then), but I've seen them go for as little as $250 with shipping on http://www.ebay.com. A large monitor lets you view more of your work in progress. Also, give your graphics view greater quality by setting the display resolution in Windows to at least 1280×1024 at 32-bit color depth. The color setting is important because 32 bit displays alpha (transparency) information when texturing. Change these settings by right-clicking on the Windows desktop; clicking Properties, Settings; and changing the Colors and Screen Area accordingly. Finally, click on the Advanced button and choose the Monitor tab. Change the Refresh Rate to the highest frequency setting that your monitor allows; doing so eliminates that interlaced flickering you might see at higher resolutions.

Caution

Be careful not to set your Refresh Rate in Windows to a value higher than recommended, or you will risk permanently damaging your monitor. Check with the documentation that came with your monitor or see the manufacturer's Web site for this information.

Configuring the Max 8 Environment

Here are some final adjustments you should perform in 3ds Max 8 before you begin placing reference art and modeling your game character:

1. **Customize keyboard.** The keyboard shortcuts that are mapped by default in Max are somewhat scattered. Over the years, I've found that remapping the most commonly used functions on the left side helps me speed up my work. Having simple operations like move,

rotate, and scale on one hand while I move the mouse with the other makes modeling swift and efficient. I've created a list of common shortcuts and remappings for Max and Photoshop in Appendix A, "3ds Max 8 and Photoshop CS2 Keyboard Shortcuts." I highly recommend becoming proficient at using them. You can also load the Custom.kbd file on the CD-ROM by clicking Customize, Customize User Interface, and clicking on Load to load this file, which contains my personal keyboard setup.

2. **Set up units.** Video games are commonly designed using the metric system as a system of measurements. Therefore, when you're creating any 3D objects intended for a game, you model them as if you are building them in real life. For instance, the character I show you how to make in this book has a height of 1.83 meters, which is exactly 6 feet tall. The grid you see displayed in Max is ruled according to the unit setup you have specified. To tell Max to use the metric system, click Customize, Units Setup, and choose Metric under Display Unit Scale (see Figure 2.2). Also, click the System Unit Setup button and change the System Unit Scale to 1 Unit = 1.0 Meters. Now you can manually enter the dimensions, in meters, for objects that you create, and you can use the home grid as a metric reference.

3. **Enable grid and snap settings.** Choose Customize, Grid and Snap Settings, click on the Home Grid tab, and change the Grid Spacing value to 1.0m. This provides 1-meter squares in the home reference grid in your viewports.

4. **Enable Transform Gizmo.** The Transform Gizmo is a moveable device with handles that appears for the X, Y, and Z axes when you attempt to move, rotate, or scale an object. Clicking and dragging the handles makes it easier to move an object along these axes. On the main menu, enable this gizmo by clicking Views, Show Transform Gizmo.

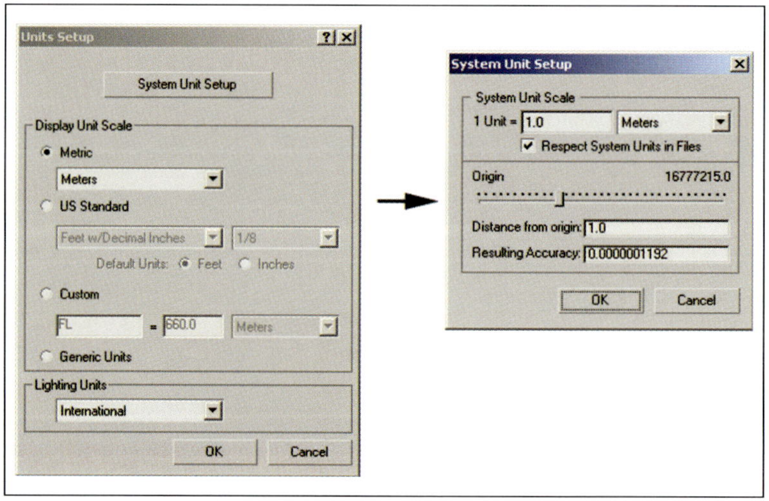

Figure 2.2
Change the Units Setup in Max to meters so that you can create your character using the metric system. Most video games base their dimensions in metric values.

5. **Zoom into grid.** With the new metric grid settings and spacing, click on any of the viewports and use your mouse wheel to scroll, or zoom, into the grid so that only two square meters are visible. This is the working space for your game character.

Orthogonal Sketch Art

Now let's get to the fun part. Before we begin modeling, we need some type of sketch art images to place on reference planes in Max. Most modeling techniques utilize front, left (or right), and top sketch art orthogonal views so that you can create the character in three dimensions. For the character in this book, I've provided some cool sketches of a military-style android that you can use to follow the examples throughout this book (but by all means, feel free to use your own sketch art). This character fits well with some of the popular games out there, like *DOOM 3* and *Half-Life 2*. It's humanoid and can carry weapons, can lip-sync dialogue, and will have realistic skins with many different texturing techniques applied, in addition to normal mapping shaders.

Figure 2.3 shows the three orthogonal sketches you can use in Max as references when building your character model. You can find them on the book's CD-ROM, named HICKS_side.tga, HICKS_front.tga, and HICKS_top.tga. They are TGA files because they each have a separate channel representing transparency information. For instance, in Photoshop, if you open any of these files and click on the Channels palette, you see a fourth channel that has a silhouette of the character in white on a black background. Max interprets the black as transparent, as you see in the next section.

Figure 2.3 Front, left, and top views of the orthogonally sketched HICKS #2A163. You'll use these images as modeling references on 3D planes in Max.

The HICKS Rebuild #2A163 Background

To understand the profile of the character we're creating, let's look into his background. This U.S. Marine cyborg, currently labeled HICKS Rebuild #2A163, was actually Corporal Dwayne Hicks from the movie *Aliens*. In *Alien*^{3}, Hicks, Newt (the little girl), and Ripley were automatically jettisoned to escape the planet. After jettison, Newt had drowned in her cryotube, and Hicks had been impaled by a safety beam. What the movie didn't show you is that Hicks' body was immediately kept in cryostasis upon discovery, and the corporation ordered his body to be reconstructed, cybernetically, and his brain reactivated. The corporation valued Hicks and Ripley because of their significant alien encounters.

Born in 2114 in the western outskirts of Belle Plaine, Kansas, Dwayne Hicks grew up in a country setting on a large farm with four older brothers and one younger sister. His parents subjected the family to labor on their farm, so he grew up with more callous than the average American. A comely and intelligent teen, he also played football in high school and was determined to join the military as soon as he was eligible. He was an unpretentious individual who should have been an officer but lacked the desire to acquire a college degree. Enlisting in the Marines was cut out for him.

Upon completion of his training at Parris Island boot camp at age 19, Hicks served two years in a ceaseless war in the Neptune region. He was stationed at a large military compound on Triton. Exhausted by this uninteresting conflict, Hicks requested transfer to the Xenomorph division, responsible for investigating and securing uncharted other worlds and eliminating potentially hostile alien organisms. Three years of service later, it was here in the XD that he was assigned to the elite unit that traveled to LV-426, the barren world whose colonists were killed by the infamous Alien species.

Corporal Hicks, now reconstructed as HICKS Rebuild #2A163, is fully reactivated in the Marine Special Forces. His mental faculty is still intact but is considered subhuman and enhanced via special neuroprocessors. Some of Hicks' critical organs have been replaced, as has his left forearm. He is rigged with combat-style support gear.

Tip

Reference art doesn't have to be sketch art. It can be something as simple as taking pictures of a real person from the front and sides. Pictures of a character model from a hobby shop can do just as well. Just make sure your character's poses are with the arms and legs spread out, because the completed model is better suited to accept the biped skeleton in this pose.

Creating Reference Planes in 3ds Max 8

Now let's use the three character sketches and place them on flat 2D planes in Max. These will be reference planes so that you can model in the X, Y, and Z directions simultaneously, thereby creating a 3D model. Most modelers put their images on three planes and go from there; I like to take it one step further and make the character sketch stand on his own with a transparent background. The planes you'll create will have the same relative length and width in meters as the pixel dimensions of each of the respective sketches.

1. In Max, click on the Create panel, select the Geometry button, and click on Plane. Click and drag in the Front viewport to create a plane. In the Plane Parameters rollout, change Length Segs and Width Segs to 1. Change Length and Width in the rollout to 1.83m and 1.74m respectively (see Figure 2.4).

Note that the dimensions of the front sketch, HICKS_front.tga, are 810×770 pixels. (You can view this in Photoshop.) What I've done is translated these measurements to meters. If the character is to be 1.83m (6 feet) tall, then 810 pixels corresponds to 1.83m (the height of the sketch). Therefore, dividing 1.83 by 810 and multiplying by 770 (1.83÷810×770) gives us the relative width of the front sketch in meters while maintaining the aspect ratio of the original sketch, which is 1.74. You can do this for the other two planes, too. This keeps the dimensions of the planes consistent with those of the sketches, and it makes the character 6 feet tall (which is the actual height of actor Michael Biehn, who plays Corporal Hicks in the movie *Aliens*).

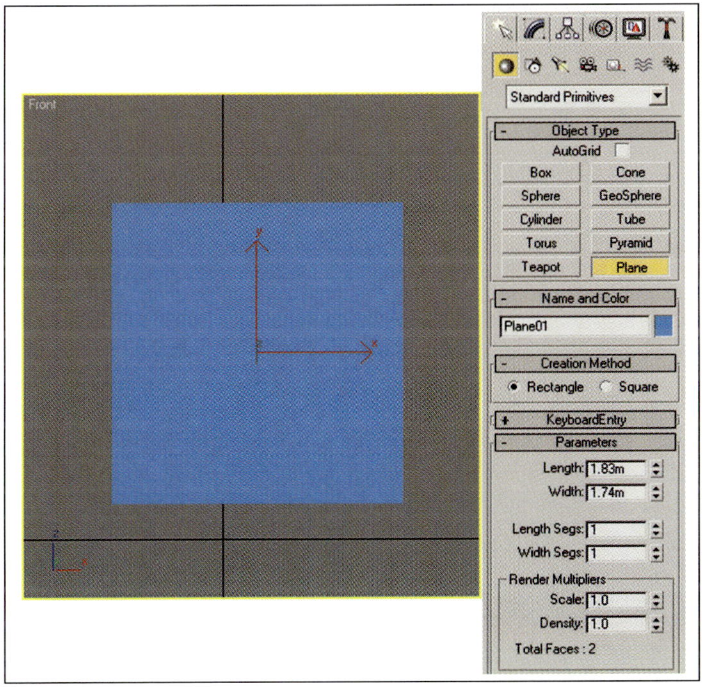

Figure 2.4 Create a plane in Front view with a length and width of 1.83m and 1.74m to match the dimensions of the HICKS_front.tga sketch.

2. Open the Material editor (press M) and select the first material slot in the top left. In the Blinn Basic Parameters rollout, click on the button to the right of Diffuse. In the Material/Map Browser screen, select Bitmap. Browse to the Chapter 2 directory of the CD-ROM and select HICKS_front.tga to load this texture into the first material slot.
3. Click on the Go To Parent button to return to the Blinn Basic Parameters rollout.

4. Click the Show Map in Viewport button, and then click the Assign Material to Selection button. This adds the texture to the plane (see Figure 2.5).
5. In the Blinn Basic Parameters rollout, set the Self Illumination spinner to 100. This fully illuminates the texture regardless of any lights present in the scene.
6. In the Blinn Basic Parameters rollout, click on the button to the right of Opacity. In the Material/Map Browser screen, select Bitmap. Browse to the Chapter 2 directory of the CD-ROM and again select HICKS_front.tga. This texture file also contains a separate alpha channel, viewable in the Channels palette in Photoshop, that represents areas of the texture that are to be transparent.
7. In the Bitmap Parameters rollout, select Alpha in the Mono Channel Output section. Your character sketch should now be floating in Max without a background, making it easier to model (see Figure 2.6).

For your information, TGA and TIF files are capable of storing alpha channels that represent transparency information for both modeling programs and video games. If you open the HICKS_front.tga file in Photoshop and open the Channels palette, you see a separate alpha layer that contains a black-and-white silhouette of

Figure 2.5 In the Material Editor, add the HICKS_front.tga texture to a material slot and assign it to the plane object.

Figure 2.6 Use the same HICKS_front.tga file as an opacity map in the Material Editor to make the character sketch background transparent.

the character sketch (see Figure 2.7). Max interprets the 100 percent black areas as fully transparent and the 100 percent white areas as fully opaque.

8. Now repeat steps 1–7 to create additional planes in the Left and Top viewports. Using empty slots in the Material Editor for each texture, use HICKS_side.tga (810×214 pixels) for the Left viewport plane, with Length equal to 1.83m and Width equal to 0.483m. Repeat with HICKS_top.tga (217×770 pixels) for the Top viewport plane, with Length equal to 0.49m and Width equal to 1.74m. When you're finished, use the Move tool to position all three planes so that their edges meet and form a modeling studio, as I have done in Figure 2.8.
9. Finally, it's helpful to freeze each plane so that you don't accidentally move them when modeling. Right-click a plane and choose Properties. In the Object Properties screen, check Freeze. Then uncheck Show Frozen in Gray. Click OK, and repeat for the other two planes. If you need to unfreeze these planes at any time, just click on the Display panel, and in the Freeze section, select Unfreeze by Name.

Note

You can see the completed virtual studio setup by opening the HICKS_studio.max file located on the book's CD-ROM in the Chapter 2 folder.

Figure 2.7 The transparency channel located in HICKS_front.tga tells 3ds Max what portions of the texture should be transparent. These are the 100 percent black areas in the channel as viewed in Photoshop.

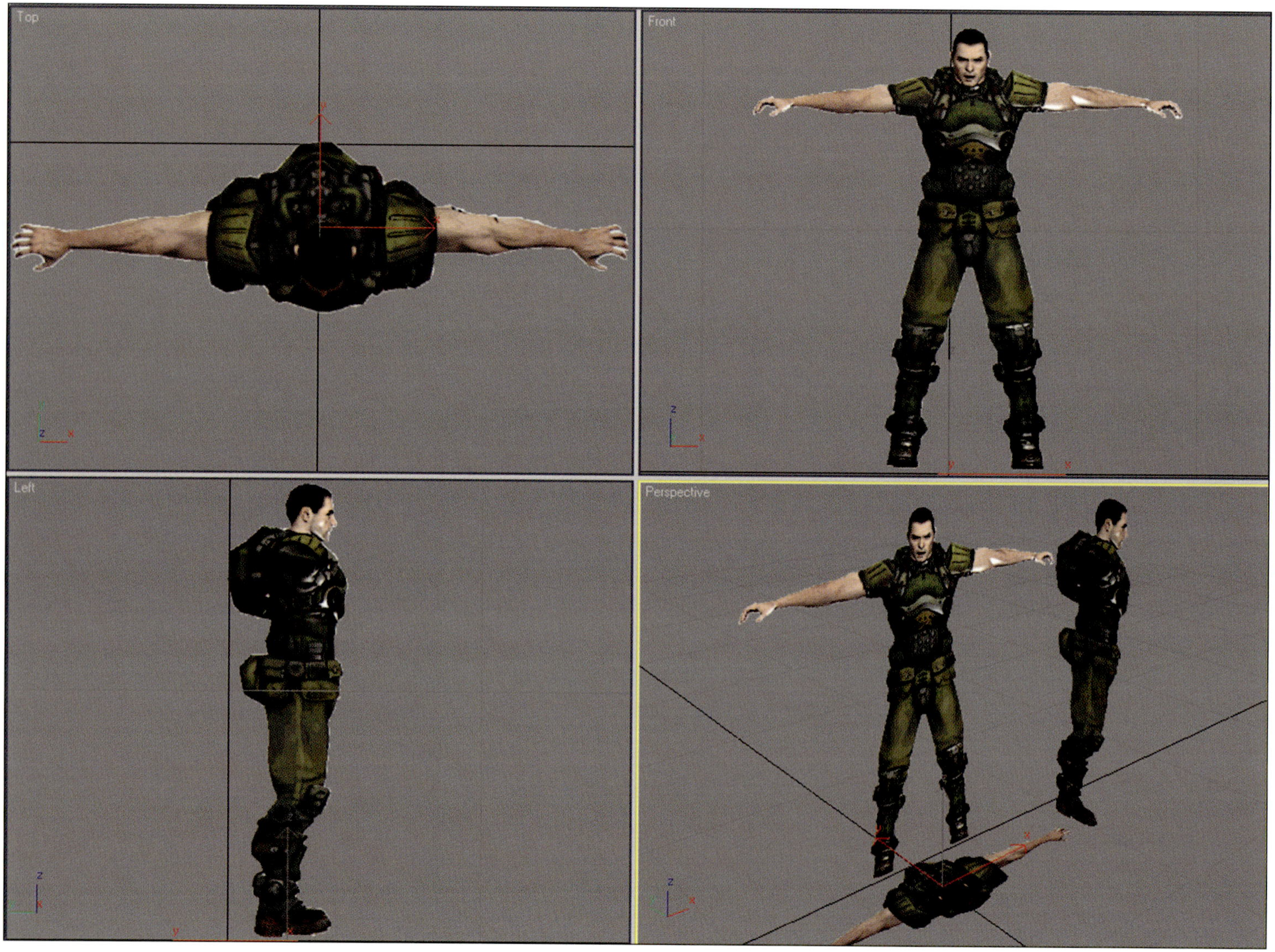

Figure 2.8 Create two more planes in the Left and Top viewports, and repeat steps 1–7 to texture them using HICKS_side.tga and HICKS_top.tga. This completes your modeling studio.

At this point, your Max modeling environment should be properly set up and allow you to begin modeling in the next chapter.

Summary

Before modeling any object in Max, it is important to have your graphics environment adjusted not only to optimize your viewing area and quality but also to provide Max with the ability to display some advanced rendering techniques you'll be using later in this book. In this chapter, I covered some hardware and software recommendations that make it easier to model. In addition, I presented the settings in Max that are helpful to set before you start modeling. Then I showed how to create a virtual modeling studio that consisted of three reference planes containing orthogonal sketches of the game character that will be created in the following chapters. Sketch art allows you to accurately and efficiently create a 3D model using these orthogonal images as references when modeling.

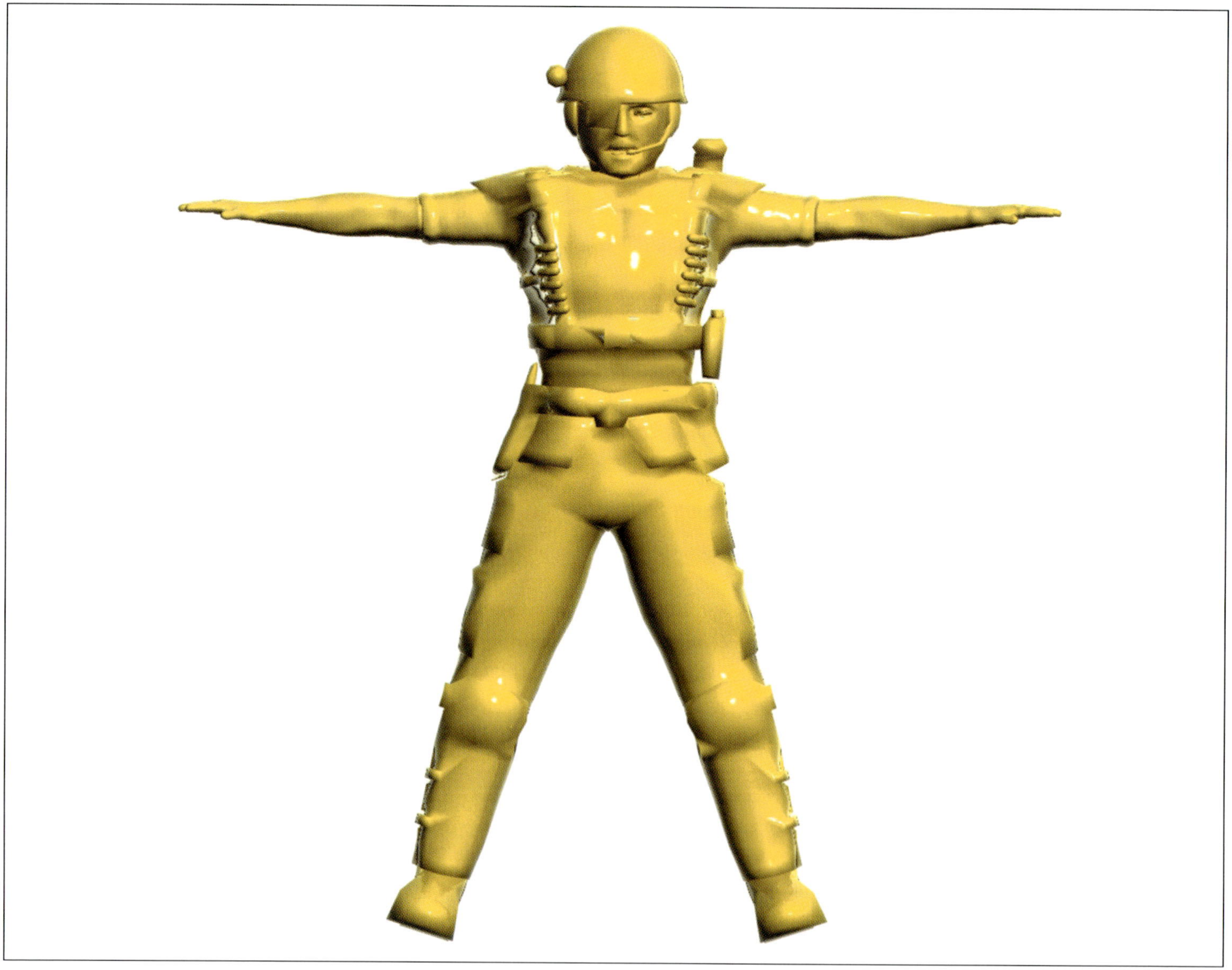

I saw the angel in the marble and carved until I set him free.
—*Michelangelo*

Chapter 3

Box Modeling in 3ds Max 8

This chapter represents the focal point of the entire book. I will show you how to model the entire Hicks character using box modeling, a simple technique that is particularly common in the game development industry. This technique offers ease of modeling with high detail and low polygon count; however, note that the level of detail (LOD) of this model will be fairly high for the texture baking process later on in this book. The final polygon count for the game-ready character will be about 50 percent less than the model created in this chapter, after you apply the MultiRes modifier. We'll target a character in the 5,000–7,000 polygon range after we've optimized the mesh and lowered the resolution. See Chapter 4, "Mesh Optimization in 3ds Max," for more details on the MultiRes modifier.

In this chapter, you will

- Create the Hicks character using the easy box modeling technique, a standard practice for creating 3D game characters in the video game industry
- Build the character from the ground up in 3ds Max 8, starting with a Box primitive and extruding and manipulating faces
- Use the orthogonal Hicks character sketches as a reference while you model
- Build one-half of the lower and upper portions of the character and then use 3ds Max's Symmetry modifier to mirror the other half

- Extrude polygons around the model to form military detail such as pockets, utility belt items, backpack, and backlight
- Create a face from a Box primitive, complete with eyes that you'll animate later
- Complete the head with primitive objects by shaping and attaching them to the face
- Generate a completed character mesh that consists of the lower body (legs and boots), upper body, head, and eyes

Environmental Considerations Before You Begin

Chapter 2, "Preparing to Model: Configuring 3ds Max and Referencing Sketch Art," showed you how to set up a 3D modeling studio for your character, but there are a few other things you can do to make modeling easier.

Try some of these settings:

- In the Name and Color section of the Control Panel, click on the color you see there to open the Color palette. If you uncheck Assign Random Colors and select a highly visible color such as bright yellow (255, 255, 0), each time you create an object, it will be that color instead of annoyingly changing colors every time.
- You'll be working in both Editable Poly and Editable Mesh modes, but every time you create an object, right-click it and convert it initially to Editable Poly. We're trying to deal mainly with quad faces and not triangles, although occasionally we might have to manipulate the mesh in Editable Mesh mode. Editable Poly's tools are impressive and extensive.
- I always center my pivot point in the Hierarchy panel after I've made all my changes to the object. Then, in the Utilities panel, I select Reset Xform. This adds that modifier to the stack, which I then collapse. I collapse it because certain modifiers you use screw up because they base themselves on the transformations of the object (scale, rotation, and so on).
- When you're finished with an object, freeze it. This way you won't accidentally manipulate it while building something else. If you right-click the object and click Properties from the quad menu, check Freeze but uncheck Show Frozen in Gray. Doing that will help you to see the object.

Modeling the Boot

Box modeling is wonderfully unsophisticated for game modeling. I will disagree for the interim with cinematic characters, however, because they involve complex spline modeling. In the world of game development, box modeling represents choppy polygonal modeling, completing a model with fairly high detail but low polygon count. When you model using this technique, take your time. This is supposed to be a fairly complex model because it's the lead character in a game. Although it looks rough at first, later on we'll add some detail and then apply a Smooth modifier to make it look awesome.

1. Create a Box primitive with the length, width, and height segments set to 1. Right-click it and convert it to Editable Poly. Move and scale it to conform to the top and side viewports (see Figure 3.1). Expand the Editable Poly item in the Modifier panel to select things like Edge, Vertex, and Polygon so that you can manipulate and shape the box.
2. In Polygon Edit mode, select the front polygon of the box and use the Extrude tool (located in the Modify panel) to extrude face forward. In Figure 3.2, I've extruded a face, adjusted the corner vertices in Vertex Edit mode to follow the shape of the reference image, and continued extruding. This becomes easy, and you'll end up building almost the entire character this way. If you need to add more detail, enter Edge Edit mode, select two opposing edges by Ctrl+clicking them, and select Connect from the Modifier panel. This adds a new edge between them. Then just select that new edge and move it to conform to the reference images.

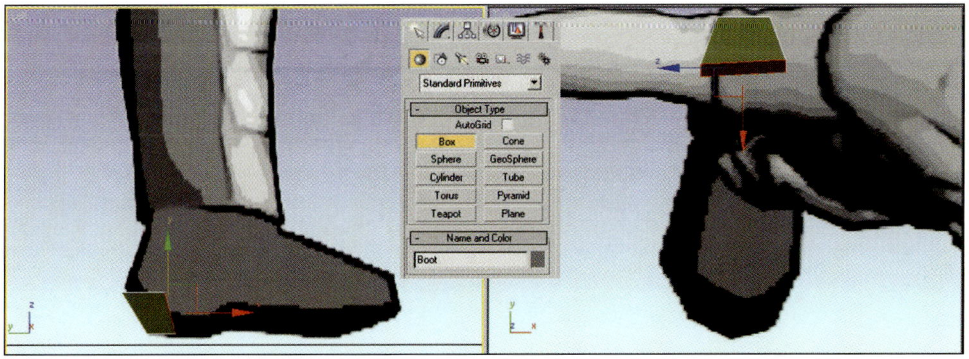

Figure 3.1 Create a Box primitive and adjust its shape according to the reference images.

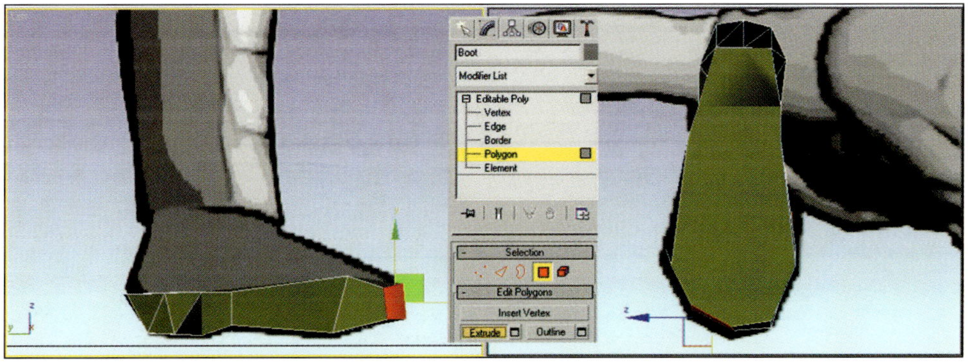

Figure 3.2 Select the front polygon and extrude it. Continue shaping and extruding the boot to conform to the image.

3. Continue extruding polygons from the top. In the Top viewport, while you're in Polygon Edit mode, hold down Ctrl, select several polys, and extrude them. As before, add more edges to polygons and move the new edges and vertices to detail the boot. As you approach the top of the boot, try to make it more circular (see Figure 3.3).
4. At this point, apply a Cap Holes modifier to close up the boot. Then apply a Smooth modifier to preview your work (see Figure 3.4). Not bad, huh? This will look great when you texture it later in the book. You can remove the Smooth modifier when you're done.

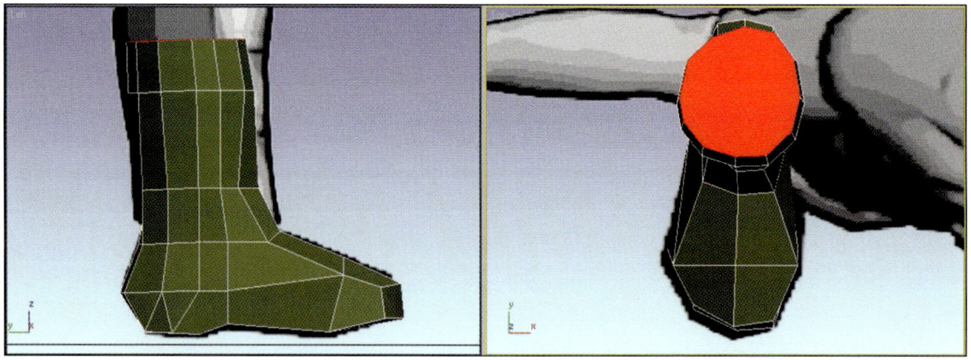

Figure 3.3 Continue extruding polygons on the top of the boot. Try to round out the top so that it can conform to the leg.

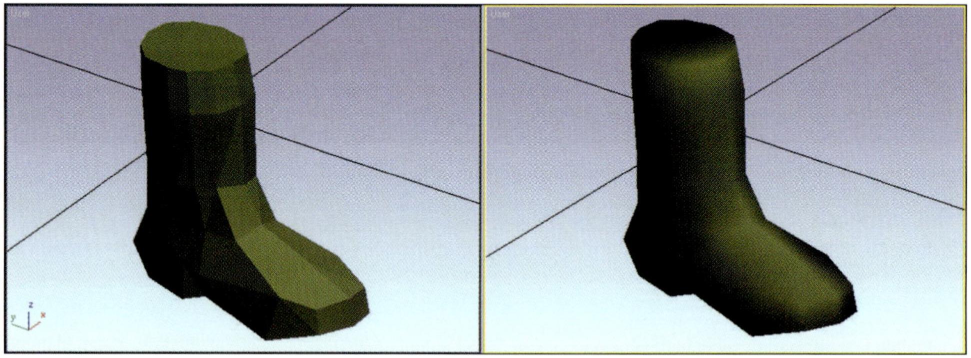

Figure 3.4 The completed boot with a Cap Holes and Smooth modifier applied.

Caution

Be sure that every object in your model is completely closed (there are no open faces) by using the Cap Holes modifier after you shape an object. Closing objects helps you avoid runtime errors when a game engine tries to incorporate your model. See Chapter 4 for more on adjusting, fixing, and optimizing your model.

Shaping the Pants (Lower Body)

The pants are baggy in keeping with military style. They also include shin and knee guards, like the marines in *Aliens*. A leg is basically a slowly extruded cylinder primitive all the way up to the torso. After you've tweaked one entire leg, you apply a Symmetry modifier, making a mirror copy of it.

Note

The boot and pants, which constitute the lower body, will be a single mesh entity with its own UV, texture, and normal maps.

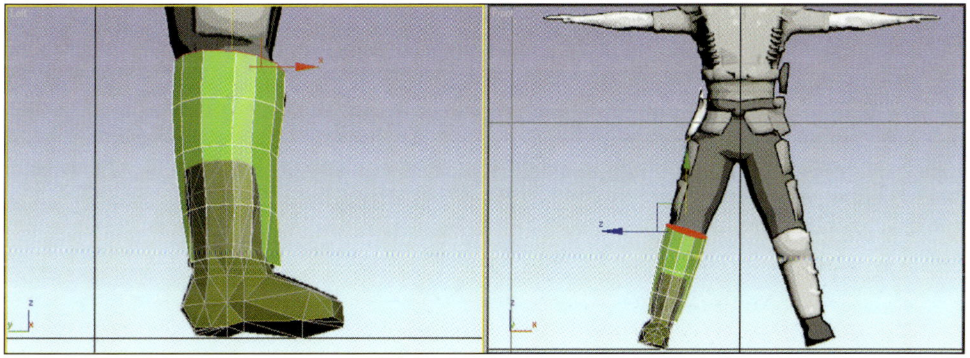

Figure 3.5 Rotate the boot to match the sketches, and then add a Cylinder primitive. I prefer to select the top face of the cylinder and extrude it continuously up the leg, moving and scaling it all the while.

1. Because the pants have shin guards going all the way down to the laces of the boot, they are wider. In Figure 3.5, I rotated the boot to conform to the image and then added a Cylinder primitive. I then scaled and rotated the Cylinder primitive into position and I extruded the top face over and over, adjusting each extrusion to generally conform to the sketches. Some people prefer to make one long cylinder with many segments and then adjust each segment, but I prefer to extrude and move each segment into place before continuing.
2. Continue to extrude the top face of the leg up to the waist. Try to scale and rotate each extrusion to conform to the shape of the sketch (see Figure 3.6).

Tip

If you're lacking detail along the length of the leg in one area, select an edge. Then, while holding down Ctrl, click on the Ring spinner, which is located in the Command Panel. This selects all parallel edges around the character. Then click the Connect button to add a new edge that runs perpendicular to the selected rings of edges. To adjust an individual segment, enter Edge Edit mode, select an edge, and click Ring in the Modify panel. This selects the entire segment, which you can move, scale, and rotate.

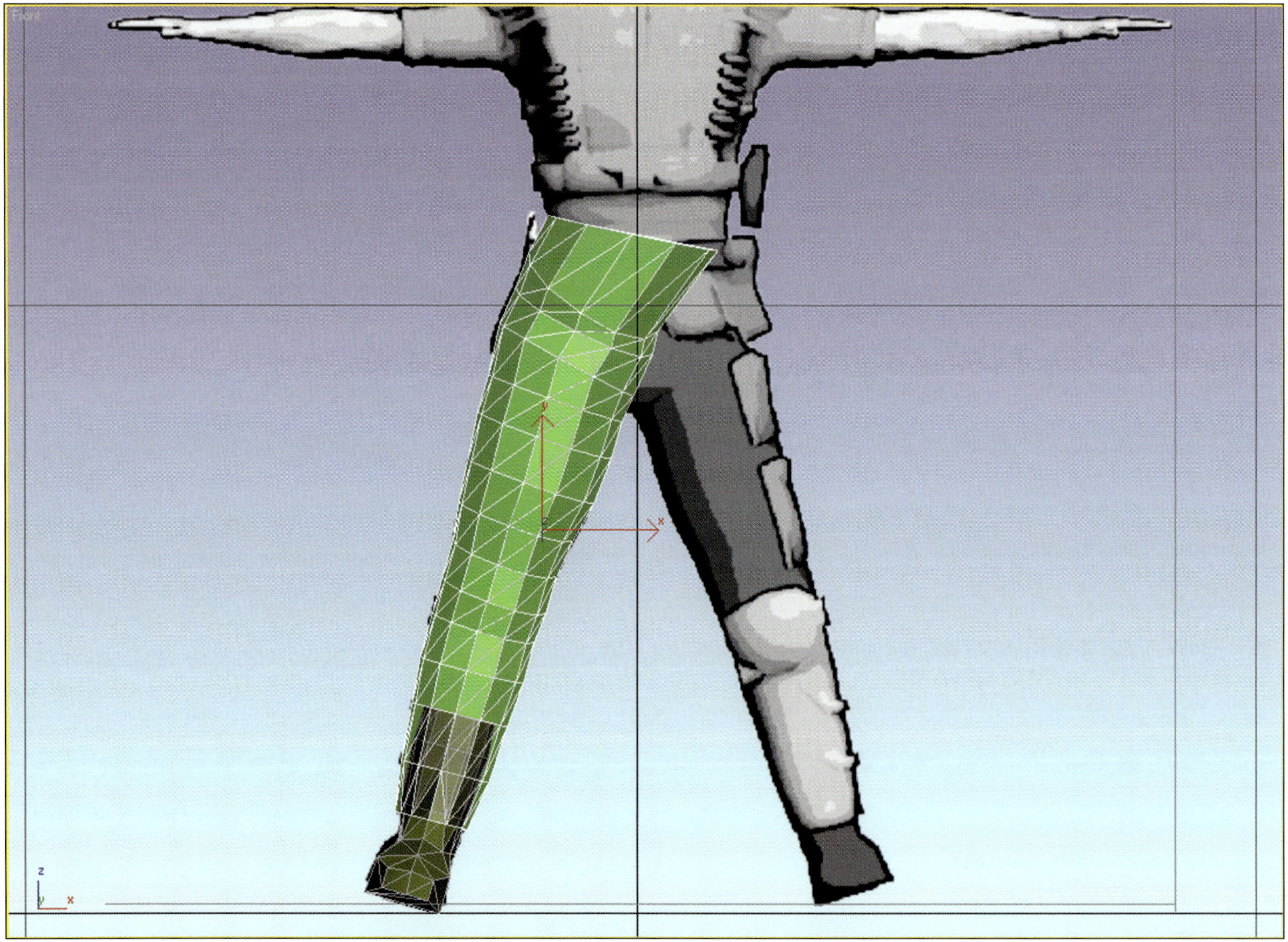

Figure 3.6 Continue extruding the top face of the leg up to the waist.

3. The base portion of the right leg is finished. Now it's time to manipulate polygons, edges, and vertices. This book isn't big enough for me to show you all the steps I took to do this, but it's not difficult—just time consuming! Take a look at the side and front of the leg in Figure 3.7. To make shapes like the shin guards and pockets, I manipulated individual vertices, while extruding certain faces. For instance, for the shin and knee guard, I selected polygons on the front of the leg to cover what will be the guard. Then I carefully extruded them. Finally, in Vertex mode, I slowly moved them to create the shape I wanted. I did the same for the pockets. (Remember that the completed model is on the CD-ROM in the Chapter 3 folder if you need a better visual reference.)
4. Next, we'll use the Symmetry modifier to the existing leg to create a duplicate. There's more detail that we could add, such as the belt and front pockets, but the Symmetry modifier can be tricky in the sense that the front (groin) area of the resultant operation is somewhat deformed and would affect further modeling performed near that area.

   This modifier works by taking on an object and merging it with an identical copy. It's sort of magnetic because as you move the copy further toward the original, the polygons try to attach themselves from one part to the other in a magnetic way. I've found that it's best to set up your model in preparation for this modifier by offering your new leg a flat area in the inseam so that things attach nicely.

   Try this. Use the Slice modifier to chop off the inseam of your leg (see Figure 3.8). Expand this modifier, rotate and position the slice plane (turn on Angle Snap Toggle on the top toolbar so that you can rotate it to 90 degrees) like I've done, and select Remove Top. This creates a surface that mates nicely with the mirrored leg. I also used the Slice modifier for the top of the leg to make it flat.

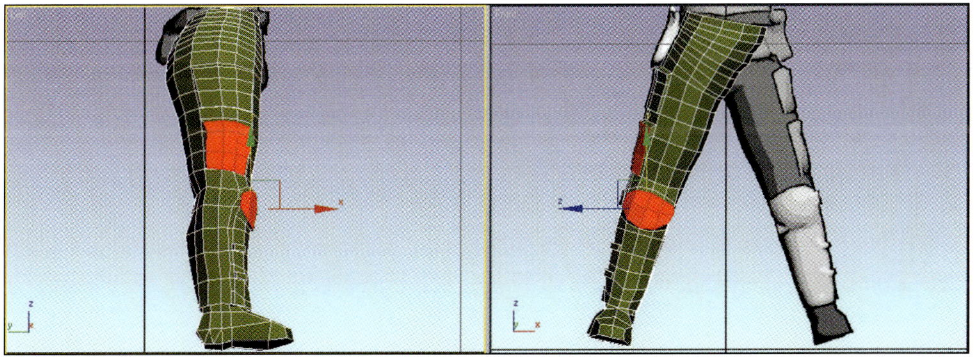

Figure 3.7 Take your time manipulating the leg mesh at the subobject level. This means moving around edges and vertices and extruding polygons to create those emerging shapes.

5. Now it's time for the Symmetry modifier. First—and most importantly—go to the Tools panel and perform a Reset Xform; otherwise, the Symmetry modifier will perform its operation based on the leg's intrinsic alignment. After you've applied it, you can collapse the Modifier stack by right-clicking it and selecting Collapse All. Now, with the leg selected, add a Symmetry modifier. In this modifier's rollout, click the X-axis, and check Flip. Expand the modifier and select Mirror. This allows you to move the mirror horizontally. When the duplicate leg is in position, right at the seam, you can collapse this modifier (see Figure 3.9). Note that if you adjust the Threshold command to something like 0.02, you'll have better results.

Caution

Collapsing the Modifier stack is something you should do only if you feel you don't need to go back to any one point in the stack to make changes to your model. I tend to collapse the stack frequently, but this is bad practice. The stack is named as such for just that reason: to enable the user to revert to previously applied modifiers and fix issues on a model.

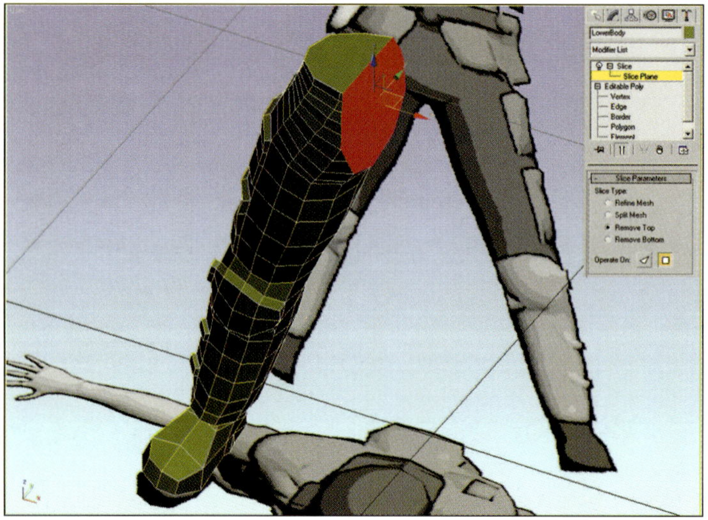

Figure 3.8 Use the Slice modifier to create a clean flat area at the inside of the waist so that the Symmetry modifier won't have problems.

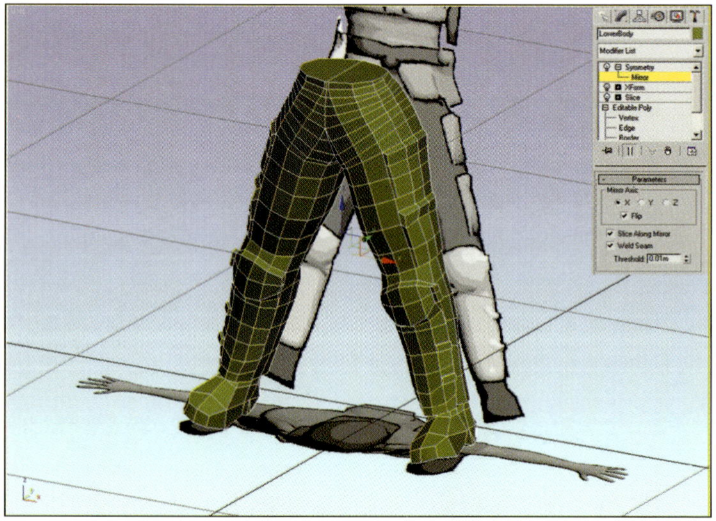

Figure 3.9 The Symmetry modifier applied to the leg.

6. The Symmetry modifier left some unusual creases in the groin and buttocks, so go ahead and manipulate those areas at the vertex level. You might have to add vertices and edges to create more definition with the Cut tool. I've added a bulge in the front, because the marines in *Aliens* have a special guard for that area.

Figure 3.10 Fix the groin and buttocks area of the model so that they flow naturally.

Note

In dealing with areas that will have extreme flexible movement (such as the crotch, knees, and armpits), you *must* have higher polygon detail to avoid kinks when the model moves. As you animate and notice these issues, know that they're not a big deal. Just go back and add the necessary detail.

Adding Some Military Detail

Here I'm going to add some miscellaneous detail (utility belt, satchels, knife, and so on) to match the sketches. However, in adding detail to a character, it's best *not* to create a separate object and then just attach it. Adding details by extruding the existing mesh has several advantages, mostly in speeding up rendering time because it reduces polygon count, and also for texturing purposes. I'm going to briefly go over some of the details I've followed along with the sketches. Basically, it's all just a matter of shaping some of the existing polygons on the model and extruding them.

Here are some things I've done to manipulate the existing polygons on my marine model:

1. I've entered Polygon Edit mode, and while holding down Ctrl, I've clicked on the polys around the beltline of the character. I've also selected polys on the right side of the hip to form the knife holder (see Figure 3.11). After using the Extrude tool to raise them out, I entered Vertex Edit mode and spent time adjusting the vertices appropriately. Note that I've had to convert the model to Editable Mesh so that I could select some individual triangles instead of quads to refine my selections; if you do so, just remember to convert back to Editable Poly.
2. On the backside of the character, I extruded out part of the left section to make the large satchel (see Figure 3.12). At first it comes out boxy, but I moved

Figure 3.11 Use the Polygon tool to select polys wherever you want to create an object; then extrude them. Adjust their shape with the Vertex tool active.

Figure 3.12 Using the existing polygons on the rear of the character, I selected several, extruded them, and adjusted their vertices to make a nice satchel. Temporarily applying the Smooth modifier makes it look great.

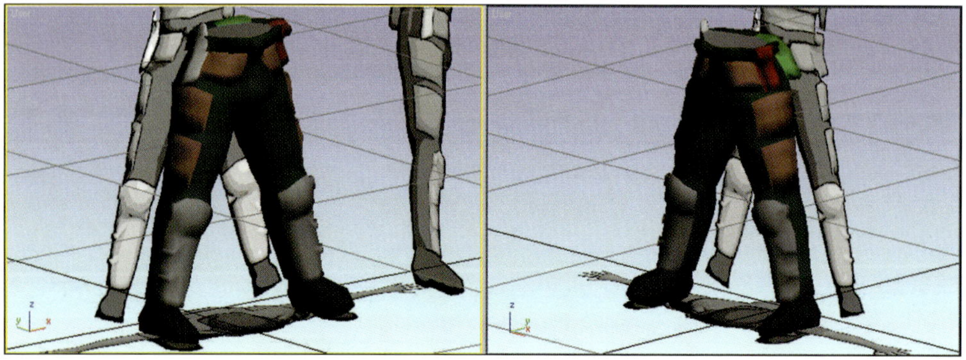

Figure 3.13 Continue extruding polys around the belt to form items to match the sketches. This will complete the model's lower half.

around some corner vertices and smoothed it out. Apply a Smooth modifier for some awesome results.

3. The rest of the utility belt and pants are now routine extrusions like before. In Figure 3.13, I've extruded a single polygon from the top of the belt above the knife to make a knife handle. (I've selected all polygons representing an individual component and then colored them by applying a Multi/Sub-Object material to the mesh using the Material Editor. Each component has a different Diffuse Color setting.) On the left side of the belt, I've extruded more polys to make a flashlight. If you have difficulty forming any item, just remember to refine the area you're extruding by connecting two edges, or add vertices by clicking the Insert Vertex button on the Modifier panel and then clicking on an edge.
4. Remember to attach any objects that are free from the lower half (such as the boots, and the forward end of the flashlight, which is a simple cylinder). Do this by selecting the Attach button in the Modifier panel, and then click on all free objects to make a single lower half. Name this single object LowerBody in the Modifier panel and save your scene.

Creating the Upper Body

Because the upper body is more complex than the lower, I've used a few more techniques such as Boolean operations to remove one object from another to quickly create an appropriate shape. However, as before, there will be a lot of extruding and manipulating of subobjects. In all, it will seem difficult, but it is just time consuming, so don't fret. Again, I'll move along in the text somewhat rapidly while highlighting any areas where I did something special. Just do your best and take your time!

Note

The upper body consists of the torso, arms, hands, and other attached objects that will end up being a single mesh entity with its own UV, texture, and normal maps.

Forming the Torso

The torso is fairly quick and easy. It is essentially a cylinder with multiple segments, with each segment uniquely adjusted using the sketches as a reference. I'll show you this technique, but you could just as easily continue extruding the lower body's top polygon all the way up to the neck.

1. First select and freeze the lower body so that you don't accidentally select it. Do this by right-clicking the lower body and clicking Freeze Selection from the quad menu. Begin the torso by creating a cylinder with 14 sides and 18 segments. You'll want a decent amount of polygons to play with so that your model will not only have good detail for the texture baking

process but also will make creation of other miscellaneous torso details easier. The arms will also be high in detail because you'll be dealing with an organic shape.

Size and position the cylinder according to the sketches (see Figure 3.14). After they're in position, begin selecting individual segments (in Edge Selection mode, click a segment edge and then click Loop on the Modifier panel) and sizing them using the sketches as a reference.

Note

The torso section is actually armor covering the entire torso with front and back sections that snap together. The armor will not be very organic in shape, which is why it looks somewhat awkward and shell-like. I spent a while watching and pausing shots of some of the marines in the movie *Aliens* to generate detail of the sketches and the model.

2. Using both Front and Side views, finish the basic torso shape up to the neck. The torso armor will look much better if you rotate some of the segments in the Side view to match the flow of the upper body (see Figure 3.15).

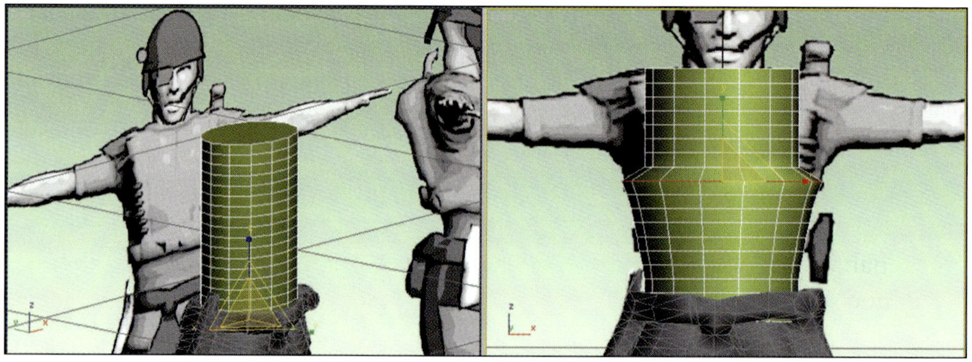

Figure 3.14 Begin the torso by creating and sizing a Cylinder primitive with 14 sides and 18 segments. Select individual segments and size them using the sketches as a reference.

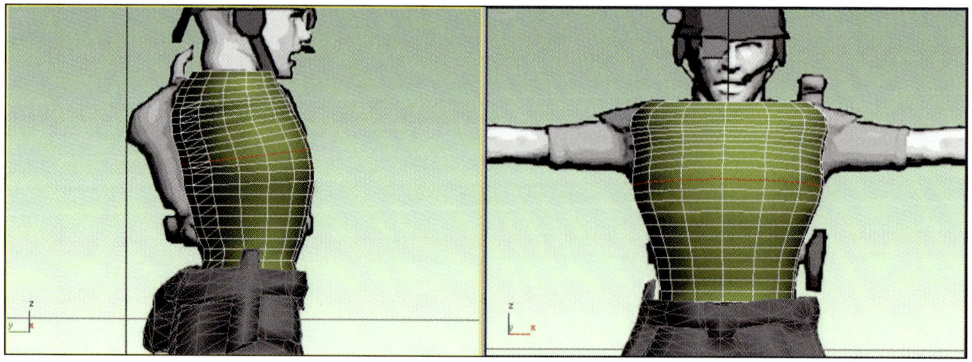

Figure 3.15 Continue sizing the segments according to the Left and Front sketches. Rotate some of the segments in the Side views to match the flow of the upper body.

3. To create the basic neck depression area, you could subdivide the top polygon of the torso and spend time manipulating vertices to create an appropriate shape. I opted to use a quick Boolean operation to do this. First, split the mesh in half using a Slice modifier, as you did with the pants earlier. This assists the operation by reducing the number of vertices and enables you to make a uniform model after you apply a Symmetry modifier.

4. Create an 18 segment Sphere primitive and scale, rotate, and position it as shown in Figure 3.16. By removing the sphere from the torso, you can create the neck area.

   Click on the torso to select it, and from the Create section, select Compound Objects from the drop-down list. Click Boolean. Then in the Modifier panel, be sure Subtraction (A-B) is selected and click Pick Operand B. Click on the sphere object to subtract it.

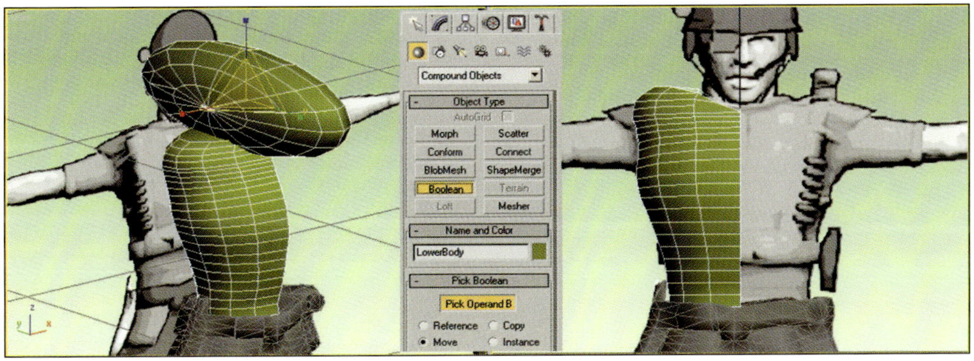

Figure 3.16 Create the neck portion of the torso by subtracting a Sphere primitive from it using a Boolean compound object.

5. The Boolean operation can be slightly unclean, especially when the polygon counts aren't high. After you've performed the operation, you might have to create new edges and polygons. Observe your model in wire frame and shaded modes (press F3 to toggle back and forth) to discover any holes in the mesh, and fix them appropriately using the different edit modes. When your half-torso is somewhat decent, go to the Utilities panel and click on the Reset Xform tool. Select Reset Selected and collapse the stack. Now you can use the Symmetry modifier along the X-axis with Flip enabled to create the other half of the torso, like you did when creating the pants earlier (see Figure 3.17). Remember that this modifier works best if the Threshold value is small, like 0.01m. In Figure 3.17, I also spent a little more time fixing any odd geometry resulting from the Symmetry modifier.

6. Shape a circular opening that will form the base of the neck. If you look at Figure 3.18, I accomplished this by creating polygons in Polygon Edit mode, slowly working from the shoulder areas inward. (Note that the neck area is initially completely open; no Cap Holes modifier is applied.) After I had built up enough polygons to form a rough circular area in the middle, I manipulated vertices in Vertex Edit mode to form a nice circle. We'll further refine this area later so that it mates nicely with the head.

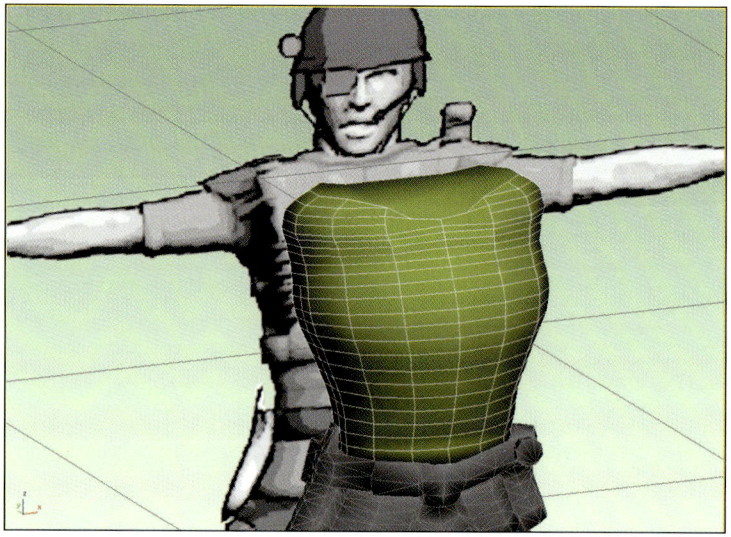

Figure 3.17 Fix any poor geometry resulting from the Boolean operation, and then apply a Symmetry modifier to the torso.

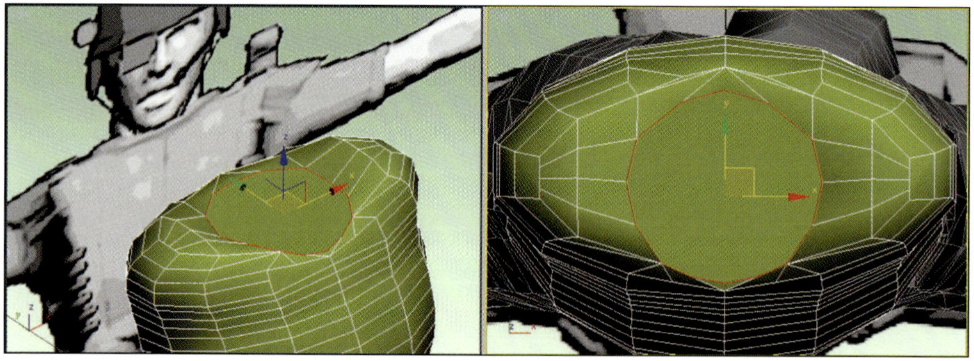

Figure 3.18 Create polygons in Edit Poly mode in the neck area, beginning with the outermost regions by the shoulders. Continue filling in polygons until you have a nice rounded area, forming the base of the neck where the head will join later on.

Forming the Shoulders and Arms

When I showed you the leg creation process, I applied a Symmetry modifier after I'd built one leg. In this case, because we are building a pair of symmetrical arms that extend off of a cylinder, we can apply a Symmetry modifier first and have Show End Results set to On. This way, as we build one shoulder, arm, and hand on one side of the model, the other side is dynamically built every step of the way. You can, of course, apply the modifier at the end, but applying the Symmetry modifier to one side at a time is cool because it helps you to preview your work as you go along.

1. First apply a Slice modifier up the middle of the torso, collapse the stack, and apply a Symmetry modifier along the X-axis, with Flip enabled and Threshold set to a low value, such as 0.01m. Join the mirrored half of the torso, and when you're satisfied, click on the Editable Poly item (the torso) just beneath the Symmetry modifier. Toggle the Show End Results button to On at the top of the Modifier panel. When you're working on the upper body from now on, be sure to keep the Symmetry modifier on top of the stack while you're working on the mesh.
2. Now switch to a side view to begin creating the shoulders. Remember that everything you do to the base torso half (not the symmetrical side) is automatically done on the other half of the torso. Using the side sketch as a basic reference, in Polygon Edit mode, select polygons around the area where the arms should protrude and delete them (see Figure 3.19). Enter Vertex Edit mode and move the inner vertices to form a nice rounded area. This will be where the armor of the torso ends and the character's military fatigues begin.
3. The remaining part of the armor that you need to create is similar to an American football player's shoulder pads. Referring to Figure 3.20, create the pads by pulling edges or vertices from the top portion of the torso in either Edge or Vertex Edit mode. Make the shape of the pads arch a bit on top, and keep them rounded at the

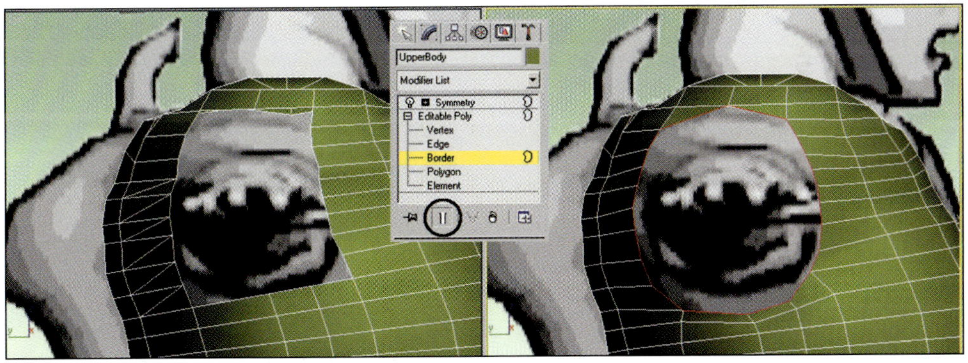

Figure 3.19 Apply a Symmetry modifier to one-half of the torso. Begin building the shoulder areas by deleting polygons and manipulating vertices to form a nice rounded starting point for the shoulders and arms.

ends. It's easiest to use the Top and Front views for this.

4. The opening of the armor for the arms begins as a simple circle-shaped area. Initially it is a fairly large area so that the character's arms can move around freely. Start creating small polygons in Polygon Edit mode at the bottom of the armor, making sure the new polys are angled outward more and more, forming the player's fatigues. If you look at Figure 3.21, I've built up a bunch of polygons in the armpit region and then around the entire circumference to create a rounded area that will dictate the beginning of the arm. Take your time doing this, and be sure to keep the polygon count fairly high, particularly in the armpit region. The high polygon count there ensures that this area will deform properly (that is, no kinks will occur) when animated.

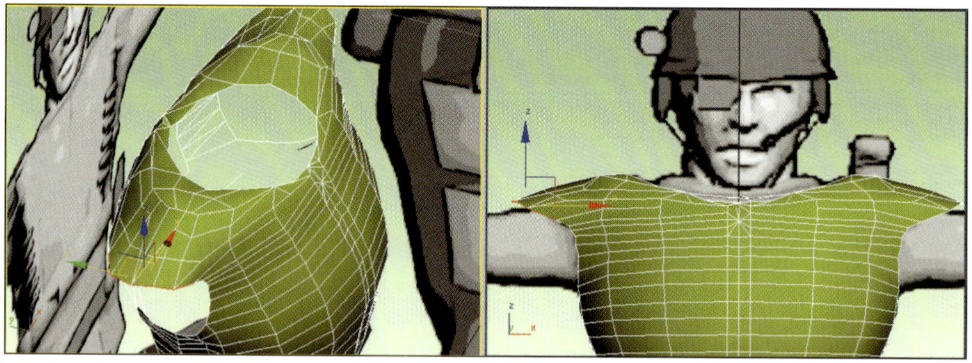

Figure 3.20 Create shoulder pads on the armor by pulling edges or vertices at the top of the armor where the arms will begin.

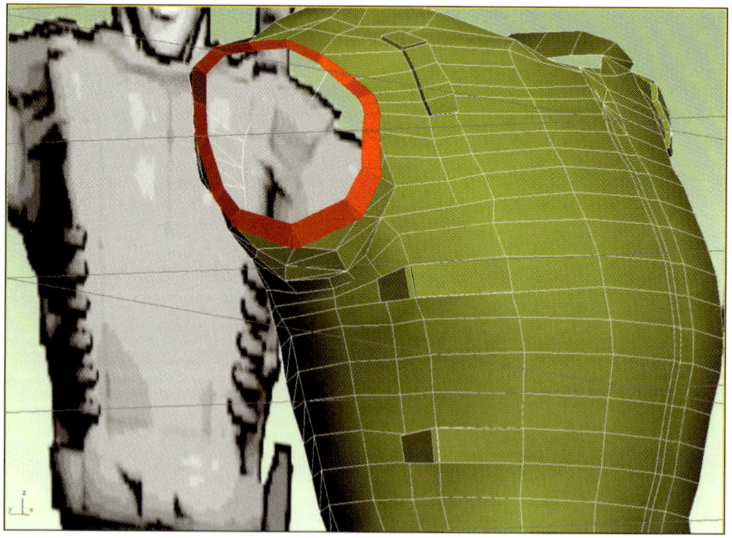

Figure 3.21 From the armor, create small polygons around the inside of the arm and armpit region. A higher polygon count in this area is recommended for proper deformation during animation.

Also note that in Figure 3.21, I extruded some polygons on the front of the armor to simulate snaps or buckles where the armor shells come together.

5. When you're satisfied with the base of the arm, it's time to extrude like we did when creating the legs. In Polygon Edit mode, select the outermost polygon (or edge) and begin extruding in small sections, scaling and rotating the sections as you move along the length of the arm. The sketches don't offer a ton of detail, so tweak these segments intuitively as you go (see Figure 3.22).

Tip

When you're modeling any organic part of a human character, such as the arms or the face, it helps to use pictures or high-quality drawings of actual human subjects. When I modeled my character, I used my *Atlas of Human Anatomy* as a reference to produce some fine mesh detail. This detail, of course, gets whittled down after you reduce the polygon count later, but the high-res version makes the normal map look great on the low-res model.

6. Looking at the sketch, the Hicks model has his shirt fatigues rolled up at the end of the upper arm. Extrude several segments and scale each one up a bit, forming this shape as I did in Figure 3.23.

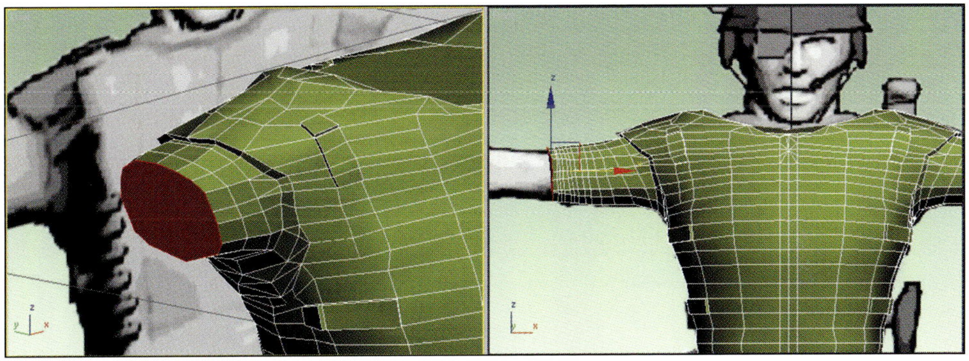

Figure 3.22 As when constructing the leg, begin forming the arm by extruding the outermost face in small segments, adjusting each extrusion to match the top and front sketches.

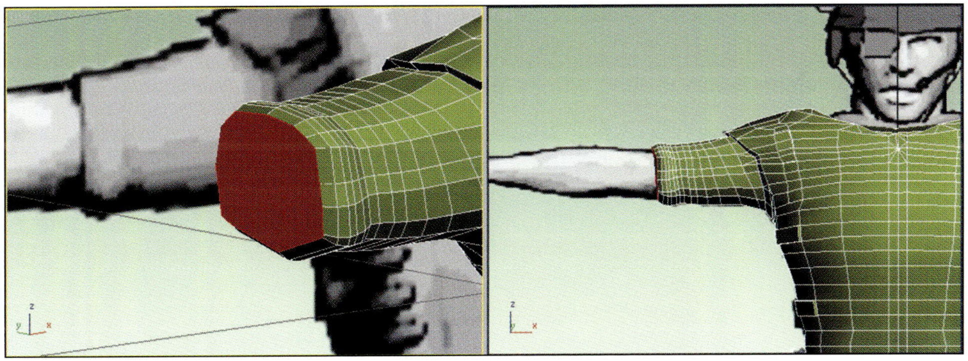

Figure 3.23 Scale up some new segments at the end of the upper arm to form a shape that depicts the shirt sleeve rolled up.

7. The rest of the arm to the wrist is going to be a bit difficult and time consuming because we're now dealing with our first raw organic shape. The sketches don't offer a ton of intricate detail, so you'll have to stretch out your arm or use a picture of a real forearm to get this right. In Figure 3.24, I slowly extruded out many small segments. Using the orthogonal viewports, I finely adjusted each one, including moving individual vertices around to produce a nice realistic shape.

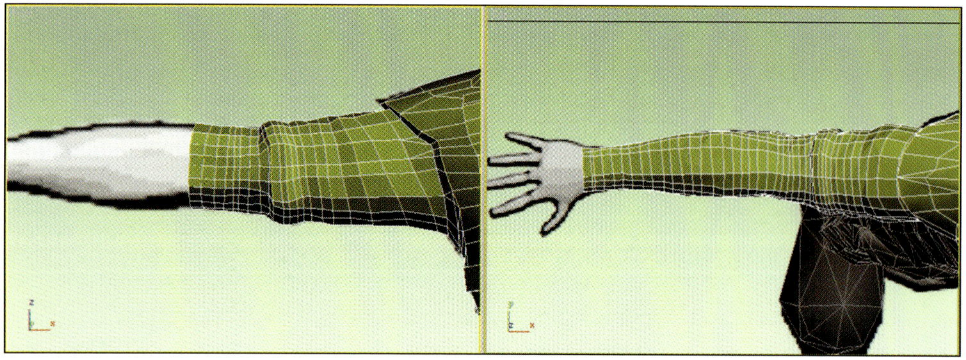

Figure 3.24 Continue extruding the forearm up to the wrist. Because the sketches don't depict intricate detail, you'll have to make many extrusions, carefully adjusting each one, using your own forearm or pictures of a real forearm for a decent reference.

Forming the Hands

The hands are also organic, but the Hicks character is wearing fingerless gloves, so you won't need too much detail for the palms. Again, this is just an extrusion process. Like the beginning of the arms on the torso, you'll have to knock out polygons to create the openings for the five fingers. It will also help you to visualize the hands as you model using your own hands as a reference.

1. Continue extruding the wrist, shaping the palm as I did in Figure 3.25 (left). After you've extruded up to the base of the fingers, select polygons in Polygon Edit mode and delete them. On the right side of Figure 3.25, I moved around vertices in Vertex Edit mode, rounding the openings of the fingers. When I was satisfied, I applied a Cap Holes modifier to seal the finger openings in preparation for extruding the fingers.
2. Extrude the fingers using the background sketch as a reference. Looking at Figure 3.26 (left), I've initially extruded a thick base representing the end of the glove and then continued to the tips of the fingers.
3. The thumb is a bit more difficult because it's not a straight shot and has a thick base. Use your own hand as a reference. Figure 3.27 depicts the end result of the finger extrusions I did, thus completing the hand.

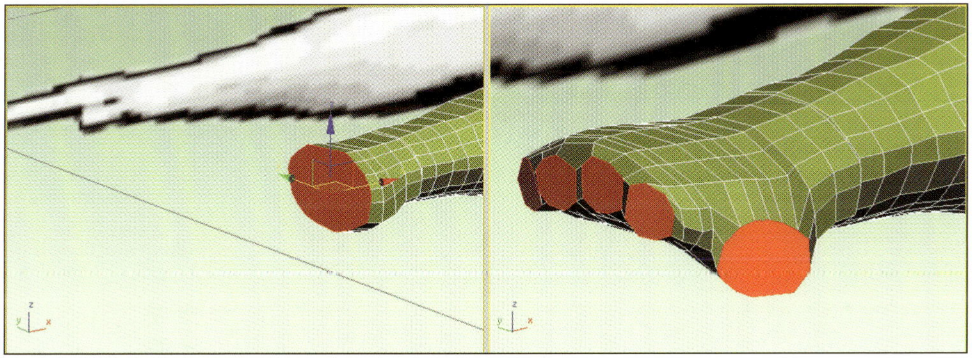

Figure 3.25 Extrude the wrist to form the palm, scaling and rotating segments as you go. In Polygon Edit mode, select polygons to represent the base of the fingers and delete them. Move around vertices to round out these shapes.

Figure 3.26 Extrude the fingers using the background sketch as a reference.

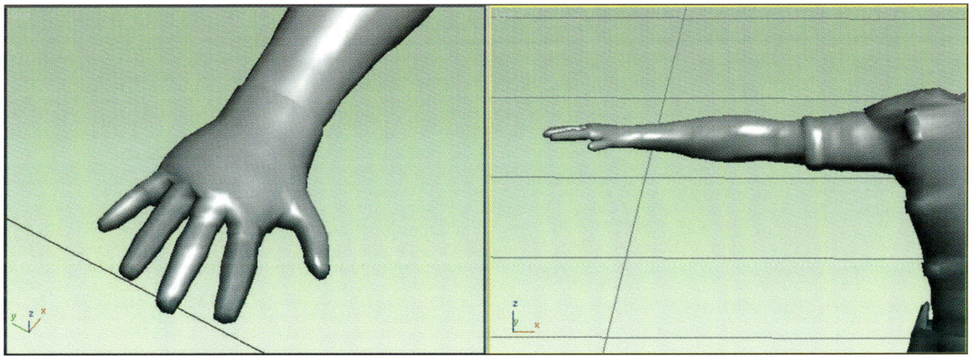

Figure 3.27 The completed hand. The thumb was a bit more difficult because it has the classic opposing angles compared to the rest of the fingers. I used my own hand as a reference.

Detailing the Torso

In this final section, you will finish the upper body by adding details to the model according to the sketches. Again, this will be simple extrusions of polygons and manipulations of the resultant vertices to shape the belts, Alice pack (backpack), and whatnot. Some other items that the Hicks model possesses, such as ammo and the canteen, are separate 3D objects that I created and attached to the torso.

1. Let's finish the top of the shoulders into the neck area now that we have good upper body symmetry going. At this point, you can collapse your stack (remember to save your file first) because the remainder of the torso detail won't be very symmetrical. Referring to Figure 3.28, pull some of the vertices on the shoulder pads upward to make them more rounded, and go along the neck region and round out the edges.
2. The shoulder light that the marines had in *Aliens* stood high and away from them and looked a bit goofy. I opted for Hicks' light to be part of his Alice pack so that it would flow more naturally from his body. Do this by extruding a square patch of polygons from the upper-left side of Hicks' back and shaping them. From Figure 3.29, I finished the light by extruding a single polygon in Polygon Edit mode. For each extrusion, I rotated the face until the light curved up and faced forward. The end of the light is hexagonal, so I inserted a couple of vertices on two edges and moved the new vertices outward. To insert a vertex, just enter Edge Edit mode, and on the Modifier panel, click Insert Vertex. Then click on an edge to add a new vertex. You have to be in Vertex Edit mode to manipulate the new vertex.
3. The sketches also depict the Hicks model having a satchel belt that goes around the waist and a harness that goes from the belt to the upper portion of the armor in the front and back. You can quickly form this by selecting polygons around the beltline and up the length of the torso and extruding

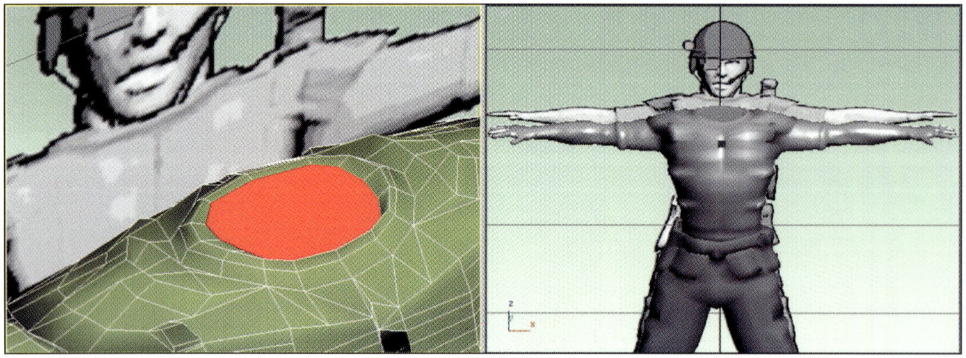

Figure 3.28 Round out the shoulder pads and neck regions by pulling and manipulating the vertices in those areas. You might have to add new polygons around the neck to accomplish this.

Figure 3.29 Create the shoulder light by extruding and shaping polygons on the upper-left portion of the character's back, using the sketches as a reference.

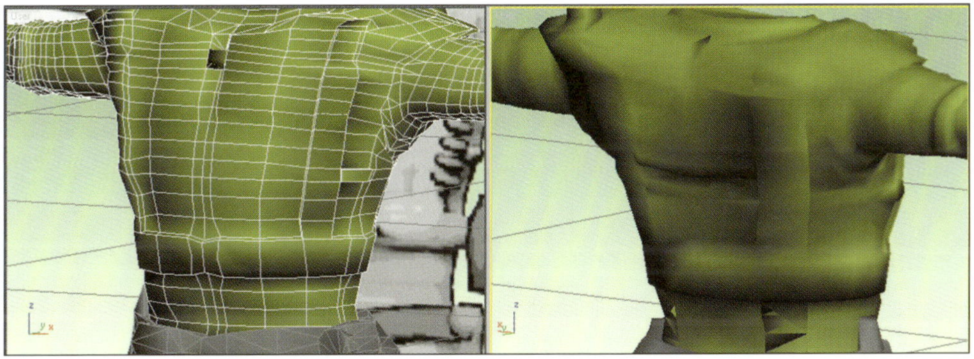

Figure 3.30 Create a satchel belt and harness around the torso by selecting multiple polygons representing these objects and extruding them.

them all at once in a small amount, as seen in Figure 3.30. You might have to create some new edges for better shape selections.

Note that in this figure, some polygons do not appear smoothed. I was going to fix this, but I decided that I would rather illustrate a situation. Errors like this are a result of bad geometry or newly created geometry *after* you've applied a Smooth modifier. If you reapply this modifier and it still doesn't smooth out, you need to fix the geometry. Most likely, the problem is duplicate vertices or polygons that somehow are not fully attached to the model. See Chapter 4 for more on this.

This is a good time to get creative. Adhering to the basic shapes depicted in the sketches, I went around the ammo belt and extruded small portions of polygons to form miscellaneous storage units that a marine might have, shaping them a bit randomly as I went around the waist. Occasionally I applied a Smooth modifier to preview the work and then removed it and continued. The Alice pack was nothing special either; it's just another large polygon selection that was extruded and shaped (see Figure 3.31).

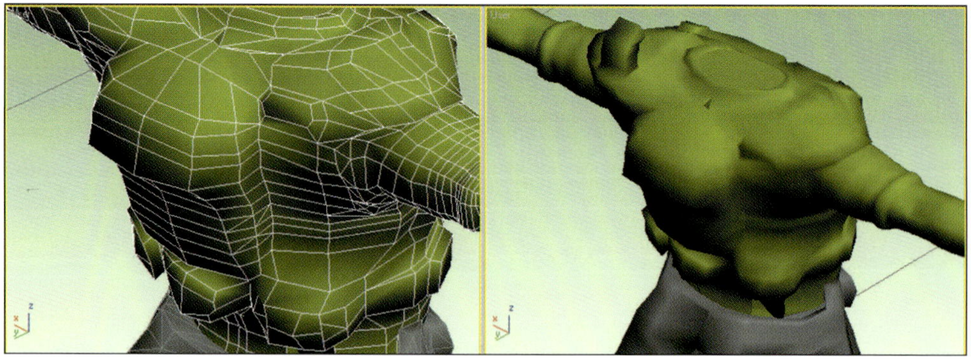

Figure 3.31 Create several miscellaneous objects around the ammo belt and an Alice pack by extruding small handfuls of polygons and shaping them. Use the Smooth modifier to preview your work as you go.

4. Finish the upper body by creating and attaching bullets along the left and right sides of the harness and a canteen on the side. The bullets are just a Capsule primitive located in the Extended Primitives section in the Create panel. Remove one end of the capsule to make a bullet, and then scale and position it at the bottom of one of the harnesses. To clone the bullet, hold down Shift and click and drag the bullet to make a copy.

   The canteen object was just a Box primitive with a Cylinder primitive attached to the top. After you've attached all objects to the mesh, you're done with the upper body (see Figure 3.32).

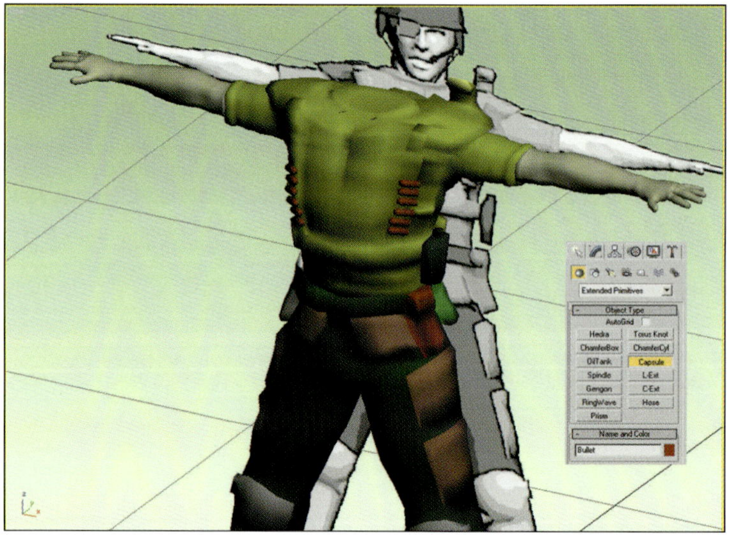

Figure 3.32 The completed upper body with bullets and a canteen attached to the harness.

Creating the Head

The head consists of several attached components: the neck, face, teeth, eyes, headgear with microphone, helmet, and a helmet camera. As with the lower and upper body meshes, the head will ultimately be a single mesh object with its own UV, texture, and normal maps.

Making the Face

The face is the last organic feature to model. Despite its small surface area, it's quite possibly the most difficult object to mesh. Take a look at 3D models in movies—ever notice how realistic *every* animal in the animal kingdom can be modeled, yet doing a human face always seems slightly artificial? That's because our faces aren't coated with thick fur, and we have hundreds of tiny muscles beneath our skin that are used for communication and projecting emotion. That's something that is difficult to model, especially at a low resolution.

There's no easy way to explain how to create the mesh of the face, so you're going to have to be creative and use front and side images of real human faces. I'm going to show you how to go about box modeling a face, but the technique involves slowly and carefully tessellating (subdividing) polygons and manipulating vertices to generalize facial features. Also, I'm only going to be modeling the left half of the face and head and then applying the Symmetry modifier. Ears won't be necessary because headgear will cover them.

1. Create a Box primitive with Length and Width segments of 1 and a Height segment of 2. Extrude the back face of the top segment to match the general shape of the left part of the face using the sketch as a reference (see Figure 3.33).

Figure 3.33 Begin the face and head using a simple Box primitive with two segments. Extrude the back face of the top segment to roughly match the sketch.

2. Enter Polygon Edit mode and click on a polygon at the front where the eyes and nose will be. On the Modifier panel in the Edit Geometry section, click on Tessellate. Then enter Vertex Edit mode to view the newly subdivided surface. Manipulate the new vertices to start matching some of the general contours and facial features of the Hicks sketch (see Figure 3.34).

   Note that I've also deleted the polygons on the top, bottom, and inside of the Box primitive. This creates sort of a mask with which to work and eliminates some of the clutter when modeling the face.

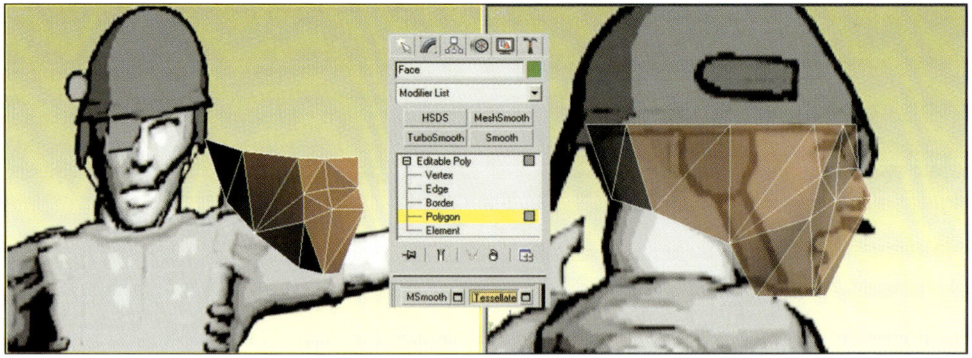

Figure 3.34 Click on a front polygon in Polygon Edit mode and click Tessellate on the Modifier panel to subdivide this surface. Adjust the vertices to start matching the general shape of the face.

3. In Figure 3.35, I've further tessellated polygons around the face and added some new vertices along the inside of the Box primitive. Following the sketch in a Left viewport, I've moved the new vertices to trace the contour of the face (brow, nose, lips, and chin). If you do it this way, you can work from the inside (middle) of the face outward, like modeling with clay.

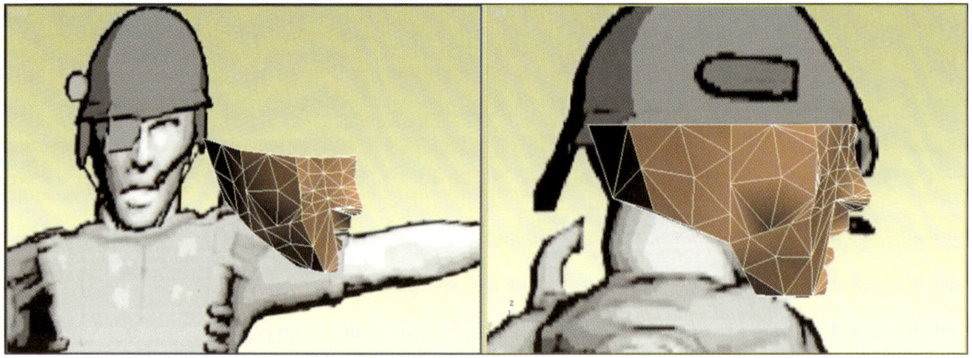

Figure 3.35 Continue tessellating polygons around the front of the face and adjusting vertices. Add and move vertices along the inside of the face to match the contour of the HICKS_side.tga sketch.

Don't worry about having too many polygons for now; we'll optimize the mesh later.

4. After you've spent a while (a few hours?) detailing the face, you should end up with a decent facial shape like mine in Figure 3.36. This isn't something easily explained in text; here is where your artistic prowess needs to shine. Such a small piece of geometry can be so difficult! It also will help to have a Smooth modifier on top of the stack with Show End Results toggled to On to help you to visualize your work, again like modeling with clay. It also really helps to have reference images of several faces that you can look at as you model.

   In Figure 3.36, look in the ocular area. There are a lot of polygons that helped me to shape this area and gave me something to work with when I created the eyelids. When I was satisfied, I knocked out polygons where the eyes would be and closed the knocked out region back up with a single polygon in Polygon Edit mode.

   Look also at the mouth. I grabbed a bunch of vertices at once (Ctrl+clicking them) and pushed them into the face, creating a cavity. Make the mouth gape open so that you can add teeth and allow the chin to move up and down for lip-sync animation. The polygons around the eye and mouth should form concentric rings to help the face deform correctly when animated.

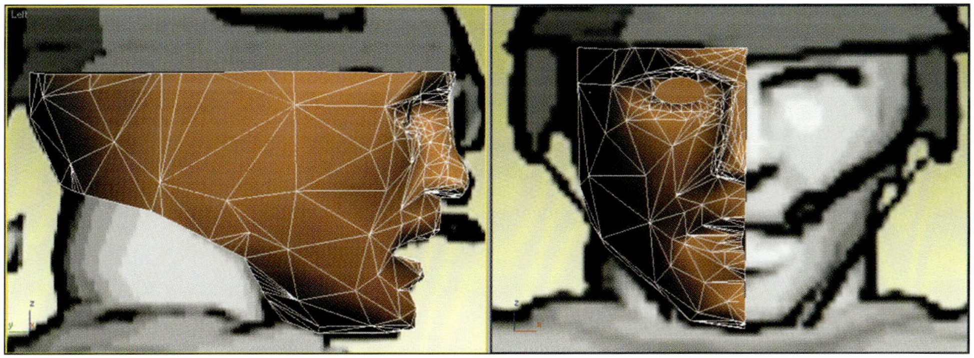

Figure 3.36 Add more detail and spend a while carefully shaping the face. Use even more detail around the eyes to shape the eyelids. Push some of the vertices inward in the mouth area so that the character can lip-sync later on.

5. When you're satisfied with the overall shape and look of the face you've created, add an Optimize modifier to the stack above the Editable Poly item in the Modifier stack (see Figure 3.37). This modifier will kill superfluous vertices, edges, and whatnot that won't affect the shape of the mesh. After I added this modifier, I collapsed my stack and spent a little time going around the face looking for vertices that were close together, selecting them using Ctrl+click, and clicking Weld in the Modifier panel. This further optimizes the model without sacrificing detail.
6. Now it's time for the eyes and teeth. First perform a Reset Xform in the Tools panel, and in

the Modifier panel, collapse your stack. Then add a Symmetry modifier to complete the face.

We could use simple Sphere primitives for the eyes, but that would add numerous polygons to the model that we would never render. Instead, in Edge Edit mode, Ctrl+click the edges around the right eye socket area, and on the Modifier panel, click Create Shape from Selection (see Figure 3.38). Name this new shape R_Eye, and for Shape Type, select Linear. This shape will be an Editable Spline. Select it, and in the Modifier panel, right-click it and choose Convert to Editable Poly. This new shape won't be closed, so add a Cap Holes modifier to close it. Repeat for the left eye. Now you'll have separate eye entities that will have their own textures and "bones," which will allow you (and programmers) to animate the eyes separately from the rest of the face. Look at Figure 3.38. I tested out shifting the eyes left and right by moving their pivot points in the Hierarchy panel and then rotating the eyes around this new pivot. The pivot points were moved to near the center of the head.

For the teeth, I chose polygon selections around a Cylinder primitive, which I detached, positioned inside the mouth, and reattached to the face.

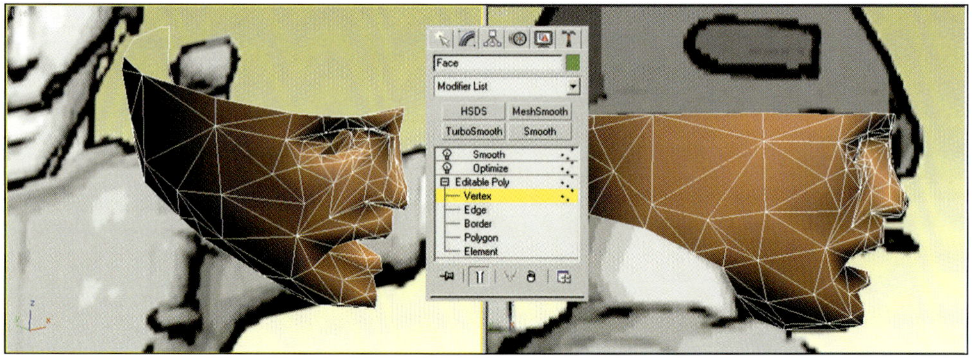

Figure 3.37 After you're finished shaping the face, add an Optimize modifier to reduce unnecessary polygons on your face object. Spend some time welding together vertices that are close to one another to reduce unnecessary polygon count.

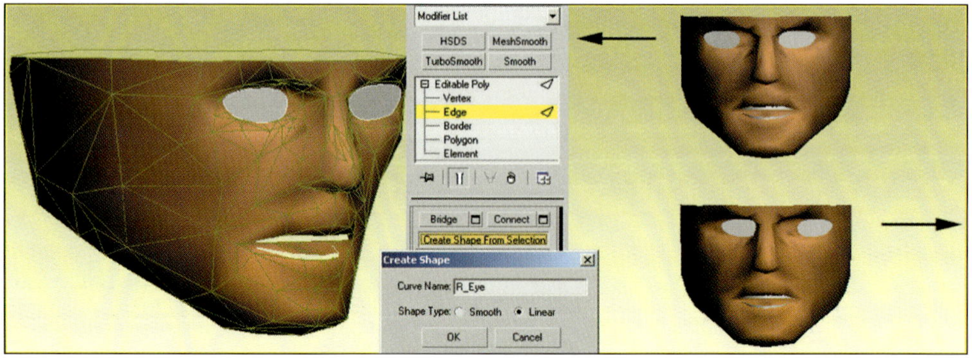

Figure 3.38 Create eyes by selecting the edges around the eye socket area and clicking Create Shape from Selection. You'll animate these curved planes separately from the head. You can make teeth from the curved surface of a Cylinder primitive.

Finishing the Head

The rest of the head is easy. It's just a few primitives that are sliced, manipulated, and attached. For the helmet, create a Capsule primitive from the Extended Primitives section in the Create panel, and convert it to Editable Poly. Remove one end of it, and in Vertex Edit mode, select all vertices around the bottom edge and scale them up to match the shape of the helmet in the sketches. With the vertices still selected, you can flare them by scaling the selection outward a bit.

In Figure 3.39, I went around the helmet and moved some of the vertices up and down to make the edge of the helmet curved. (I also went to some Army depots online and used pictures of helmets as a reference.) When you're satisfied with the shape of the helmet, close it up with a Cap Holes modifier.

In *Aliens*, the helmets that the marines wore had a neck protection flap that extended from the back side of the helmet. I created this by selecting some polygons at the back, extruding them down, and then shaping them. This is also visible in Figure 3.39. Don't worry about a chinstrap for the helmet at this time; we'll add faux detail for this in Chapter 6, "Skin Texturing with Photoshop CS2."

The front of the helmet has an infrared eyepiece that drops down from the helmet. Create this by extruding one or two polygons from the edge of the helmet downward and adjusting the end vertices to shape it (see Figure 3.40).

The earpieces are just Sphere primitives that are cut in half, scaled flat along the X-axis, and attached to the helmet where the ears of the character would be. If you look to the left earpiece, I've extruded a single polygon several times, bending each extrusion around to the mouth to create a microphone. After you apply a Smooth modifier, this will look great and have a low polygon count.

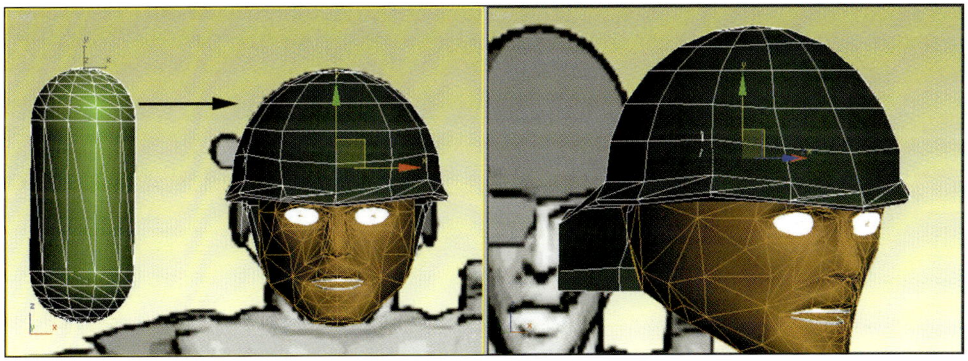

Figure 3.39 Create a helmet using a Capsule primitive. Remove the bottom of the capsule and shape the helmet using the sketches as a reference.

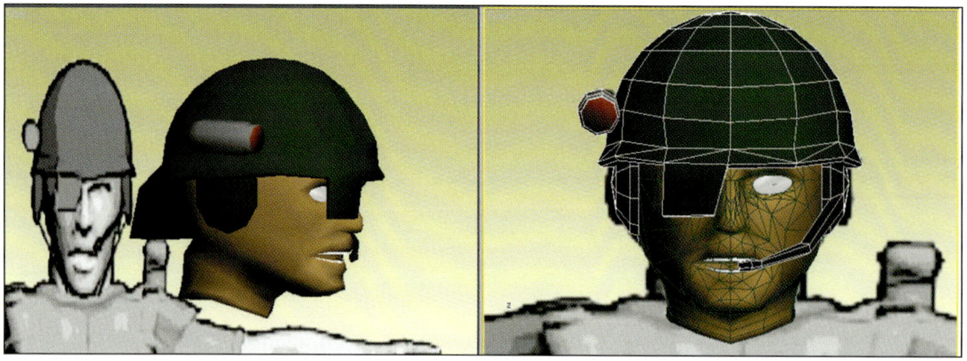

Figure 3.40 Finish the head by adding an infrared eyepiece to the front of the helmet, earpieces on both sides with a microphone, and a helmet camera. You can attach these new objects to the face, leaving the eyes unattached for animation. Extrude polygons from the head to form a neck.

Now create a helmet camera as in *Aliens* by using another Capsule primitive with one end chopped off and capped. I've attached mine to the helmet after I scaled and rotated it at a slight downward angle.

The bottom of the head has a large hole where the neck needs to attach. I manually capped this hole by creating polygons in Polygon Edit mode. (Simply adding a Cap Holes modifier would create awkward geometry.) Then I selected all these new polygons and extruded them several times, scaling and rotating each extrusion, thus shaping the neck. This completes the head. At this point, you can attach everything that constitutes the head except for the eyes. The eyes need to be free for movement and will be controlled by bones separate from the biped skeleton. (See Chapter 7, "Rigging a Character with Biped in 3ds Max.") Add a Smooth modifier to preview your work.

Finalize the head by adding a Reset Xform modifier from the Tools panel and collapsing the stack. (You might also want to add a Reset Xform modifier to the upper and lower body.) In your scene, you should now have five components dictating your model: the head, two eyes, upper body parts, and lower body parts. This will complete the model. However, don't attach everything until Chapter 7 because you'll be optimizing and texturing individual components in the next few chapters. Figure 3.41 shows the Hicks character at the completion of this chapter.

Note

After I completed my model, I attached everything to make a single mesh entity so that I could view the overall polygon count. If you do this, right-click the mesh and choose Properties from the quad menu. On the top left is the number of faces contained in the mesh. With the mesh still an Editable Poly object, you should have something in the ballpark of 5,000–7,000 polygons. However, this is not the true face count. Right-click the Editable Poly object in the Modifier panel and convert it to Editable Mesh. Go back to the Properties screen, and the face count should be double that amount. Mine came out to about 11,500 polygons, as predicted, but will be reduced by about 50 percent when we optimize the model and apply a MultiRes modifier.

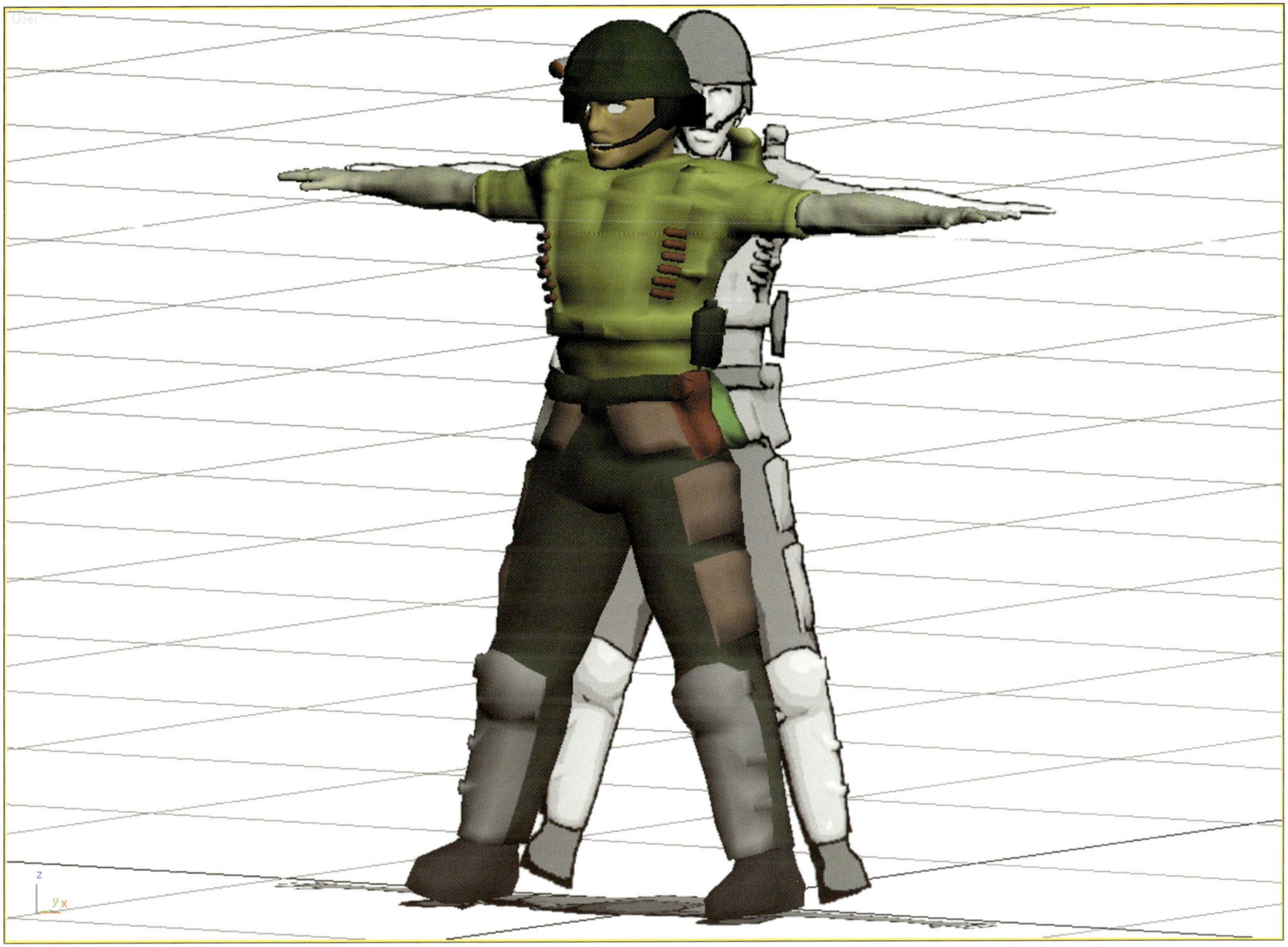

Figure 3.41 The completed Hicks model consisting of five components: the head, two eyes, upper body parts, and lower body parts.

Summary

This chapter was dedicated to creating the 3D mesh of the Hicks character using the industry standard box modeling technique, employed primarily for ease of modeling with a high quality and low polygon count ratio. You generally perform this technique by creating a simple Box primitive in 3ds Max and extruding and manipulating polygons, edges, and vertices from that base primitive.

Using three orthogonal character sketches, we built the character from the ground up, forming a boot from a Box primitive that turned into one-half of a pair of lower legs. Then we completed the other half of the lower body by using a Symmetry modifier that created a mirrored copy of the first half. After that, we added detail to the pants by extruding and manipulating more polygons around the lower body to create items like pockets, shin guards, a knife, and miscellaneous utilities.

We generated the upper body in a similar manner with box modeling, although it began with a Cylinder primitive. Through use of a Symmetry modifier, we extruded polygons from one side of the upper portion of the cylinder to create an arm and a hand. This modifier was active on the Modifier stack so that we generated the other arm dynamically as we built the first. Then we added more detail to the rest of the torso just as we did the lower body, by extruding and shaping polygons around the utility belt, a backpack in the middle of the upper portion of the torso, and a backlight object near the top. Some items like bullets and a canteen were simple primitive objects that we attached to the upper body mesh instead of as polygon extrusions.

The head was the most difficult and time consuming object to model given its inherent anatomical intricacy. However, we also box modeled it using a simple Box primitive, whose faces we carefully subdivided, manipulated, and shaped using the sketches as a reference. We finished the remainder of the head entity by creating separate eye objects that we'll individually animate later in this book, and we made a helmet with a camera, earpieces, and a microphone from Capsule and Sphere primitives. The final outcome of the model consisted of five parts: the lower and upper body, the head, and two eyes.

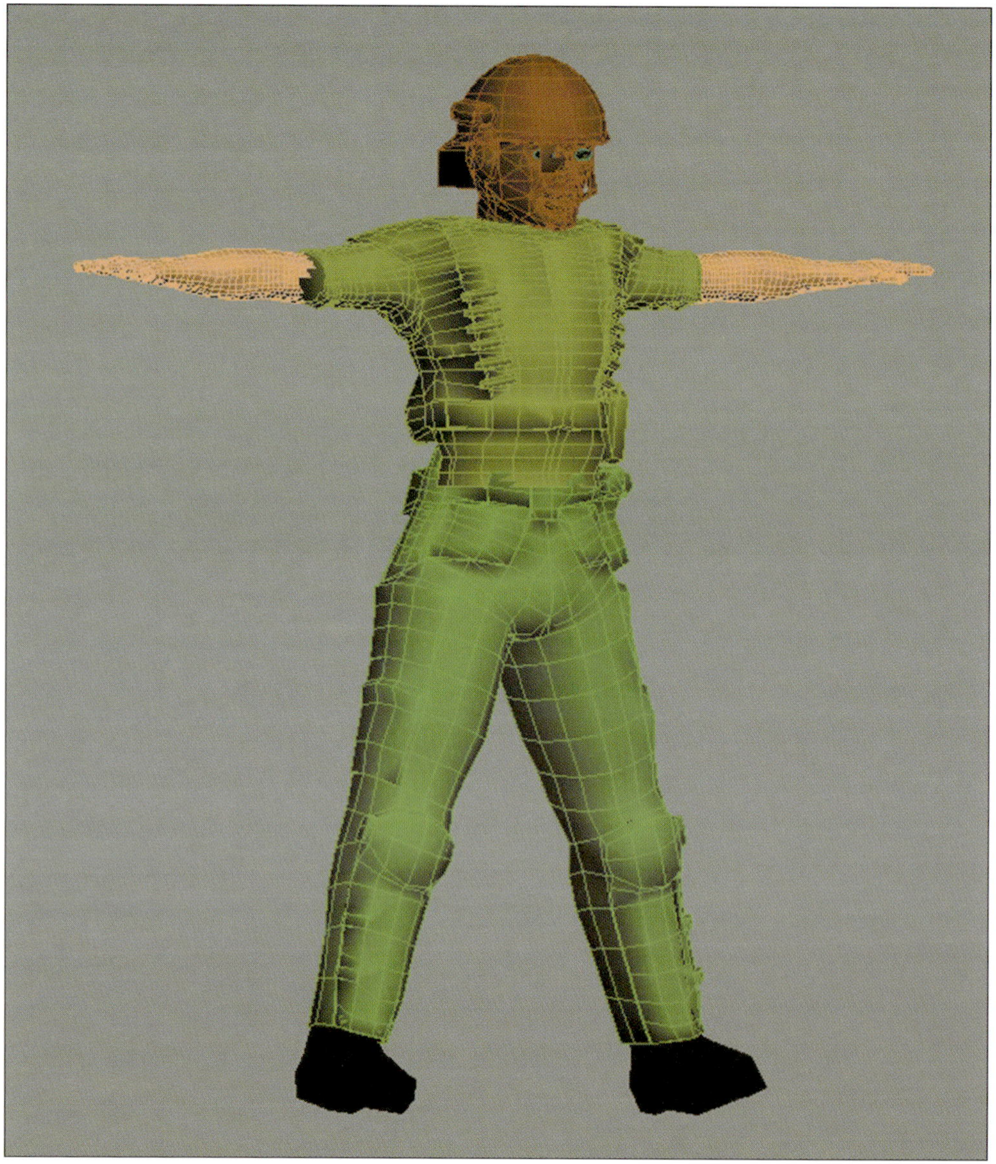

Have no fear of perfection—you'll never reach it.
—*Salvador Dali*

Chapter 4

Mesh Optimization in 3ds Max

Before you proceed with UV and texture mapping your character mesh, you must correct errors and make final adjustments to the geometry so that the mapping processes go smoothly. You can use several modifiers to accomplish this quickly, but you'll have to fix other errors manually. In this chapter, you will

- Analyze the entire mesh for errors using an STL Check modifier
- Separate your character into individual elements
- Use the STL Check modifier on each element, and fix the geometry
- Reattach the elements into seven main character components, each eventually having its own UV, texture, and normal maps
- Test optimize your character using the Optimize and MultiRes modifiers
- Learn how to change the pivot point of your character mesh

Analyzing the Character Mesh Using STL Check

I'm doing this chapter by example because I don't know exactly what errors your mesh might have or what adjustments might be required. I'm constantly creating new subobjects (vertices, edges, faces, and polygons), moving things around, knocking out polygons, and attaching and detaching elements. All these operations inevitably lead to some type of simple geometrical error that you can quickly expose with an STL Check modifier. You can discover other errors such as crossed edges by adding a checkerboard texture map to the character, after you've created the UV map, and observing any weird distortions on the texture. (See the next chapter for information on adding a checkerboard map.) You can fix all these errors fairly easily, usually by capping holes, creating new polygons, and moving or welding vertices.

Note

STL stands for Stereo Lithography, which is a file format that enables a computer to drive a laser that will build a 3D model from scratch, based on an STL file. If the STL Check modifier in 3ds Max finds errors, the computer-laser system can't properly build a 3D model. If your mesh's geometry passes this check, most likely a game engine can render the mesh without crashing.

To quickly check all the errors in your mesh, first save your scene to a MAX file because you have to reload it after this step. Select one mesh object in your scene, such as the torso, and in the Modifier panel, click the Attach List button to the right of Attach. Select all objects in the list that represent the entire character, and click Attach. You should now have a single mesh entity.

Then right-click the mesh, and at the bottom of the quad menu, select Convert To Editable Mesh. In the Modifier panel, add an STL Check modifier. In this modifier's options, make sure the option Everything is selected, and click Check at the bottom (see Figure 4.1). Press F3 to toggle between solid and wire frame modes. In wire frame mode, note the errors highlighted in red around the mesh. (My mesh had just over 600 errors.) Don't be frightened by this; fixing one problem area, like a single bad polygon, usually corrects a multitude of errors at once.

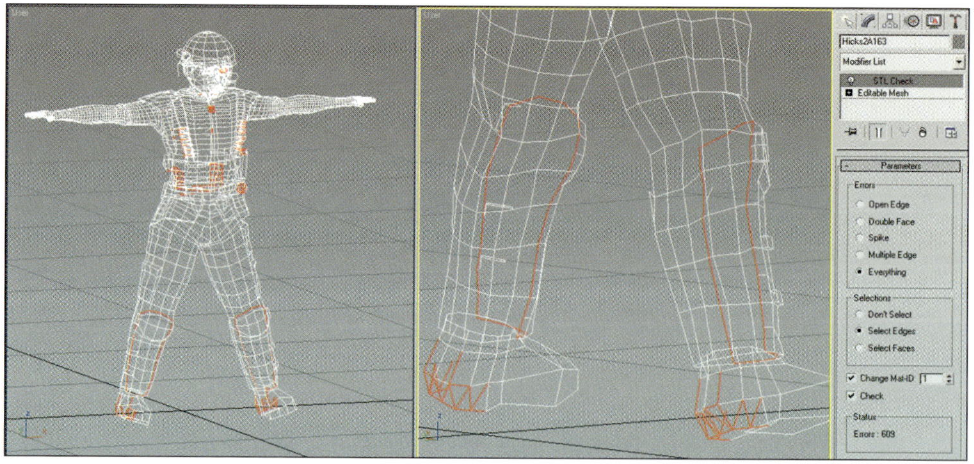

Figure 4.1 With all elements of the mesh attached, add an STL Check modifier to the stack to view errors in your mesh. (Mine are highlighted in red.)

You can view the errors by category by selecting the following in the STL Check modifier's options:

- **Open Edge.** Indicates an object—either an element or a polygon—that is not closed. For instance, if you created a simple Sphere primitive and then deleted a face or polygon, the STL Check highlights all edges around the open area. You typically resolve this by creating a new polygon or adding a Cap Holes modifier.
- **Double Face.** Indicates that the vertices defining the triangle that constitutes the face actually consist of multiple vertices per vertex position. If you enter Vertex Edit mode and click+drag on what appears to be a single vertex, the Modify panel shows more than one vertex selected. Many times you can resolve this by selecting these vertices and clicking on Weld, which welds them into a single vertex. If Weld does not resolve the problem, you must delete and re-create the faces or edges in that area.
- **Multiple Edge.** Indicates two or more edges occupying the same space. This is similar to the Double Face error. You resolve it by welding vertices or deleting edges and creating new polygons.

Tip

Clicking on Selected Edges in the STL Check modifier shows only the edges of polygons that have the problem. This helps clarify the areas on which you need to focus.

Isolating Mesh Elements

Before you begin to fix your mesh, isolate your character into individual elements so that you can operate on them separately. Reload your saved mesh that has no STL Check modifier and is still in Editable Poly form. Working from the boots upward, isolate your elements. For instance, enter Element Edit mode, and select the entire boot. Make sure all subobjects that constitute the boot are selected, and click Detach on the Modifier panel (see Figure 4.2). Name the object Boot. In the Hierarchy panel, click Affect Pivot Only and center the pivot to the object.

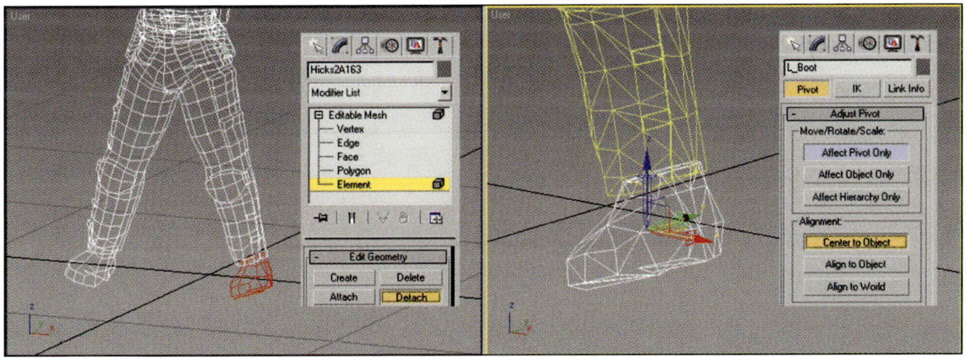

Figure 4.2 Beginning with the boot, detach it in Element Edit mode and center its pivot.

Do this for all the elements in the character mesh. In Figure 4.3, notice that I've detached 20 different main elements, which will help me unwrap them during the UV unwrapping process in Chapter 5, "UV Mapping the Character in 3ds Max."

Fixing Mesh Errors

Now that you've separated your elements, you can reapply the STL Check modifier to each item and correct its errors. I like to keep this modifier on top of the stack and work on the mesh below it, with Show End Results toggled to On. Beginning with the boot, look for the errors and zoom in on them. In Figure 4.4, I saw some multiple-edge errors, so I clicked and dragged over a single vertex in Vertex Edit mode. The Modify panel showed three vertices selected, which means that area has duplicate subobjects.

To fix this error, I can usually just click Weld on the Modifier panel to weld them together as a single vertex, but in this case, there were multiple vertices with this same problem. Instead, I applied a Weld Vertices modifier with a Threshold value of 0.01m, just below the STL Check modifier. This automatically welds all vertices in the mesh element that are within the immediate 0.01m vicinity of one another. This modifier cured all ailments in the boot according to the STL Check (see Figure 4.5).

Continuing throughout the character's mesh elements, first try the Weld Vertices modifier to fix problems. If errors persist, you have to further

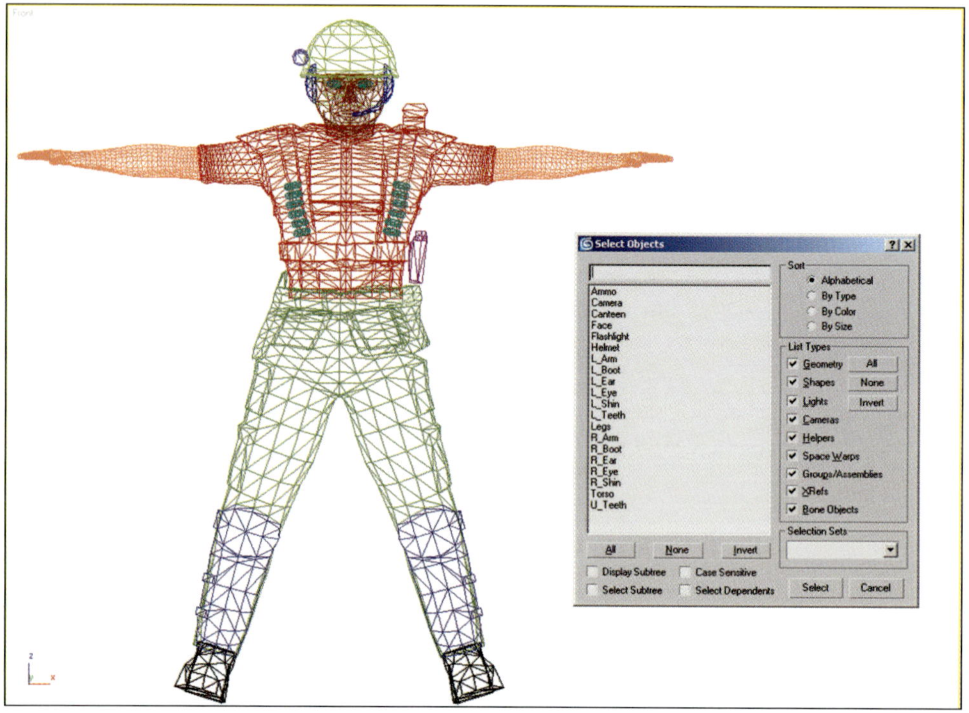

Figure 4.3 Isolate all main elements in the rest of the mesh. In this figure, I've separated 20 items, which will help me during the UV unwrapping process in the next chapter.

analyze the mesh. Look at the bad geometry and see if deleting and re-creating faces helps, or look for crossed or duplicate edges. In Figure 4.6, I found a couple of crossed edges by looking at Vertex Edit mode. The edges cross, and there are no vertices at the intersections. Sometimes you can move vertices around to uncross them. Deleting the geometry and re-creating the faces also resolves the issue.

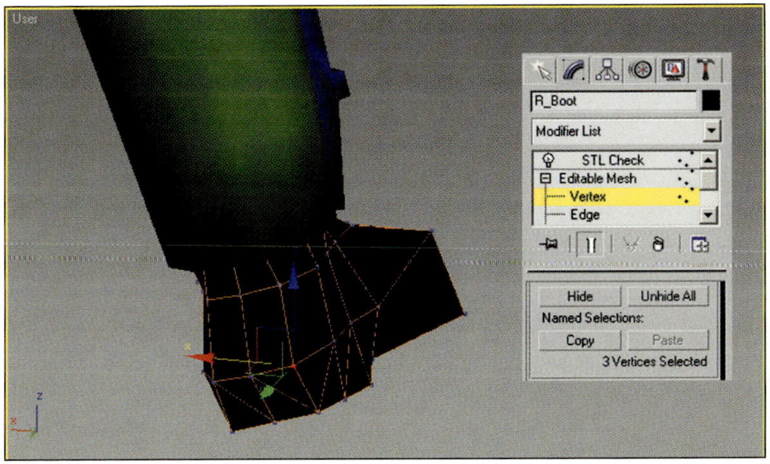

Figure 4.4 Add an STL Check modifier to the boot element. Here I selected a single vertex, but it turned out to be three vertices occupying the same space. This indicates a multiple-edge error.

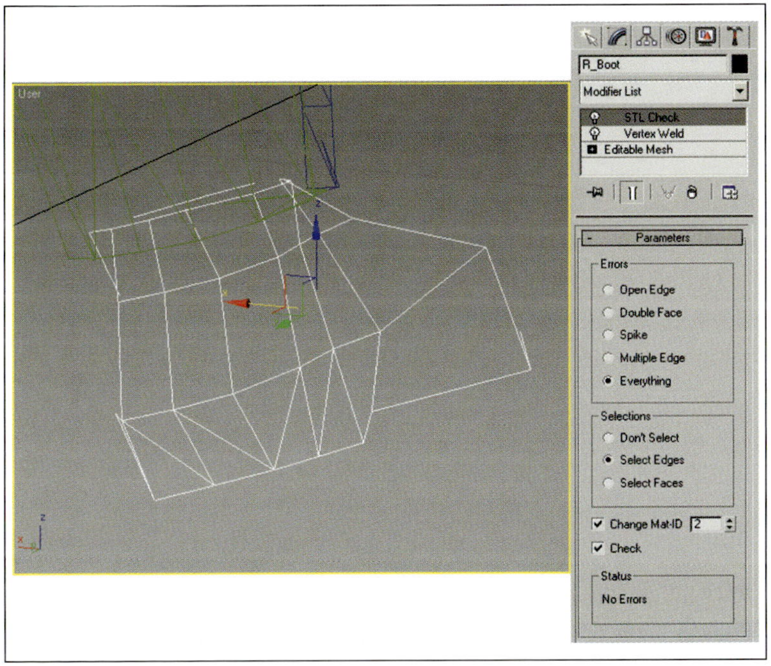

Figure 4.5 Applying a Weld Vertices modifier to the boot element fixes any errors in its mesh.

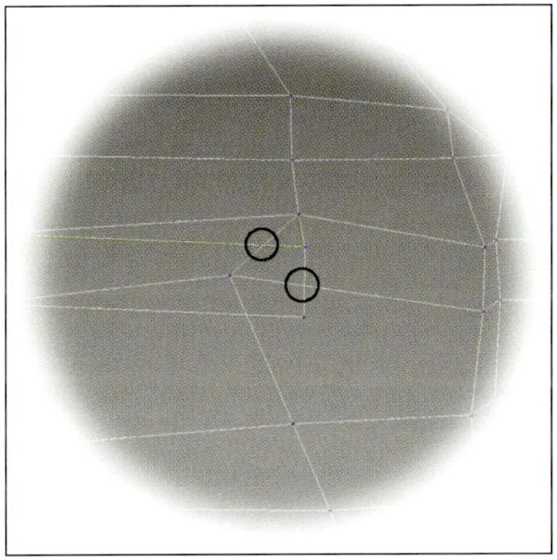

Figure 4.6 If a Weld Vertices modifier doesn't fix the geometry, look for crossed vertices or other bad polygons and either move the vertices around or delete and re-create the geometry.

Reattaching Elements and Test Optimizing

After you've finished fixing your mesh, your STL Check should issue no errors. The character mesh should now be attached into the following seven components, each having its own texture map. (During the UV unwrapping process, you can still select individual elements in Element Edit mode.)

- The head, consisting of the helmet, camera, headset and microphone, and face
- The two eyes (separate objects)
- The torso, consisting of the upper body, canteen, and ammo
- The arms and hands (separate objects)
- The lower body, consisting of the waist, flashlight, legs, and boots

After I attached my components, I reapplied an STL Check to each one to double-check the mesh for errors. Then I centered the pivot points for each.

You can perform a quick optimization and polygon reduction just to see how your mesh will look in the end. Note that this is only a test. Be sure to save your work, because you'll be working at the highest polygon count until you've created and applied the texture and normal maps. First reattach everything to form a single mesh, and then apply an Optimize modifier (see Figure 4.7). Looking at the Before/After section in the Modifier panel, my mesh went from 10,762 faces to 8,290 without changing the shape of the mesh. The target face count will eventually be between 5,000 and 7,000.

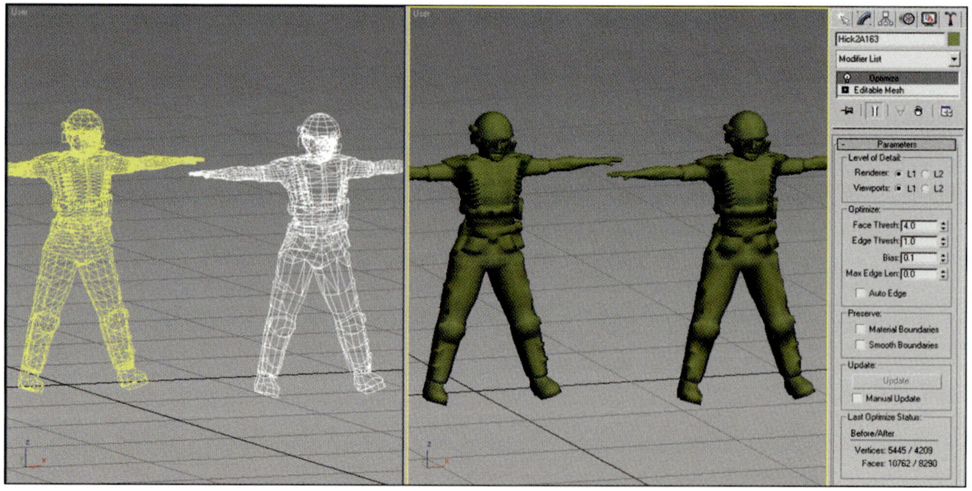

Figure 4.7 Applying an Optimize modifier to the entire mesh dropped the face count from 10,762 to 8,290 without changing the shape of the mesh.

Delete the Optimize modifier. Then apply a MultiRes modifier, and in its Options panel, click Generate. At the top of the panel, change the Vert Percent from 100 percent to 50 percent. My mesh now has 5,316 faces and still maintains most of its shape (see Figure 4.8). This modifier is great for creating multiple Levels of Detail (LODs) for video games. It isn't necessary for characters to have the same face count as they diminish in distance from the player's view. If characters maintained the same count, the computer would attempt to display inviolable detail and slow down graphics processing.

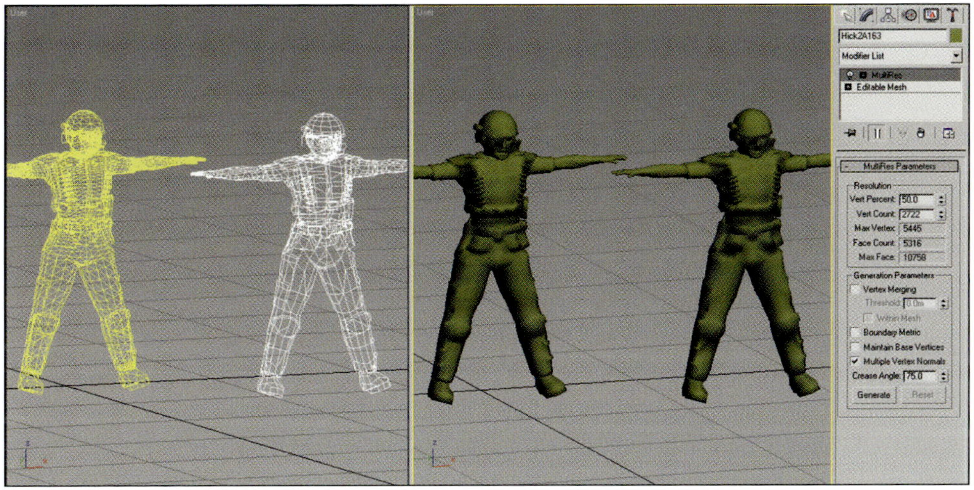

Figure 4.8 Using a MultiRes modifier at a 50 percent face count reduces my count from 10,762 to 5,316.

Changing the Character's Pivot Point

Notice that the mesh's general axis displays the Z-axis pointing up, the X-axis to the left, and the Y-axis to the rear. Game engines will specify the axial orientation; many times this is default, but some will say to have the Y- or Z-axis pointing forward. To change the pivot point, rotate the entire mesh 180 degrees about the Z-axis with Angle Snap toggled to On (see Figure 4.9). Then, in the Utilities panel, apply a Reset Xform. Now the mesh has the Y-axis pointing forward.

After you've done the optimization and pivot tests, remember to reload the original fixed mesh with the seven attached components.

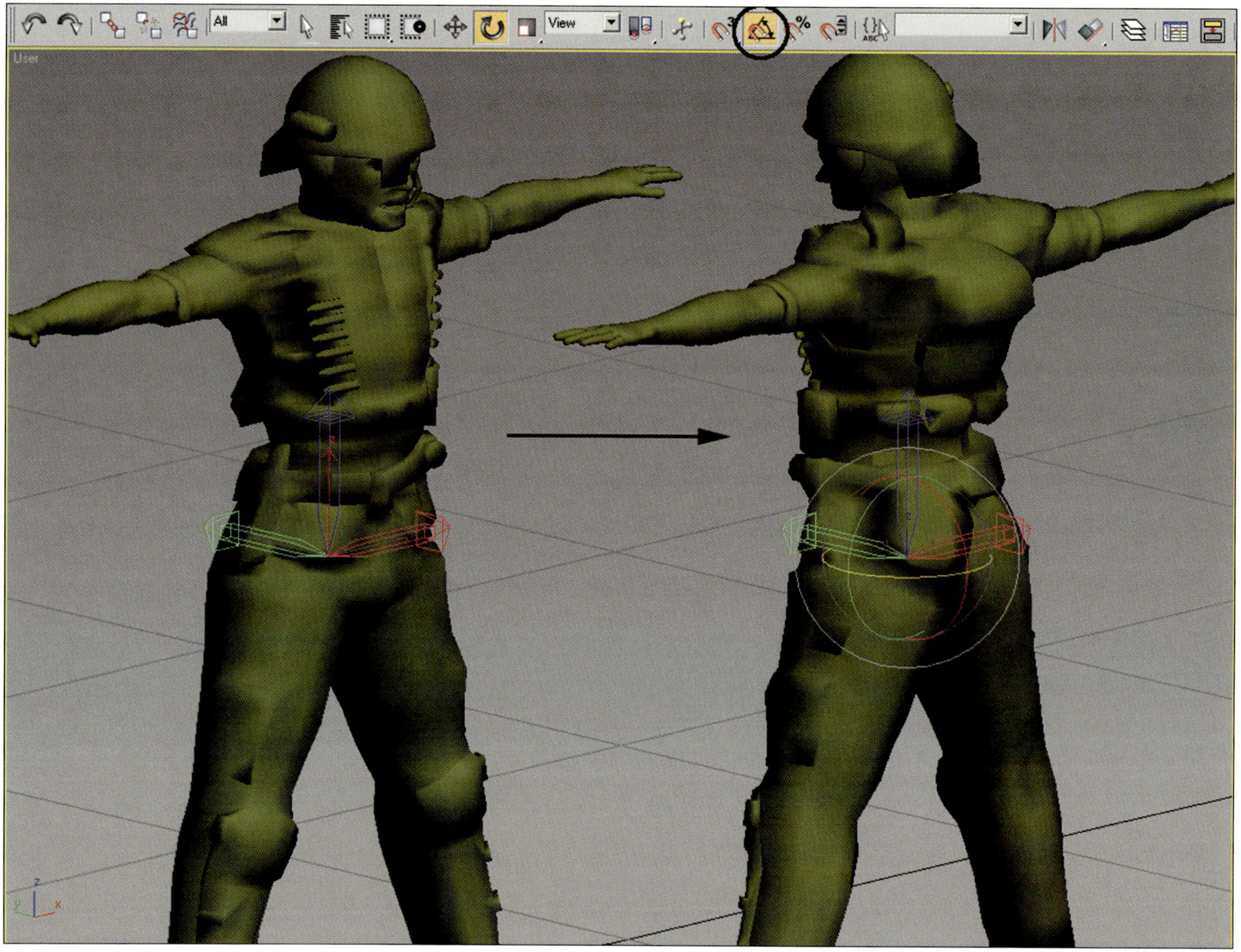

Figure 4.9 To change the character's general pivot point, rotate the entire mesh about its Z-axis 180 degrees. Apply a Reset Xform modifier to lock it.

Summary

This chapter discussed how to use the STL Check modifier to detect geometry errors in the character mesh. This modifier detects bad subobject problems, such as duplicate vertices or faces, crossed edges, and open faces or edges. By carefully analyzing the problem areas, we can usually resolve the errors by welding vertices or deleting and re-creating faces and edges. We tested optimization by applying Optimize and MultiRes modifiers, which decreased the face count dramatically from more than 10,000 faces to about 5,200, well within our final target face count. Then we attached the character mesh to seven main components—the head, two eyes, torso, arms, hands, and legs—in preparation for the next chapter on UV mapping.

Every act of creation is first an act of destruction.
—*Pablo Picasso*

Chapter 5

UV Mapping the Character in 3ds Max

With the mesh complete, cleaned, and optimized, you're ready to UV map the character. This process flattens out all the textures that make up the character so that you can paint them using Photoshop. To flatten each texture, you need to define seams. It's best to hide these seams. In this chapter, you will

- Apply the Unwrap UVW modifier to each element of the character
- Unwrap the lower body, including the legs and boots
- Unwrap the arms, including the arms and hands
- Unwrap the head and body, including the torso, face, and helmet
- Pack the final texture map
- View the resulting mappings in 3ds Max

The Mapping Process

3ds Max has several different mapping methods available to users. All of these mapping methods are available when you first apply the Unwrap UVW modifier to the object that you want to unwrap. The Unwrap UVW modifier lets you select Vertex, Edge, and Face subobjects. After you choose several Face subobjects, you can select the mapping method to use. The available default mapping methods include these:

- **Planar mapping.** Bases the mapping on a projection from a single point.
- **Cylindrical mapping.** Bases the mapping on a cylindrical-shaped object, such as the label of a can.

- **Box mapping.** Applies six Planar mappings from each direction of a box surrounding the object.
- **Spherical mapping.** Bases the mapping on a spherical-shaped object, such as an orange.
- **Pelt mapping.** Pulls each of the seam borders outward to stretch the mapping coordinates.

The mapping method to use depends on the type of body part that you are applying the texture to. Cylindrical mapping works well for legs and arms; Box or Spherical mapping is generally used for the head, torso, and feet; and Planar mapping is useful for the hands and the soles of the feet. However, for many complex objects, the Pelt mapping method combines the benefits of each of these methods.

Of all the available mapping methods, the Pelt mapping method is probably the easiest to visualize and use on characters. This mapping method splits the mapping along predefined texture seams. These seams are then aligned to a circular stretcher (see Figure 5.1) and pulled until all the vertices are exposed, creating a flat, stretched mapping of UVs. Pelt mapping lets you pull the seams of the object, causing all the interior faces to be stretched flat. For most of Hicks' parts, we'll use the Pelt mapping method. Pelt mapping is similar to the way the skinned fur of an animal is stretched, thereby giving it its name.

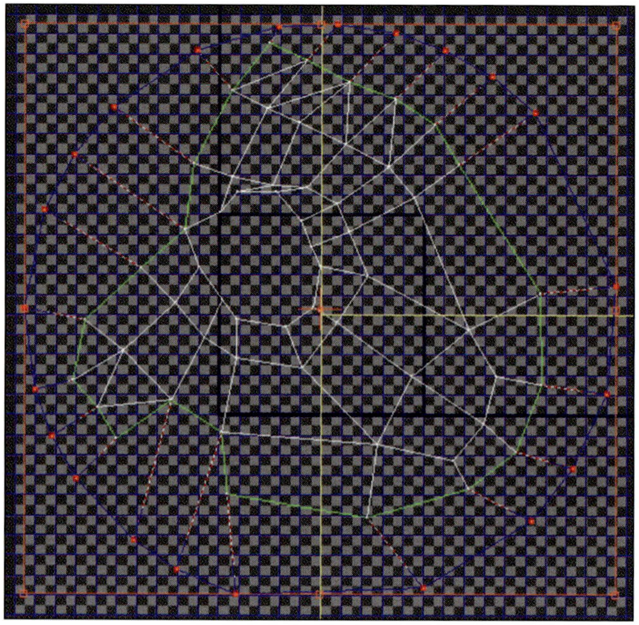

Figure 5.1 The Pelt stretcher is used to pull seam vertices away from the rest of the piece.

When you select a mapping type, a gizmo appears in the viewport. This gizmo defines how the mapping is projected, and you can manipulate it by using the Move, Rotate, and Scale tools. The Command Panel also includes several buttons to help position the current mapping gizmo, including Align X, Align Y, Align Z, Fit, Center, Best Align, Align to View, and Reset. Of these, the Best Align button is probably the most helpful. It centers the gizmo and aligns it to the boundaries of the current selection.

You can view the unwrapped UVs in the Unwrap UVW window, which you open by clicking the Edit button. This window has several menus and controls for working with the UVs.

The Edit UVWs window includes three additional mapping methods: Flatten, Normal, and Unfold. These methods are useful in certain situations. The Unfold mapping type is great for unwrapping simple geometric objects because they show all the faces.

Selecting Body Parts

In the previous chapter, we divided the Hicks character into several parts so that we could texture them separately. We can use symmetry to reduce the number of textures that we need to create, but the base list will include the following:

- Boots
- Legs (including the pelvis region)
- Torso
- Arms (including the hands)
- Head
- Eyes

For each body part that is selected, you can choose a specific set of faces to be textured separately. For example, when texturing the arms, you'll want to separate all the hand polygon faces from the rest of the arm and scale them up. In this way, you can draw the hands with greater detail than the rest of the arms.

You need to select faces before you can choose a mapping type. Whenever you select a subobject in the viewport, the same subobject selection is also selected in the Edit UVWs window, and vice versa. This provides two ways to select the appropriate subobjects.

The Command Panel also includes several selection controls. When Ignore Backfacing is disabled, it selects all subobjects that you drag over; when the option is disabled, it selects only those subobjects that face the current view. You can also select by element or select all subobjects within a given Planar angle. The Expand button has a plus sign on it. It expands the current selection and tries to stick within the given seams. The Reduce button has a minus sign and does the opposite.

Defining Seams

The important thing to remember about map seams is that you want them to run along those parts of the body where they aren't noticed. Seams are the places where one side of the texture map matches the opposite side. Photoshop includes some features for making seamless textures, but even with these, there can be some discoloring along the seams, so it's best to hide the seams when possible.

The Unwrap UVW modifier includes several ways to define the mapping seams (see Figure 5.2). The Edit Seams button lets you select which edges to use as the map seam. The Point to Point Seam button lets you select beginning and ending points,

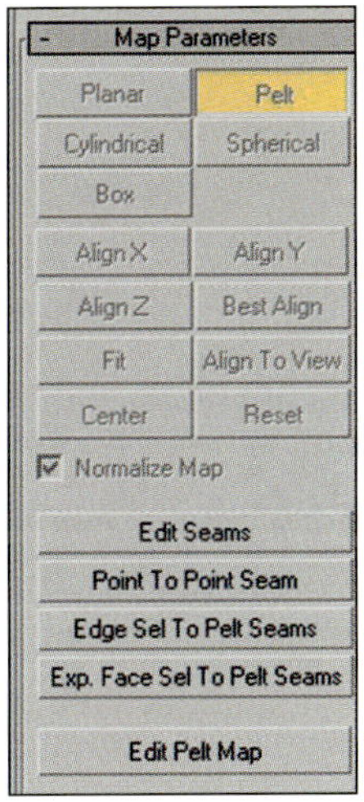

Figure 5.2 These four buttons are different ways to define mapping seams.

and the seam is automatically generated to run between these two points. The Edge Sel to Pelt Seams button lets you define a seam by first making a selection of edges and then turning it into a seam.

When you select an object, it often has seams defined by material or smoothing groups or based on the way you created it. For many objects, you can select individual object elements by selecting all the faces for a given object and clicking the Exp. Face Sel to Pelt Seams button. This button expands the face selection to the current face seams. It is also a useful way to check whether your defined seams completely separate.

If you correctly place your seams, when you apply your texture to the model, the seams are placed in the most unnoticeable location. See Table 5.1 for a quick guide on mapping techniques and where to align seams. Sometimes it's easier to create a seam running along the midline of the body than along the side. It's better to have a straight seam than one that is jagged even if it's hidden.

Table 5.1 Seam Alignment Suggestions

Mesh Portion	Seam Location
Head (normal)	Top/back
Head (oblong)	Top
Face	n/a
Body	Sides
Tail	Bottom
Arms/legs	Inside, facing body
Feet	Inside, facing body
Bottom of feet	n/a

Stretching the Pelt

After you define the seams, you can open the stretcher, which aligns all the seam vertices along the outer edge of the stretcher interface. You can see this interface by clicking the Edit Pelt Map button. This also opens the Pelt Map Parameters dialog box (see Figure 5.3), where you can set the options for the stretcher. After you set the options, click the Simulate Pelt Pulling button to have the stretcher pull all the internal vertices toward the outer edge of the stretcher.

Positioning the UVs

After you apply a mapping type to a set of faces, you should drag the mapped UVs away from the rest of the UV to keep them separate. You can also create a selection set for the mapped faces if you need to recall the selection.

At the top of the Edit UVWs window are several transformation buttons that let you move, rotate, and scale the selected mapped faces. There is also a button to mirror the selected UVs.

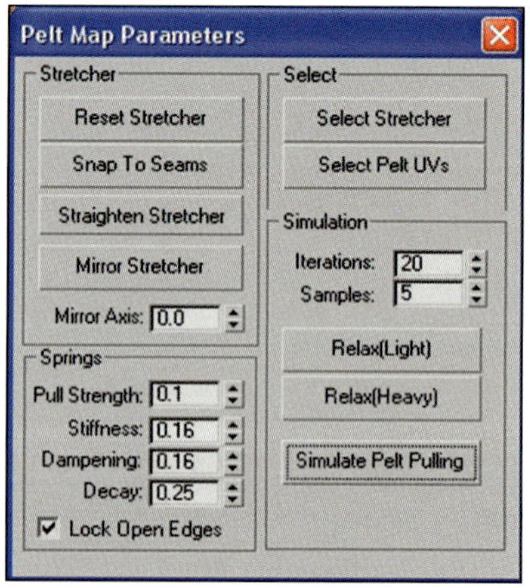

Figure 5.3 The Pelt Map Parameters dialog box includes several options for defining how to apply the Pelt mapping.

The Freeform Mode button surrounds the selection with a gizmo that you can use to move, rotate, and scale the selection with a single gizmo.

Stitching Edges

As you select faces, sometimes you accidentally miss a single face. If you don't map this missed face, it might get a strange color (or no color) applied to it. To fix a missing face, simply select the edge that is close to the selection where it should be and choose Tools, Stitch Selection. This stitches in the missing face to its matching edge. You can also use the feature to weld vertices together to close separated faces.

Packing UVs

After you've mapped all the UVs, the final step is to pack them into a condensed space. There's no sense in creating a texture that is larger than needed, and the Edit UVWs window includes a menu option that packs all the selected UVs into the given space. It doesn't always do the best job of packing UVs, so you might want to manually place the UVs before saving the mapping.

Step 1: Unwrap the Boots

We'll start with unwrapping the boots, which are separate objects. If the boots were part of the same object, we could flip and apply the resulting mapping to the opposite boot so that a single texture would cover both boots, but because the boots are separate, we need two mappings. Having two mappings lets us color the boots differently. For example, we might use a different mud splatter on each boot.

The best method for mapping the boot skin is to use Pelt mapping, but before we Pelt map the boot, we'll want to separate the boot's sole and define a seam along the back of the boot. This will leave just the surface of the boot to be stretched.

1. Select and zoom in on the left boot object. Then apply the Unwrap UVW modifier from the Modifiers, UVW Coordinates menu. Select the Face subobject mode, and disable the Ignore Backfacing option. Then drag over the entire boot in the viewport to select all the faces (see Figure 5.4).

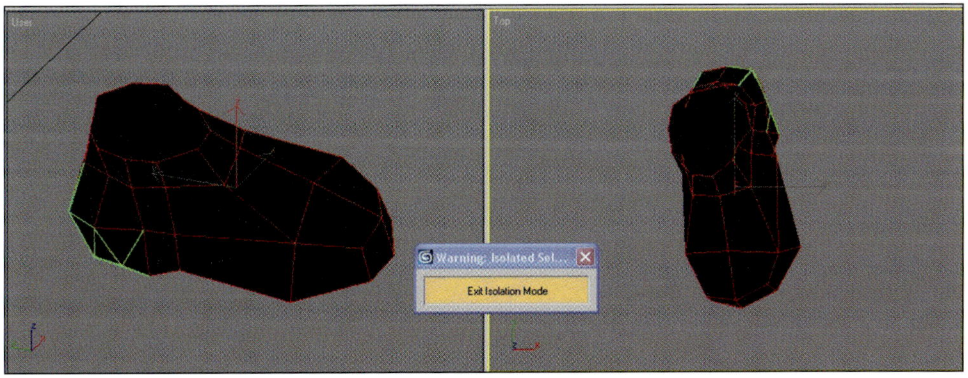

Figure 5.4 Apply the Unwrap UVW modifier and select all Face subobjects.

Tip

A quick and easy way to zoom in on the selected object is with the Isolate Selection feature. Found in the Tools menu or by pressing Alt+Q, this command hides all other objects except for the current selection and zooms in on the object in all viewports. To exit this mode, click the Exit Isolation Mode button that is floating above the viewports.

2. Rotate to the bottom of the foot, and select the polygons on the sole of the boot. Then click on the Planar button to apply a Planar mapping. This opens the Edit UVWs window. Select and scale the selected UVs and move them to the side so that they're out of the way for now (see Figure 5.5).
3. Select the remaining polygons in the Edit UVWs window by dragging over them. The faces turn red when selected and click the Pelt button (see Figure 5.6). This selects all the remaining polygon faces in the viewports. Then click on the Best Align button to orient the mapping gizmo.

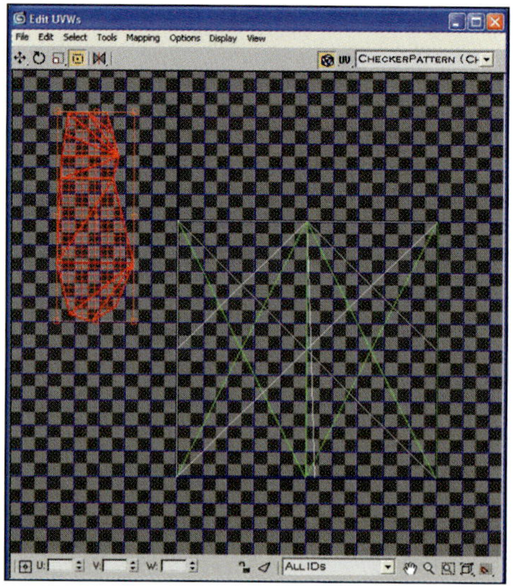

Figure 5.5 Select the polygons for the sole of the boot and apply a Planar mapping.

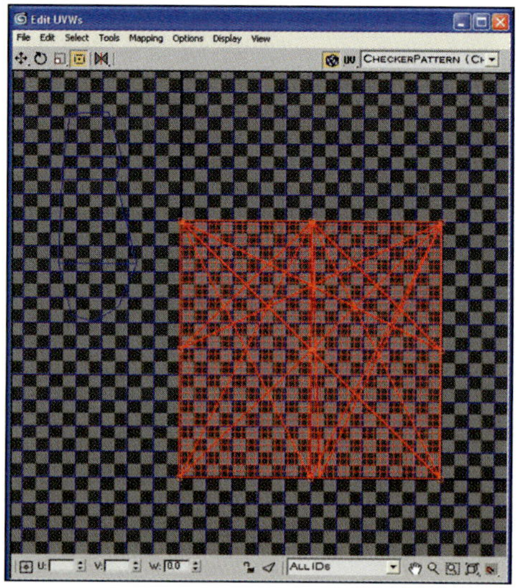

Figure 5.6 Select the remaining polygons for the boot and apply a Pelt mapping.

4. Click on the Edit Seams button, and define the boot seams along the top rim of the boot and up the back side of the boot. The seams are displayed as light blue lines (see Figure 5.7). The seam for the sole of the boot is already defined because the sole has already been mapped.
5. In the Command Panel, click on the Edit Pelt Map button. This opens the Stretcher within the Edit UVWs window. Click on the Simulate Pelt Pulling button three times to stretch out the UVs (see Figure 5.8). Then remove the Stretcher by closing the Pelt Map Parameters dialog box.
6. Click on the Pelt button to exit Pelt mapping mode. Then scale and resize the boot UVs in the Edit UVWs window (see Figure 5.9).

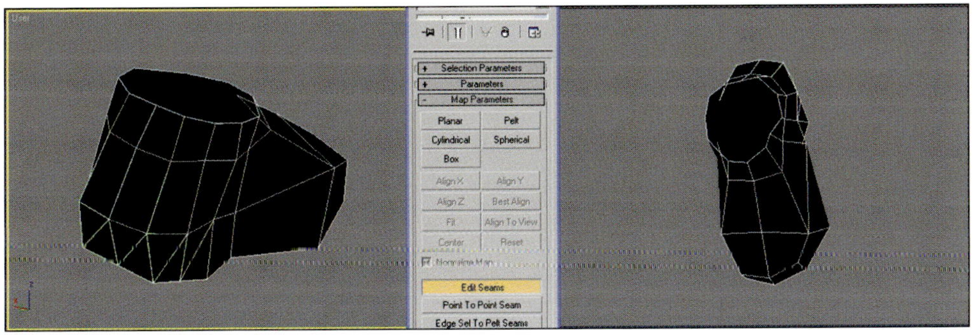

Figure 5.7 Define the seams for the Pelt mapping.

7. In the center of the boot UVs is a circular set of faces marked in green. These vertices are the top of the boot, which will be hidden by the leg and aren't needed. Select these faces and detach them from the rest of the boot UVs using the Tools, Detach command. Then scale them down and move them to the side of the other UVs (see Figure 5.10).

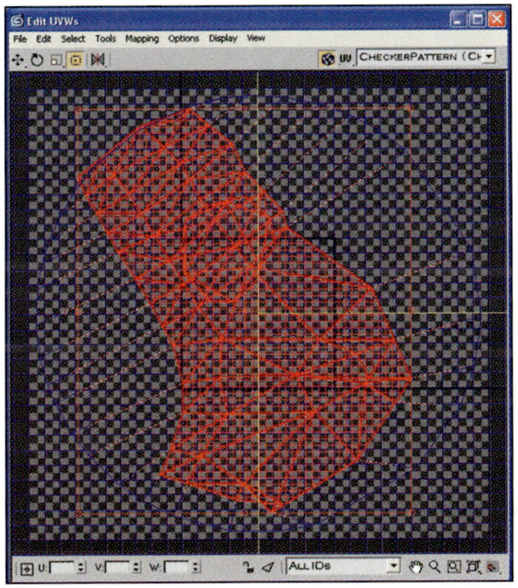

Figure 5.8 Stretch out the Pelt mapping with the Simulate Pelt Pulling button.

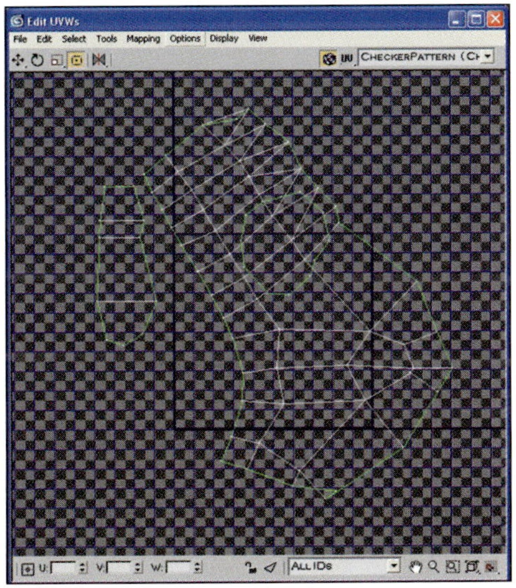

Figure 5.9 The boot UVs are scaled and positioned next to the boot sole UVs.

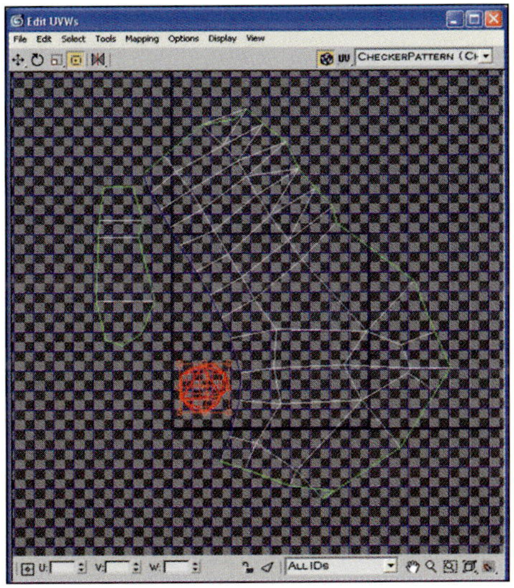

Figure 5.10 Select and detach the faces for the top of the boot.

8. In the Options section of the Edit UVWs window, set the map resolution to 256×256 and choose the Tools, Pack UVs command. This automatically rotates and scales the UVs to fit within the specified map (see Figure 5.11).

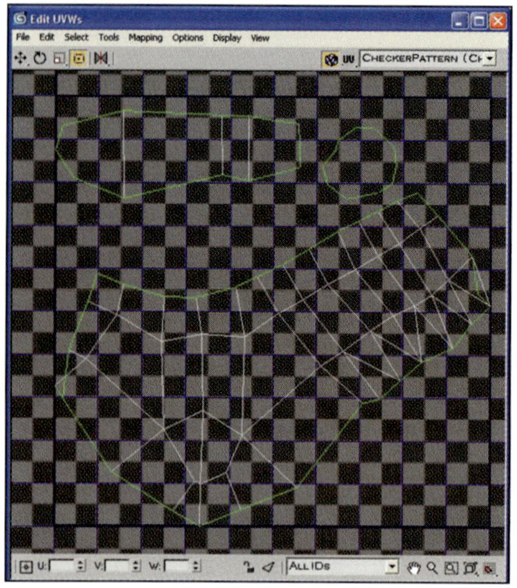

Figure 5.11 Packing the UVs automatically scales and rotates them to fit within the specified map.

9. Exit the Unwrap UVW subobject mode. Then repeat these steps for the opposite boot. With the entire character visible, select and drag the Unwrap UVW modifier from the Modifier Stack for the mapped boot, and drop it on the opposite boot to apply the same modifier to that boot. It will need to be changed, but you can reuse the selections to make the mapping go more quickly.

Step 2: Unwrap the Legs

Next we'll move onto the legs and the pelvis region. The legs are symmetrical, but the items around Hick's utility belt are different on each side, so we'll need to create a separate mapping for the pelvis region. Let's start by getting the legs unfolded and stashed away. Here we have the option of symmetrically stacking the legs for texturing or texturing each one separately. For this character and Hicks' utility belt, we'll keep the legs separate. This uses up some of the precious texture space, but it gives us a chance to add different details to each leg.

1. Select the legs body part and apply the Unwrap UVW modifier; then select the Face subobject mode. With the legs selected, choose the Tools, Isolate Selected command to zoom in on Hicks' legs. Then click the Lasso Selection tool. In the Command Panel, disable the Ignore Backfacing option so that your selection will include faces on the other side of the model, too. Draw a selection completely around the leg (see Figure 5.12).

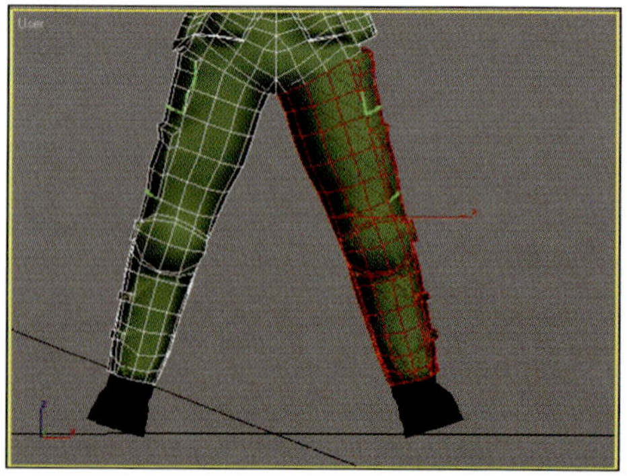

Figure 5.12 Use the Lasso tool with the Ignore Backfacing option disabled to select one of Hicks' legs.

2. With the leg faces selected, click on the Point to Point Seam button, and define a seam that circles the top and bottom of the leg and runs down the inseam (see Figure 5.13).

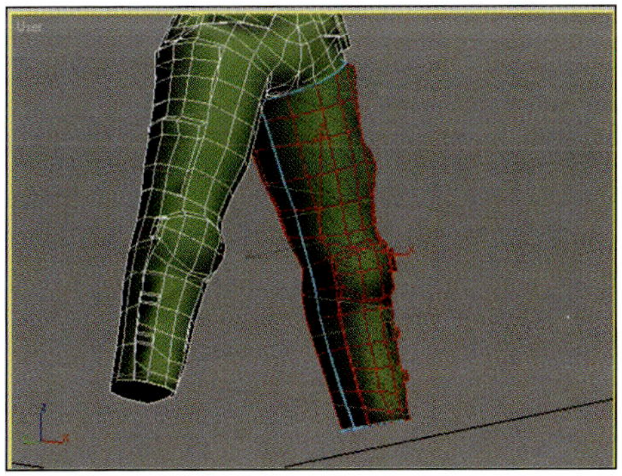

Figure 5.13 Pelt seams are defined along the top and bottom of the leg and along the inseam.

3. Click on the Pelt button in the Command Panel. This adds a Planar gizmo to the scene. Rotate, manipulate, and position the Planar gizmo so that it runs the length of the leg (see Figure 5.14). The easiest way to do this is to click the Best Align button.

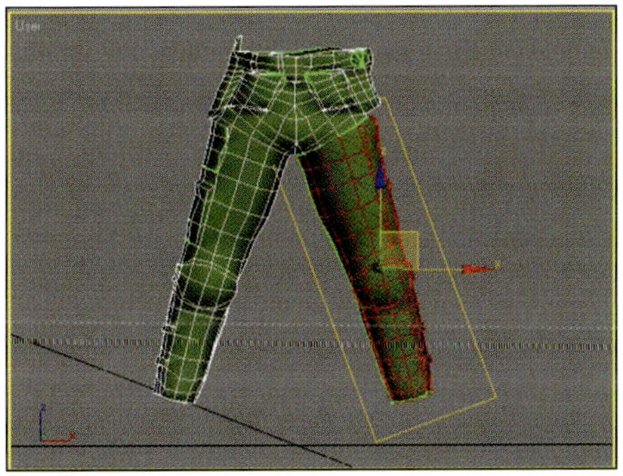

Figure 5.14 Rotate and position the Planar gizmo to run the length of the leg.

Tip

Remember that anything we do to the texture points in this program does not physically affect the vertices of the mesh model. We're only messing with the model's texture coordinates, which, before unwrapping, represent a 1:1 correspondence with the mesh's vertices.

4. Click the Edit Pelt Map button to open the stretcher for the Pelt mapping. Click several times on the Simulate Pelt Pulling button to stretch out the Pelt mapping UVs (see Figure 5.15). This stretches the entire selected leg except for the kneepad and shin area. Close the Pelt Mapping Parameters dialog box to hide the stretcher. Click the Pelt button to exit Pelt mode, and drag the UVs in the Edit UVWs window to the side, away from the rest of the UV faces.

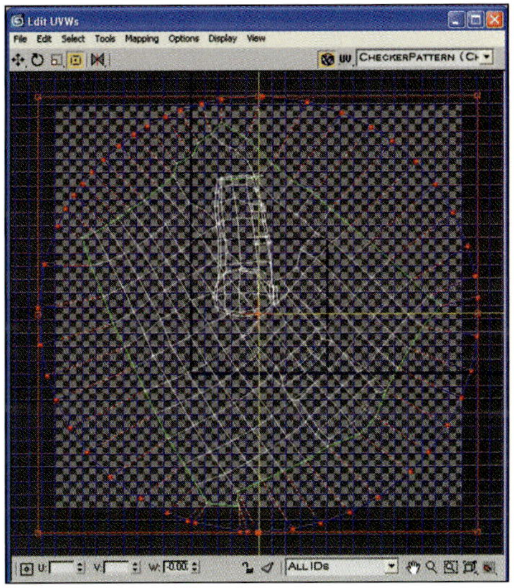

Figure 5.15 Stretch out the Pelt mapping in the Edit UVWs window.

5. Click on the Exp. Face Sel to Pelt Seams button. This selects the kneepad and shins that weren't stretched. With these UVs selected, drag them away from the rest of the leg (see Figure 5.16). Then select and separate the UVs for the bottom edge of the leg.
6. Repeat steps 2 and 5 for the opposite leg, so that the UVs for the opposite leg are also separated from the rest of the UVs (see Figure 5.17).

Tip

If two objects are symmetrical, you can match the UVs on top of one another so that you can use a single texture for both objects. This saves texture space, which can quickly use the available memory for a game.

7. Select the faces that make up the flashlight on the left hip, and apply a Pelt mapping. Then stretch out the mapping and use the Exp. Face Sel to Pelt Seams button to select and separate the cylinder at the end of the flashlight. With the cylinder selected, choose the Mapping, Unfold Mapping method. Then scale down the cylinder to be fairly small (see Figure 5.18).

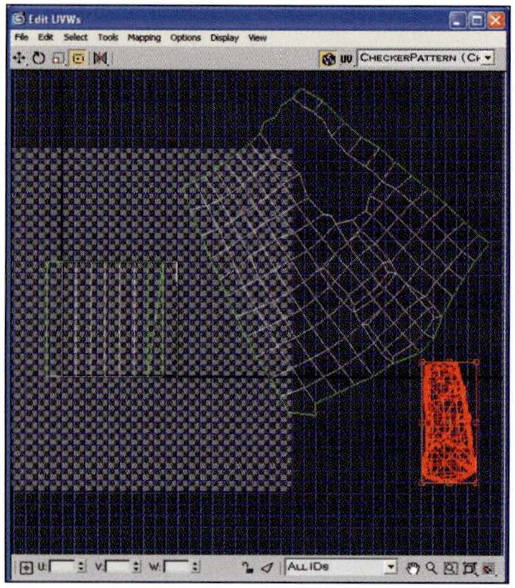

Figure 5.16 Select and drag the kneepad and shin objects away from the rest of the leg.

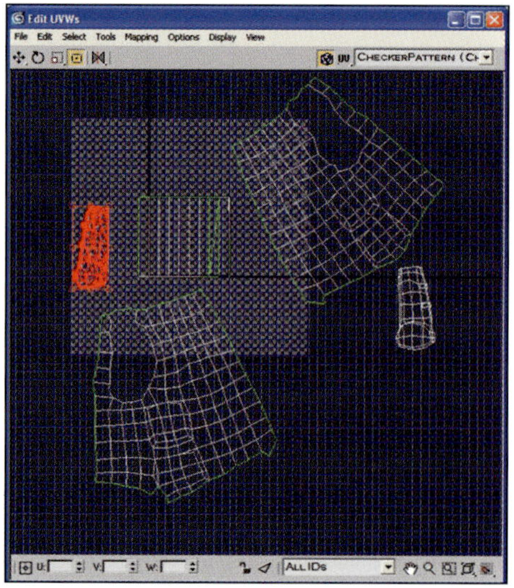

Figure 5.17 Repeat for the other leg.

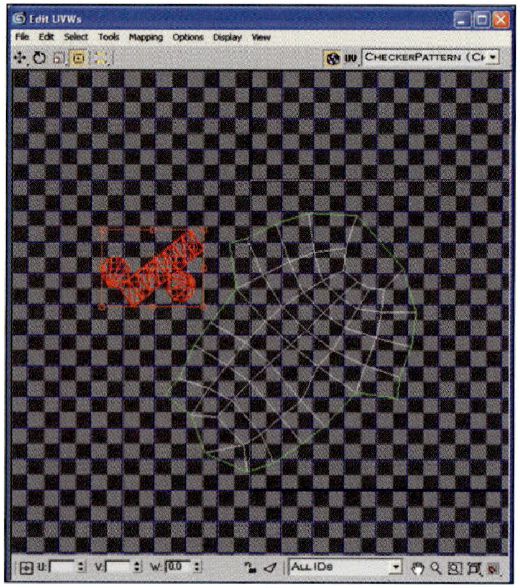

Figure 5.18 Unwrap the flashlight object, including the cylinder positioned on its front.

8. Repeat step 7 for the first aid kit on the back left hip of Hicks (see Figure 5.19).
9. Select all the remaining UVs in the Edit UVWs window. Then add the seams along the top of the pelvis and down the outer left leg along the flashlight, and create a Pelt mapping. Split the pelvis into two parts, and create a Pelt mapping for each half (see Figure 5.20).
10. After you've mapped the entire lower body, select all the UVs and choose the Tools, Pack UVs command to consolidate all the UVs into the texture area. Then move through the UVs and separate any overlapping vertices to clean the overall map (see Figure 5.21).

Caution

If at any point you try to relax your cut selection and something out of the ordinary happens (for instance, the selection suddenly becomes enormous), something is wrong with the mesh of the object. The only thing you can do is return to 3ds Max and fix the problem. Usually the problem is something as simple as an open face, an isolated vertex that's attached to nothing, or something similar. Just zoom close to the mesh, and you'll usually see the problem.

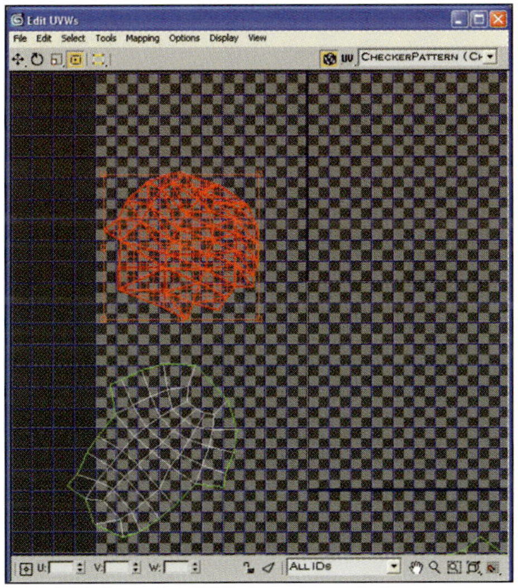

Figure 5.19 You can also unwrap the first aid kit independent from the rest of the pelvis.

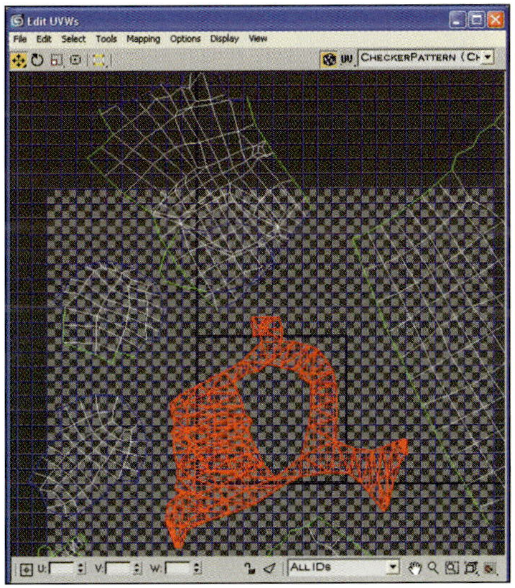

Figure 5.20 The remaining faces are split into two halves of the pelvic region.

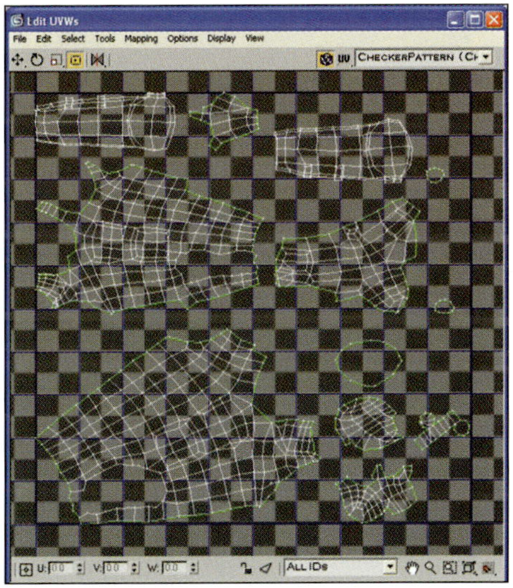

Figure 5.21 Pack and clean up all the UVs to make them easy to texture.

This concludes the leg. I think the most valuable portion of all of it was fixing the mesh. Kinda cool, yes? Now, normally I'd just say, "Repeat for the arms." However, our character's arms are quite different from those of other characters, so we'll do that next. It would also be a good idea to save your file so that you won't lose your work. Oh, and if you wanna take a little break to stretch your own legs, go ahead. I'll wait.

Step 3: Unwrap the Arms and Hands

The biggest issue I have with Hicks' arms is his fingers. There's a lot going on there with all the joints and skin folds. However, because there won't be a whole lot of texture detail on them, and most of the hand will be covered by fingerless gloves, unwrapping and texturing it won't be too hard. We can simply split the arm down its length and divide the hand in half. Sound good? Well, if you were a movie producer and needed this character in your film, that wouldn't sound good at all. In fact, digital movie characters nowadays have every point of their UVs carefully mapped and placed across multiple maps, because extreme detail is of utmost importance. But, because nobody will notice the itsy bitsy finger detail in a video game, why bother?

1. Select the arm object and isolate it from the rest of the body using the Tools, Isolate Selection command. Then apply the Unwrap UVW modifier to the arm/hand object (see Figure 5.22).
2. Select all the polygon faces for the arm from the wrist up with the Ignore Backfacing option disabled. Then deselect the object cap at the end of the arm where the elbow is. Create a seam running along the inside of the arm using the Point to Point Seam button (see Figure 5.23).

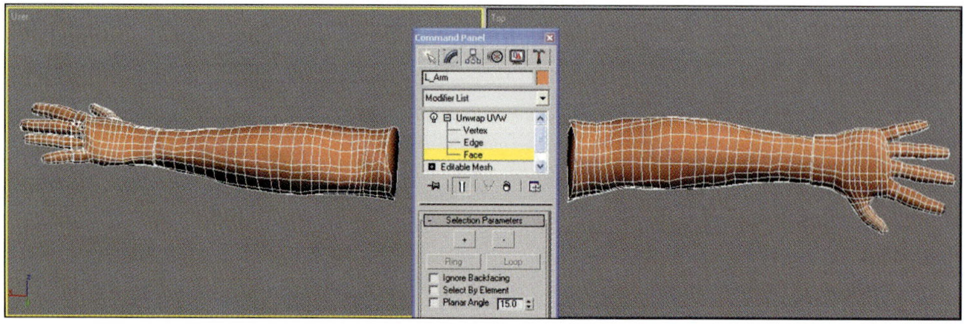

Figure 5.22 Apply the Unwrap UVW modifier to the arm object.

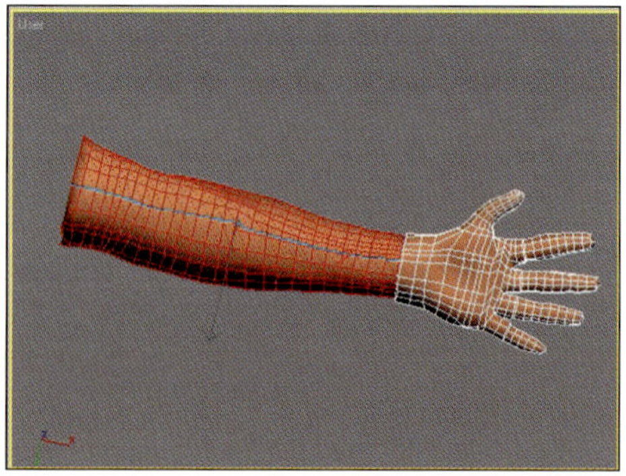

Figure 5.23 The arm is selected, and a single seam is defined that runs along the arm.

3. Click on the Pelt button to apply a Pelt mapping, and then click on the Edit Pelt Map button to view the Stretcher. Click several times on the Simulate Pelt Pulling button in the Pelt Map Parameters dialog box to smooth out the Pelt map into a square section (see Figure 5.24).

4. Close the Pelt Map Parameters dialog box, and click the Pelt button to exit Pelt mapping mode. Then drag the UVs in the Edit UVWs window off to the side and out of the way (see Figure 5.25).

5. Add a seam that splits the hand in half into a palm side and the back of the hand. You can use the Point to Point Seam button to make a seam that runs up and down each finger and down the sides of the hand (see Figure 5.26).

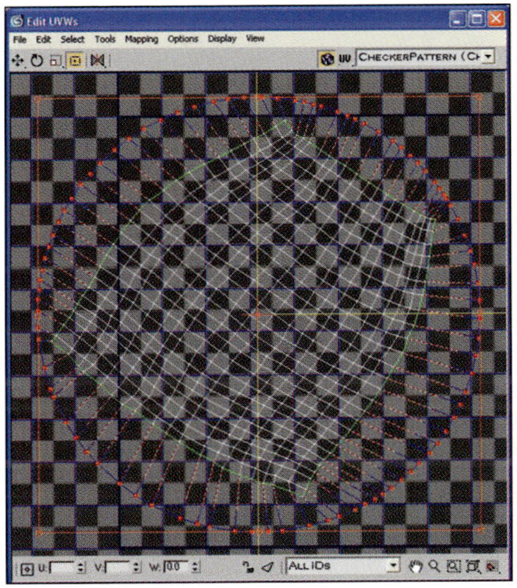

Figure 5.24 Using a Pelt mapping, the forearm stretches out to a square.

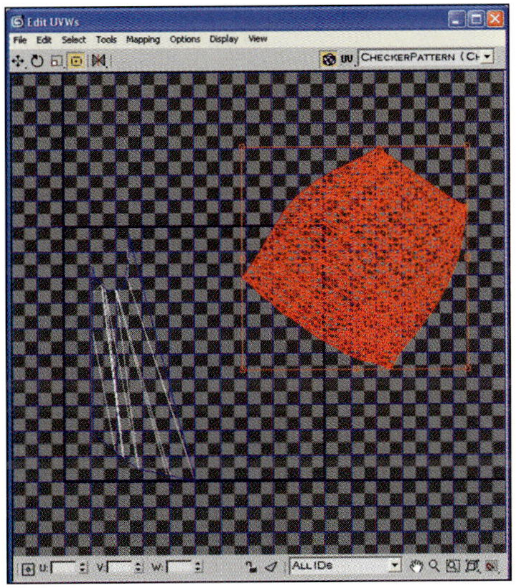

Figure 5.25 Move the UVs for the arm out of the way in the Edit UVWs window.

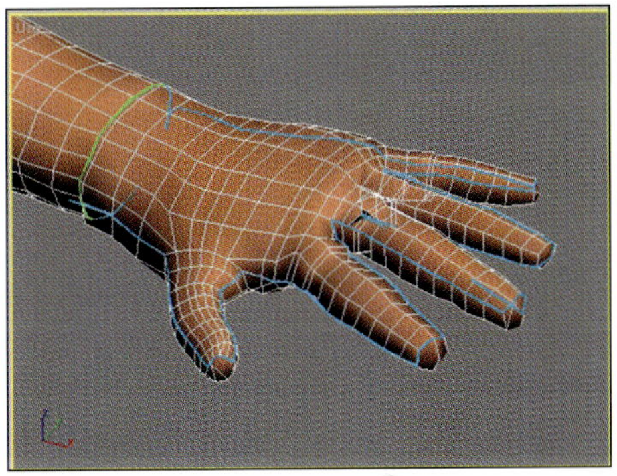

Figure 5.26 Create a seam that divides the hand into top and bottom sections.

6. With the seam in place, select all the faces in the hand object, and click the Exp. Face Sel to Pelt Seam button. This selects only one side of the hand along the seam (see Figure 5.27). If nothing happens, you have a gap in your seam. Zoom in close to the seam, and make sure it's complete.
7. With the faces selected, click the Pelt button followed by the Edit Pelt Map button. If you stretch the hand, the resulting finger UVs are pulled completely out of place. To maintain the basic shape of the hand, click on the Snap to Seams button in the Pelt Map Parameters dialog box. This makes the stretcher the same shape as the hand seams. Then scale the stretcher up, and click the Simulate Pelt Pulling button to stretch out the Pelt map (see Figure 5.28).
8. Drag over the remaining UVs in the Edit UVWs window to select the other half of the hand. Repeat step 7 for the opposite side of the hand, and drag the stretched UVs for the opposite side of the hand away from the other parts in the Edit UVWs window (see Figure 5.29).
9. Select all faces in the Edit UVWs window, and choose the

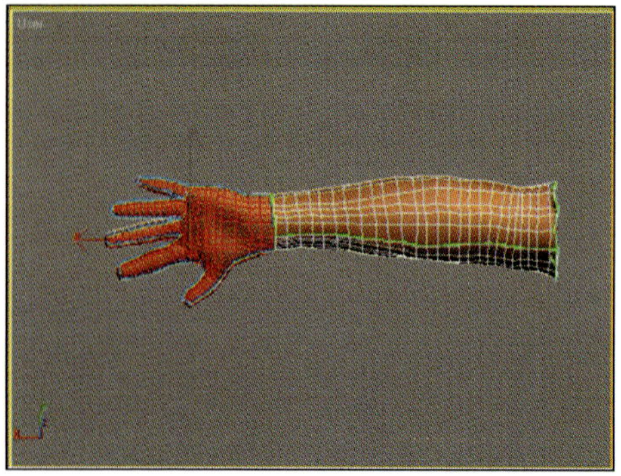

Figure 5.27 Select all the faces on one-half of the hand.

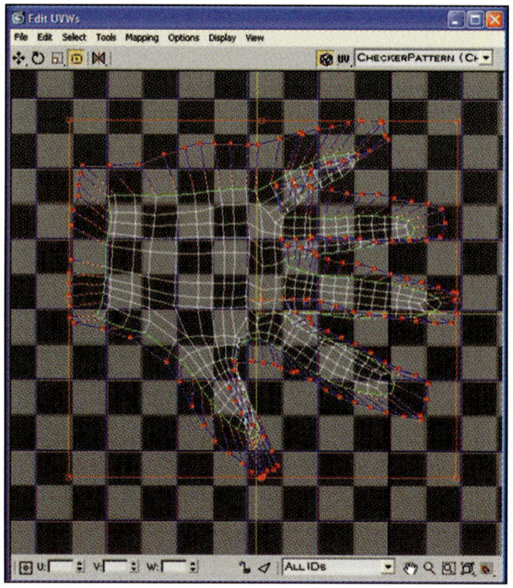

Figure 5.28 Use the Snap to Seams button to make the Stretcher be the same shape as the hand.

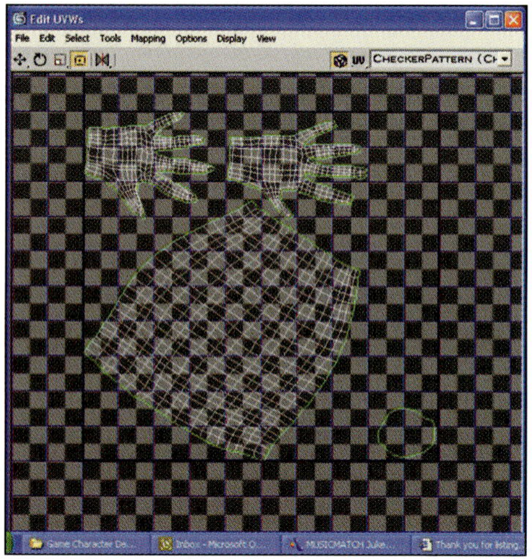

Figure 5.29 The opposite side of the hand is Pelt mapped just like the palm.

Tools, Pack UVs command to condense all the UVs together (see Figure 5.30).

10. We're done with one hand. Just repeat for the other hand. If you need to save texture space, attach both arm objects into the same object and stack the top parts of the two palms together as one piece, as well as the bottom parts. This way we can texture the top and bottom of the hand separately. You can stack the fingers in one clump.

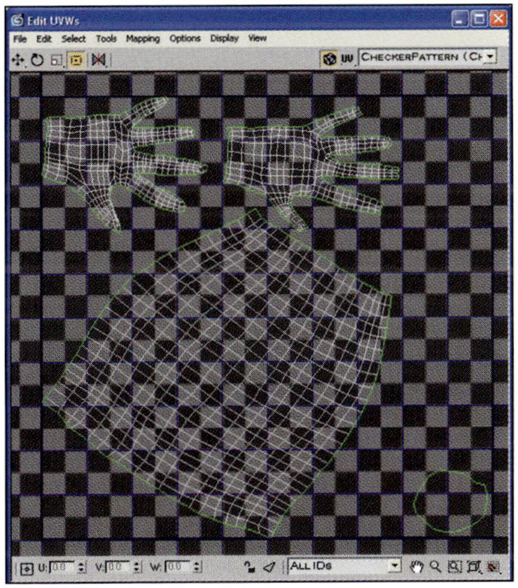

Figure 5.30 The Edit UVWs window shows the packed arm and hand UVs.

That completes the arms. Just move the components away for now, and at the end, we'll organize the map neatly. Before you continue, save your file so that you won't lose your work. Now let's move on to the body portion of Hicks.

Step 4: Unwrap the Body

The body should go fairly quickly because it includes holes where the head, arms, and legs are attached. This makes it easy to split the body into two halves and Pelt map each side like we did with the hands. The tricky part is to include separate mappings for the added attachments, such as the camera on Hicks' shoulder and the canteen on his hip.

1. Select and isolate the body object. Then apply the Unwrap UVW modifier to the object (see Figure 5.31).
2. Choose the Face subobject mode for the Unwrap UVW modifier, and drag over all the faces that make up the canteen object that's attached to Hicks.

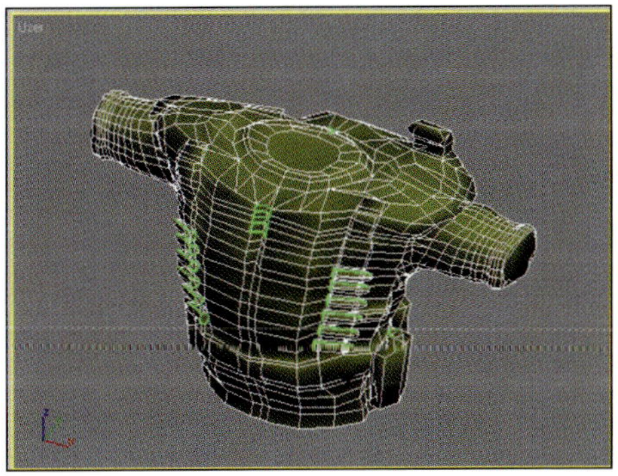

Figure 5.31 The torso object is isolated and ready to unwrap.

Click on the Cylindrical button, and position the Cylindrical gizmo so that it surrounds the canteen object (see Figure 5.32). With the canteen faces selected, choose the Mapping, Unfold mapping option in the Edit UVWs window to unfold the canteen map. Select and drag the canteen UVs away from the rest of the UVs. With the canteen faces still selected, click on the Exp. Face Sel to Pelt Seams button to select the canteen's cap. Unfold this part also, and move it away from the rest of the UVs.

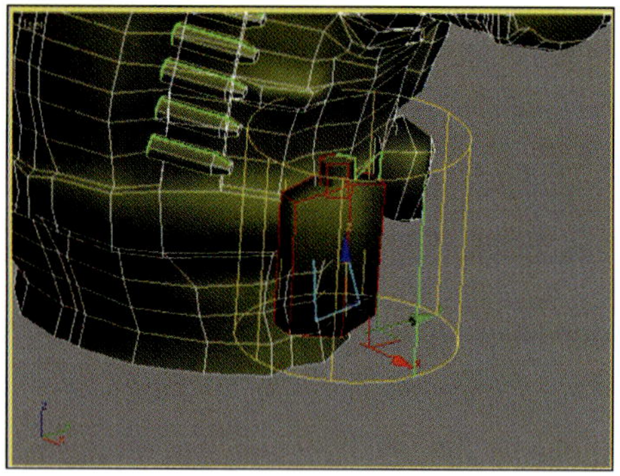

Figure 5.32 Apply a Cylindrical mapping to the canteen followed by the unfold mapping method.

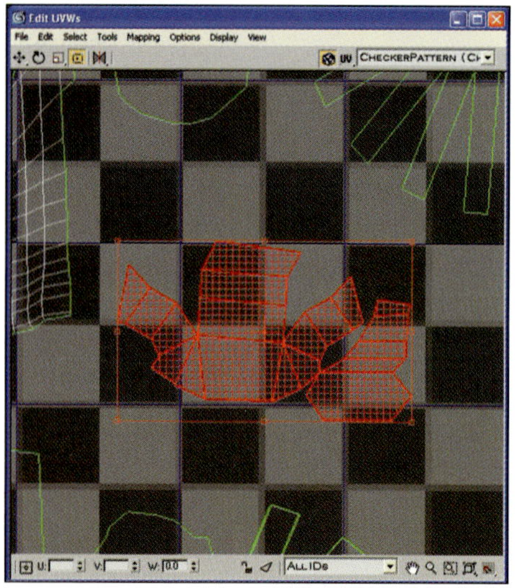

Figure 5.33 Select the shoulder camera and unfold map it.

3. Next, select the faces for the camera on Hicks' shoulder, and apply the Cylindrical mapping to this object, along with the unfold mapping. Select the UVs in the Edit UVWs window, and drag them away from the rest of the UVs (see Figure 5.33).
4. The next task is to split the remaining torso object in half. The natural seam to follow runs up the sides and across the shoulders, but first create a seam for the neck, arms, and pelvis. Then run seams up either side using the Point to Point Seam button (see Figure 5.34).
5. Select all the faces on one of the halves, and choose the Pelt mapping button. Then click on the Edit Pelt Map button. Click several times on the Simulate Pelt Pulling button to stretch out the UVs (see Figure 5.35). Close the Pelt Map Parameters dialog box, and click the Pelt button to exit mapping mode. Then drag the UVs off to the side, and separate the border vertices that represent the neck, arm, and waist holes.

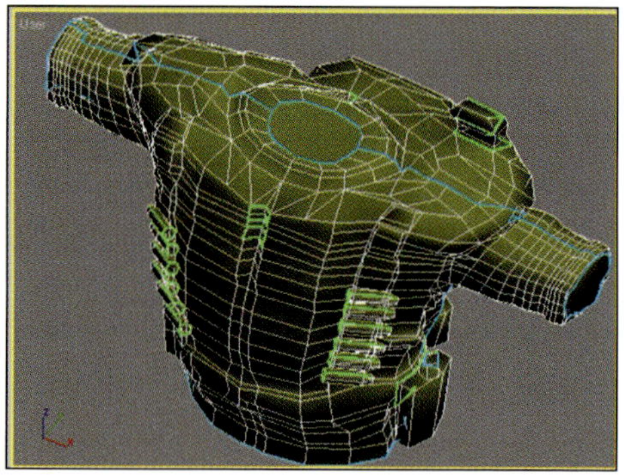

Figure 5.34 Seams run under the arms and across the shoulders dividing the torso in halves.

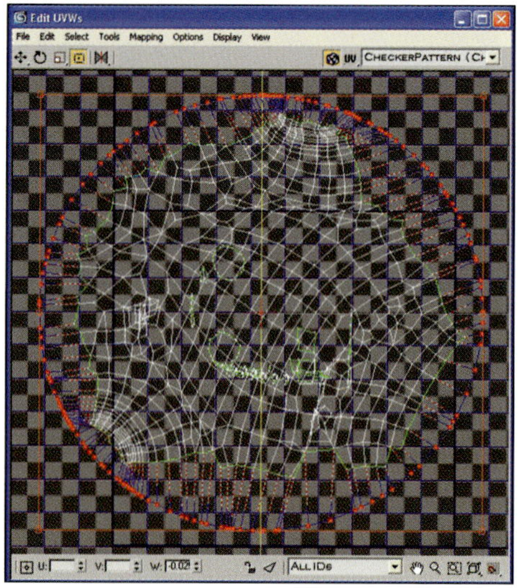

Figure 5.35 The Pelt mapping of one-half of the torso splits the torso into front and back sections.

6. For the front half of the torso, apply a Planar mapping, and use the Best Align button to line up the mapping gizmo. With the bullets on the front of the torso, this method is preferred to the Pelt mapping (see Figure 5.36). We'll check this mapping with a checkerboard texture before texturing to see how it looks in the next chapter.

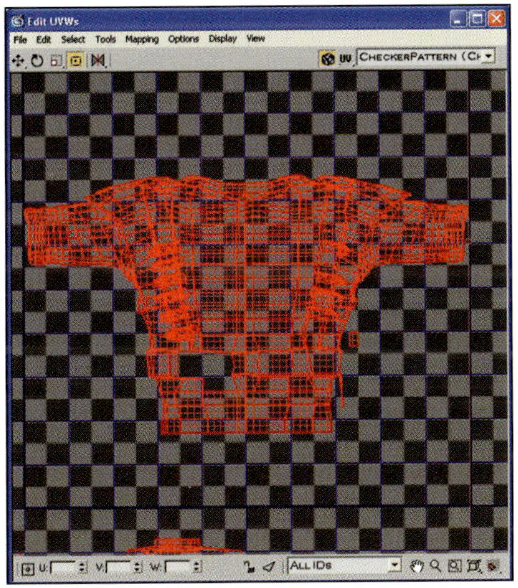

Figure 5.36 The Edit UVWs window shows the mapping for the front of the torso.

7. As a final step, select the Tools, Pack UVs command, and adjust any overlapping UVs (see Figure 5.37).

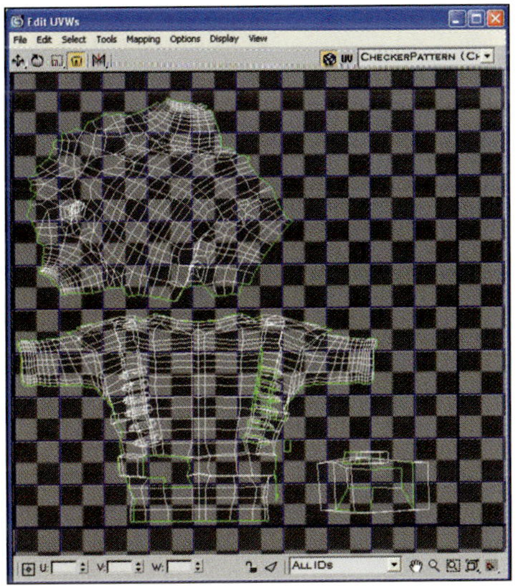

Figure 5.37 After you pack and adjust any overlapping UVs, you're ready to texture the template for the torso.

Step 5: Unwrap the Eyes

The eyes are easy to map, but they also contain a lot of detail. Even though the eyes are only a small part, they still can get a rather large section of the texture map because people notice the eyes and its details.

1. Select one of the eye objects, and apply the Unwrap UVW modifier. Select the Face subobject, and drag over the entire object. Click on the Planar button, and use the Best Align button to position the Planar gizmo so that it surrounds the eye (see Figure 5.38).

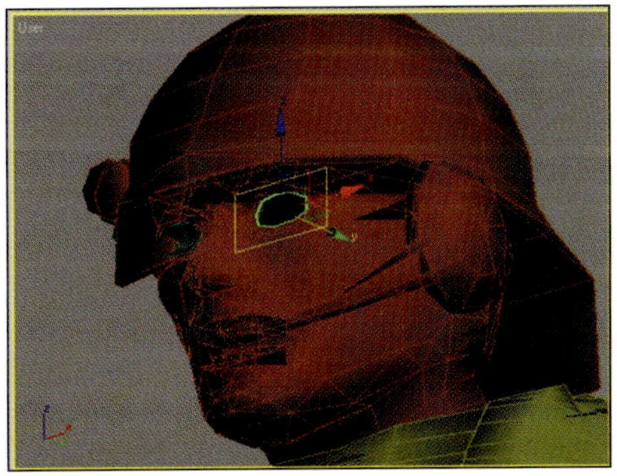

Figure 5.38 Select the eye faces, apply the Planar mapping, and position the Planar gizmo to surround the eye object.

2. Click on the Edit button to open the Edit UVWs window. The simple Planar mapping is shown (see Figure 5.39).
3. Drag the applied Unwrap UVW modifier from the mapped eye to the unmapped eye to apply the same mapping to the other eye.

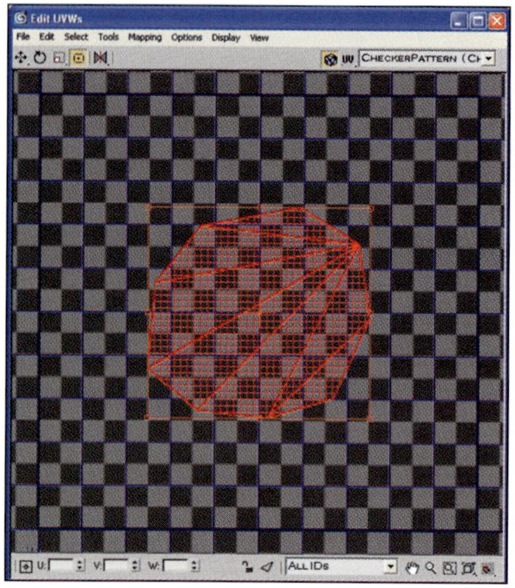

Figure 5.39 The Planar map for the eye is shown in the Edit UVWs window.

Step 6: Unwrap the Head

The head is a somewhat complex part of this character. Normal human characters have fairly spherical-shaped heads, and therefore a Spherical mapping would suffice. However, 'tis not the case for our character, which will need a combination of Spherical and Pelt mapping to deal with the helmet and face plus some cutting and stitching to get it just right. I also want to get more of the neck in there.

1. Select and isolate the head, and then apply the Unwrap UVW modifier to the object. Select the Face subobject mode, and drag over the entire object with the Ignore Backfacing option disabled to select all faces. Then click on the Exp. Face Sel to Pelt Seams button (see Figure 5.40). This selects only the camera on the side of Hicks' helmet.
2. With the helmet camera's faces selected, click the Cylindrical mapping button, and click the Best Align button to align the gizmo to the camera. Then rotate the gizmo to align with the length of the camera (see Figure 5.41). Click again on the Cylindrical button to exit mapping mode, use the Unfold mapping method, and then select and move the selected UVs off to the side.
3. Select one of the polygons on the neck guard at the back of the neck, and click the plus sign button to expand the selection area to include the rim of the helmet on the back side. Click the Planar button and then the Best Align button to align the Planar gizmo. Then click the Planar button again and move the UVs off to the right (see Figure 5.42). Repeat step 3 for

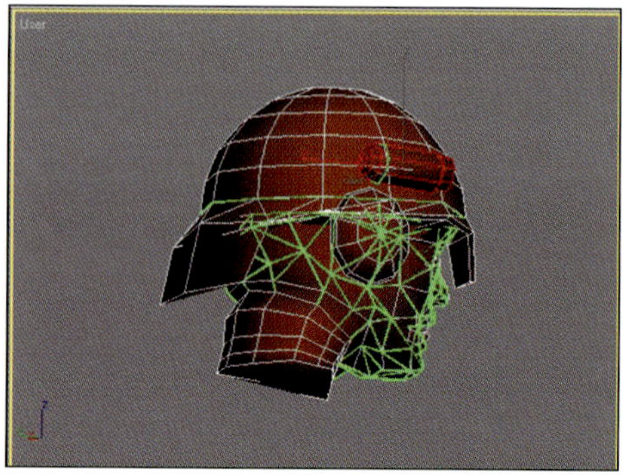

Figure 5.40 The Exp. Face Sel to Pelt Seams button isolates the helmet camera.

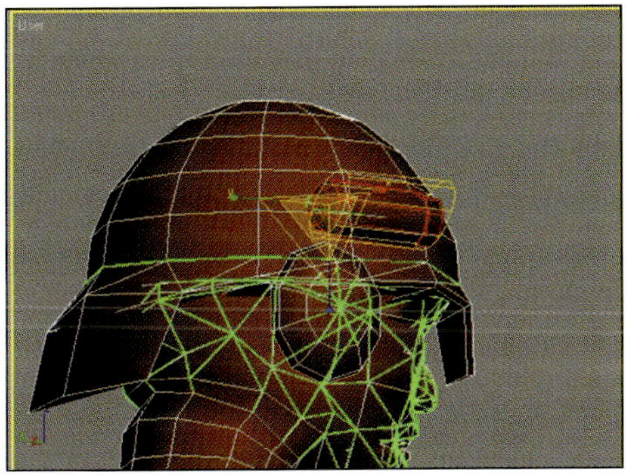

Figure 5.41 Align the Cylindrical gizmo to the length of the camera for correct mapping.

the front eyepiece. Then repeat step 2 for the microphone in front of the helmet.

4. Select the remaining faces, and define a seam that runs around the neck and along the back of the neck around the guard and to the top of the head using the Point to Point Pelt Seam button. Select all face objects, and click on the Pelt button followed by the Best Align button. This fixes the gizmo in front of the face. Click next on the Edit Pelt Map button. Then click several times on the Simulate Pelt Pulling button to stretch out the remaining head UVs (see Figure 5.43).
5. Select all UVs in the Edit UVWs window, and choose the Tools, Pack UVs command to condense all the UVs to a single template. The face and head UVs should be scaled to be larger than the rest of the UVs because they represent the most detail (see Figure 5.44).

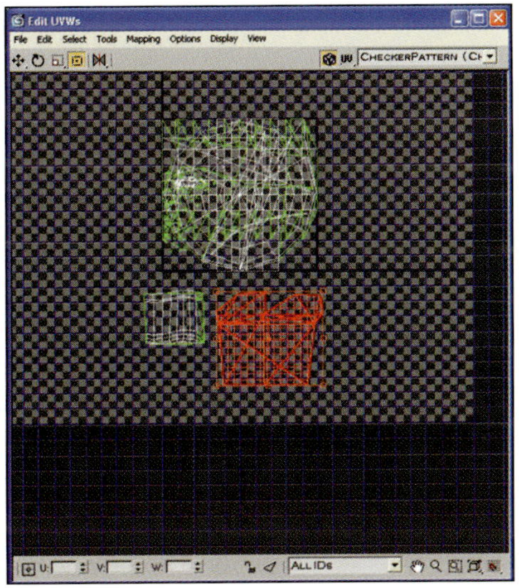

Figure 5.42 Apply a Planar mapping to the back neck guard.

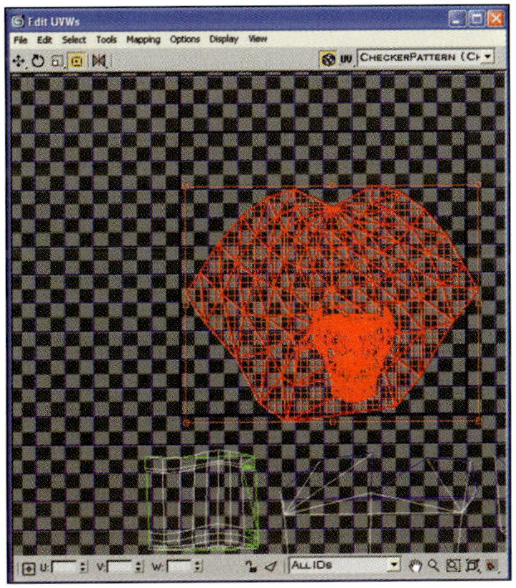

Figure 5.43 Stretch out the Pelt mapping for the remaining head UVs.

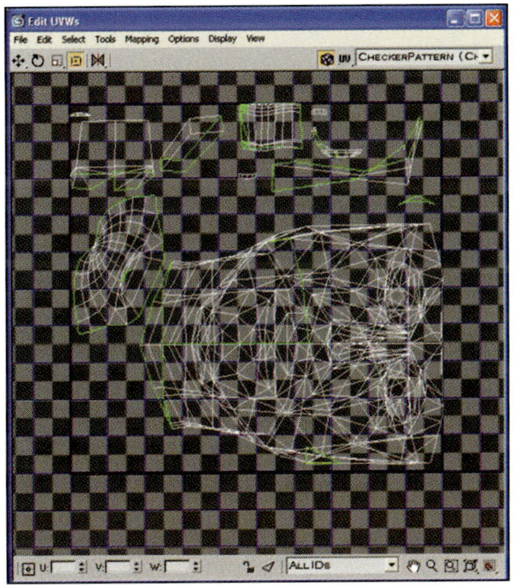

Figure 5.44 After you pack the UVs, the template is ready.

Pack the Map

As I mentioned in the previous chapter when packing these maps, it's best to do this stuff manually so that you can give preference to items that need more detail. The logic is thus: The larger the scale of an individual map item on the Material map, the more texture detail you'll be able to apply to it. Get it? For instance, if you were to scale the head portion of the map down to a tiny little piece, how much texture detail would show up when you reduced the texture skin to 256×256 pixels? Not a lot, my friend. So in this case, the pieces that need the most detail are the head, followed by the body, arms, legs, and so on.

Just remember that when you place and scale the pieces on the map, if you use Edit, Free Transform, hold down the Shift key so that the pieces scale uniformly. Otherwise, your texture bitmap distorts.

Rendering Templates

3ds Max includes a feature that renders the UV template to a bitmap that you can import within Photoshop. This is really handy and gives you the chance to draw directly on the template showing all the UV edges.

To render a UV template, select the Tools, Render UV Template command from the Edit UVWs window. This opens the Render UVs dialog box (see Figure 5.45). From this dialog box, you can specify the bitmap's dimensions and the size and colors of the edges and background.

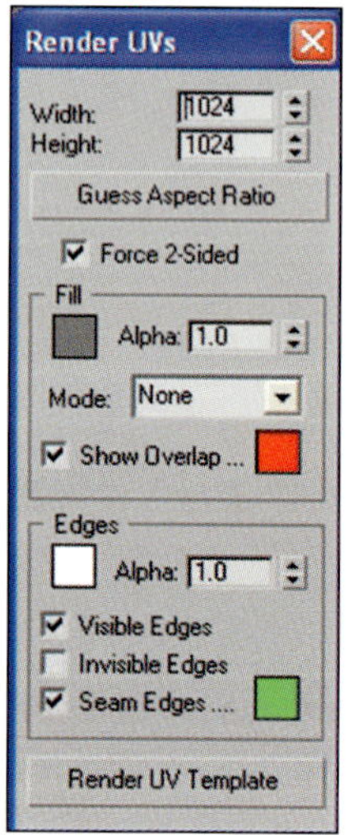

Figure 5.45 You use the Render UVs dialog box to render out the UV templates to be imported into Photoshop.

1. Open the Edit UVWs window for each defined set of UVs by clicking on the Edit button. Then select and choose the Tools, Render UV Template command. In the Render UVs dialog box, click on the Render UV Template button. This opens the Render Map window and displays the rendered UV template (see Figure 5.46).

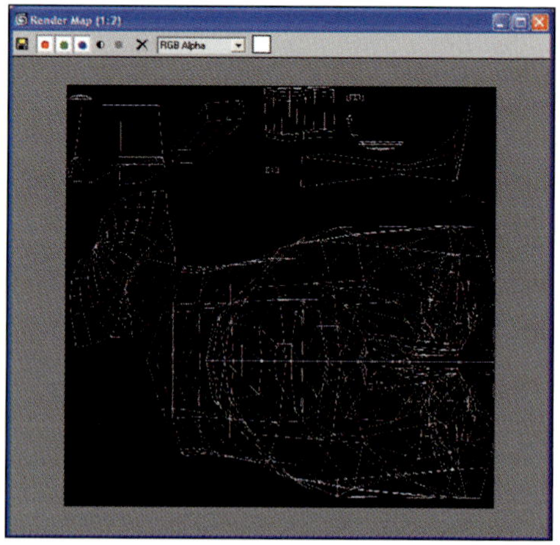

Figure 5.46 The Render Map window shows the UV template for the selected object.

2. Repeat the render template process for each object. From the Render Map window, click on the Save button, and save each template to a format that you can open within Photoshop.

Update and View the Results in Max

After you've packed your map and rendered the template, click on the Modifier tab to see the whole stack. The topmost update is the latest. To view it, add an Unwrap UVW modifier to the stack, and in its panel, click the Edit button. Now you're ready to texture Hicks. To commence this process, skip to Chapter 6.

Summary

This chapter discussed how to unwrap all the various objects required to create texture templates. The UV coordinates define how the texture map is aligned to the various 3D geometry. Correctly unwrapping the texture maps into UVs allows the textures to wrap about the 3D object without stretching and deforming.

Color in a picture is like enthusiasm in life.
—*Vincent van Gogh*

Chapter 6

Skin Texturing with Photoshop CS2

After you've defined all the UVs for your character, it's worth your time to check out the mapping for each part with a test texture. Then after you've saved out the various templates, you can pull the templates into Photoshop and proceed to paint the various textures. Photoshop lets you place the template on a background layer, making it visible without painting on top of it. In this chapter, you will

- Test the UV mappings with a checkerboard image
- Render each mapping template
- Load each template into Photoshop
- Paint the head texture
- Paint the arm and hand textures
- Paint the torso, leg, and boot textures
- Apply the textures to the character in 3ds Max
- Use the Render to Texture interface to bake the resulting textures

Thoughts on Texturing

I get many of my ideas for this kind of stuff from watching movies and reading books. I've learned to keep an eye out for interesting textures that can be applied to characters. The value of textures is in the details. The attached CD includes many interesting textures that I've gathered over the years that are featured in my other book, *The Dark Side of Game Texturing*.

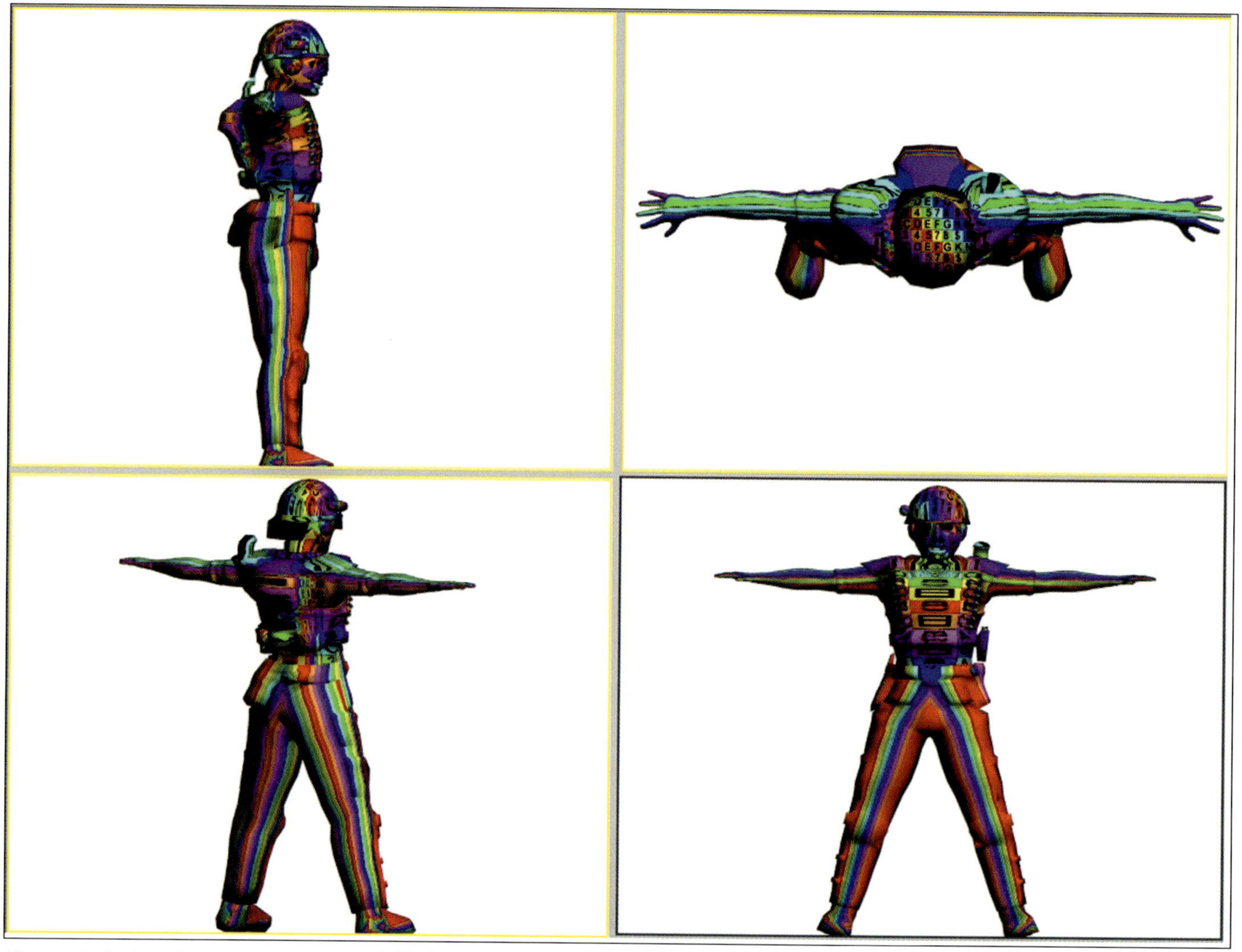

Figure 6.1 Applying a texture to a model before the UVs are defined results in textures that are inverted, smeared, stretched, and deformed.

Texturing Techniques We'll Utilize

Again, I like to make great use of many of Photoshop's filters and styles to lay the groundwork for my textures. However, the organic stuff needs a bit more traditional artwork applied, mostly with the use of dodging and burning the base texture to enhance the muscular Hicks. I don't consider myself a traditional artist in the least, because I was born, bred, and self-taught with computer graphics. However, traditional artistry becomes inherent in my work the more I do this stuff, regardless of the techniques I use.

Fixing UVs: Add a Checkerboard Map

Even though you did a careful and neat job of unwrapping and organizing the UVs, there's still a chance that the isolated UV portions of the texture map are inverted (like looking in a mirror) or that texture coordinates are crossed (resulting in smearing), overlapped (causing a duplication of texture), or not properly relaxed (causing bloating or shrinking of the texture). I can almost guarantee that at least one of the aforementioned scenarios exists in your setup, but it's not a huge ordeal—it just means we have to go back to 3ds Max and fix them. For the Hicks character, inversion is not a big deal, but we need to check for the other errors. When you apply a texture (such as a checkerboard texture) without UVs, you'll notice many of these problems (see Figure 6.1).

One outstanding way of detecting problems before you begin the texturing process is to set up a checkerboard map. By filling your texture map with a small checkerboard pattern and then applying the texture to the model, you will have a much easier time checking for errors. I like to fill the individual areas of my texture map with differently colored patterns to make a clear definition of what each of the UV sections are, and I also like to add some text to the area, which not only helps me to identify that area but displays an inverted map area, too. If inverted UVs exist, the text comes out backward.

To see what I mean, first fill in the individual UV sections of the base color layer on the texture map. I've saved a checkerboard pattern for you. Just load the checkerboard.tif file in Photoshop, located on the CD-ROM in the Chapter 6 folder. Then use the Lasso tool to create selections around the UV areas, and fill the selections with the different colored patterns using either Edit, Fill or the Paintbucket tool. Figure 6.2 shows my map. Finally, use the Type tool to position text on the separate UV

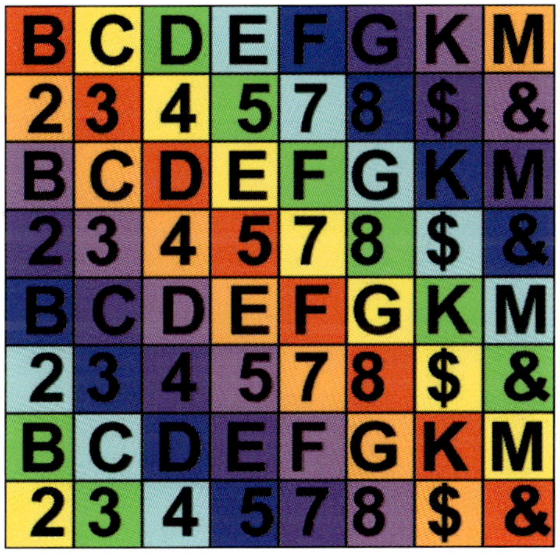

Figure 6.2 Fill the separate UV areas with different colored patterns.

areas, or put a nonsymmetrical symbol on them, so that if any particular area happens to be inverted, you'll be able to tell instantly.

Next, you need to apply the checkerboard texture to each of the various body parts. Check for any signs of smearing, overlapping, or unevenness. It is common to find the most noticeable flaws in the front of the face, where the density of the checkerboard map is less than its surroundings. This means that we should go back to the UV mapping and select the points in that area, relax them, or otherwise scale them up a bit so the coverage of the material map is even in that entire head section. Also, because we stretched and relaxed nearly all portions of the UV map, I don't expect to see any other problems with smearing (see Figure 6.3).

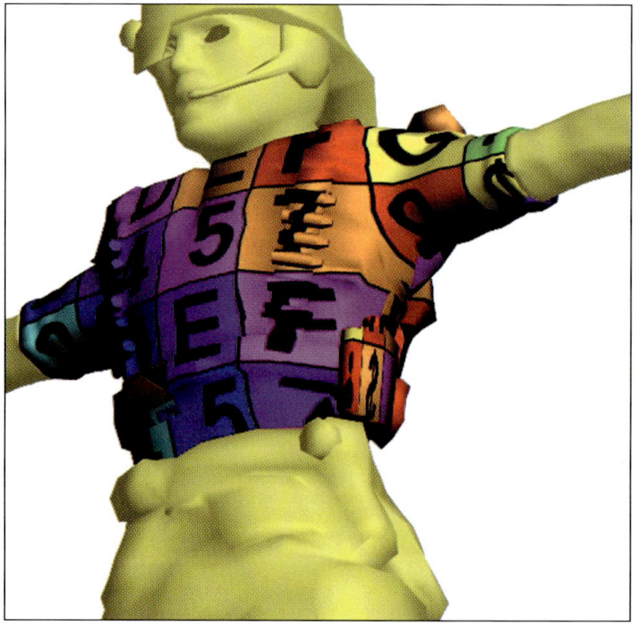

Figure 6.3 Apply the checkerboard material to the torso, and check for signs of smearing, overlapping, or unevenness.

1. Within 3ds Max, select the mapped boot object and open the Material Editor. Select one of the sample slots and name it boot. Then click on the mapping square next to the Diffuse color (see Figure 6.4) and choose the Bitmap option in the Material/Map browser. In the File dialog box that opens, select the Checkerboard.tif image. Then apply the material to the boot object.

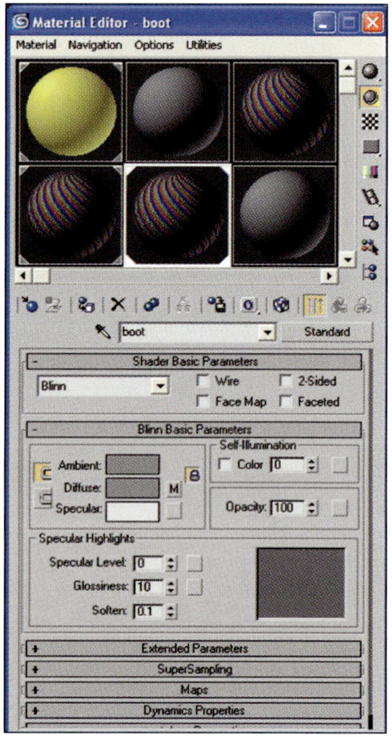

Figure 6.4 The Material Editor lets you apply materials and textures to scene objects.

2. With the top of both boots visible, do a quick render of the scene to see how the map aligns to the boots (see Figure 6.5). Then rotate the model until the bottom of the boots are visible, and rerender the scene.
3. Replace the texture maps on both boots with the standard yellow material by dragging the yellow material onto each boot object. Then select a new sample slot and name it legs. Add the checkerboard.tif map to the Diffuse color for this new material and apply it to the leg object. Then render the legs to look for any problems (see Figure 6.6). From the render, you can see that the left leg mapping is backward.

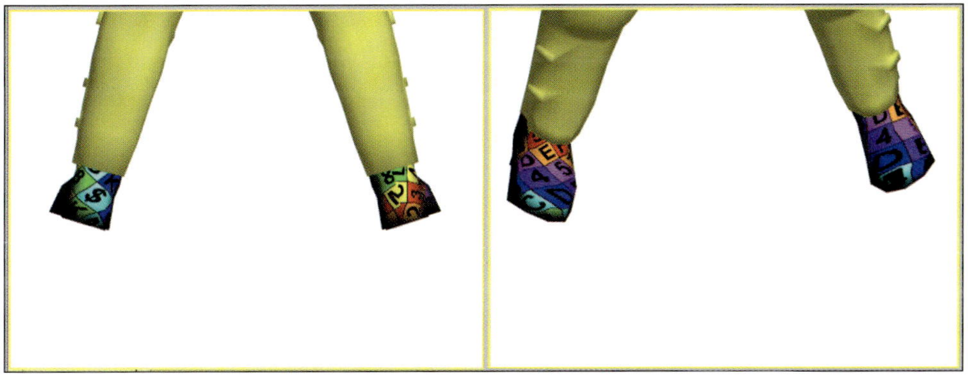

Figure 6.5 The map alignment for the tops of the boots looks fine without significant stretching.

Figure 6.6 The render for the legs shows that the mapping on the left leg is backward.

4. With the leg object selected, select all the faces for the UVs that correspond to the left leg, and select the Tools, Flip Vertical command in the Edit UVWs window. If you then rerender the legs, you can see that the problem is fixed (see Figure 6.7).
5. Drag the default yellow material from the Material Editor and drop it on the legs object. Then select a new sample slot in the Material Editor and name the new material torso. Click on the mapping button next to the Diffuse color swatch, and choose Bitmap from the Material/Map browser. Select the checkerboard.tif file from the File dialog box. Then drag the new material to the torso, and render the torso to see how the mapping looks (see Figure 6.8).
6. The front of the torso is Planar mapped, which includes the bullets on the front of Hicks' jacket. You need to separate these bullet UVs from the rest of the jacket. Also notice the set of polygons in the lower-right section of the abdomen that has some problems. Before diving into fixing these problems, check a render of the back of the torso (see Figure 6.9). On

Figure 6.7 After you flip the UVs for the left leg, the problem with backward UVs is fixed.

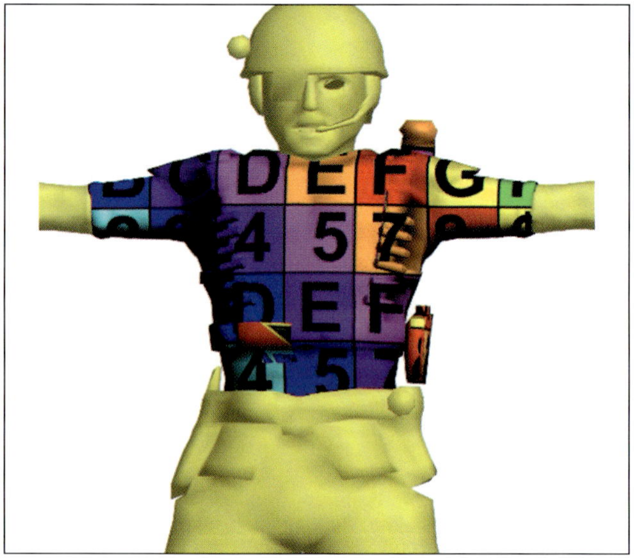

Figure 6.8 The checkerboard test texture is applied to the torso object.

the back, you need to separate the pack from the rest of the torso's UVs.

7. With the torso object selected, open the Modify panel and click on the Edit button to access the Edit UVWs window. Select all the UVs in the window, and click the Exp. Face Sel to Pelt Seams button. This selects a single bullet on the front of the torso. Click the Cylindrical button followed by the Best Align button. Then choose the Mapping, Unfold Mapping menu and click on the Cylindrical button again to exit mapping mode. Then select and drag the bullet mapping away from the rest of the UVs. Repeat this step for all the remaining bullets. You'll find that there are three different unfold mapping types. You can stack similar types on top of one another (see Figure 6.10).

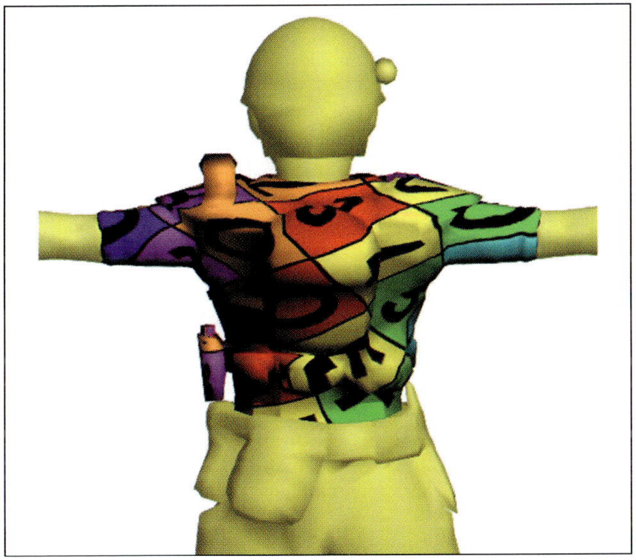

Figure 6.9 The back of the torso reveals that the UVs for the pack need to be separated from the rest of the torso's back UVs.

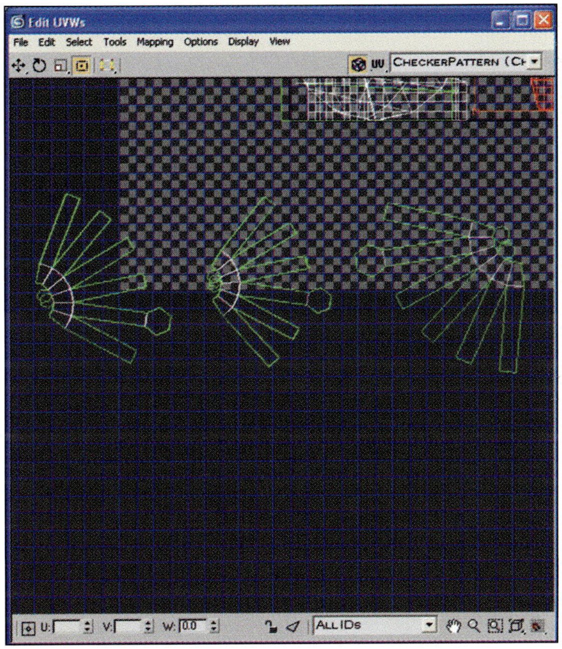

Figure 6.10 Using the Unfold mapping method, you can separate each of the bullets from the rest of the UVs.

8. To separate the pack's UV on the back of the torso, select all the pack's faces and apply a Pelt mapping. Then stretch out the Pelt mapping. I've also separated the arms and divided the torso into halves using the front seam instead of the sides. The front seams run vertically in a straight line. (Creating a seam along the side would require a jagged seam.) The resulting mappings from the front seams are much cleaner, as shown in the test render (see Figure 6.11). On the back, you need to separate the pack from the rest of the torso's UVs.
9. Apply the default yellow material to the torso. Select a new sample slot in the Material Editor, and name the new material arms. Then apply the checkerboard.tif test texture as the map for the Diffuse color, and drag the new material to both arms. After rendering, you can see that the mapping for the left arm is fine, but the right arm's mapping is stretched (see Figure 6.12).

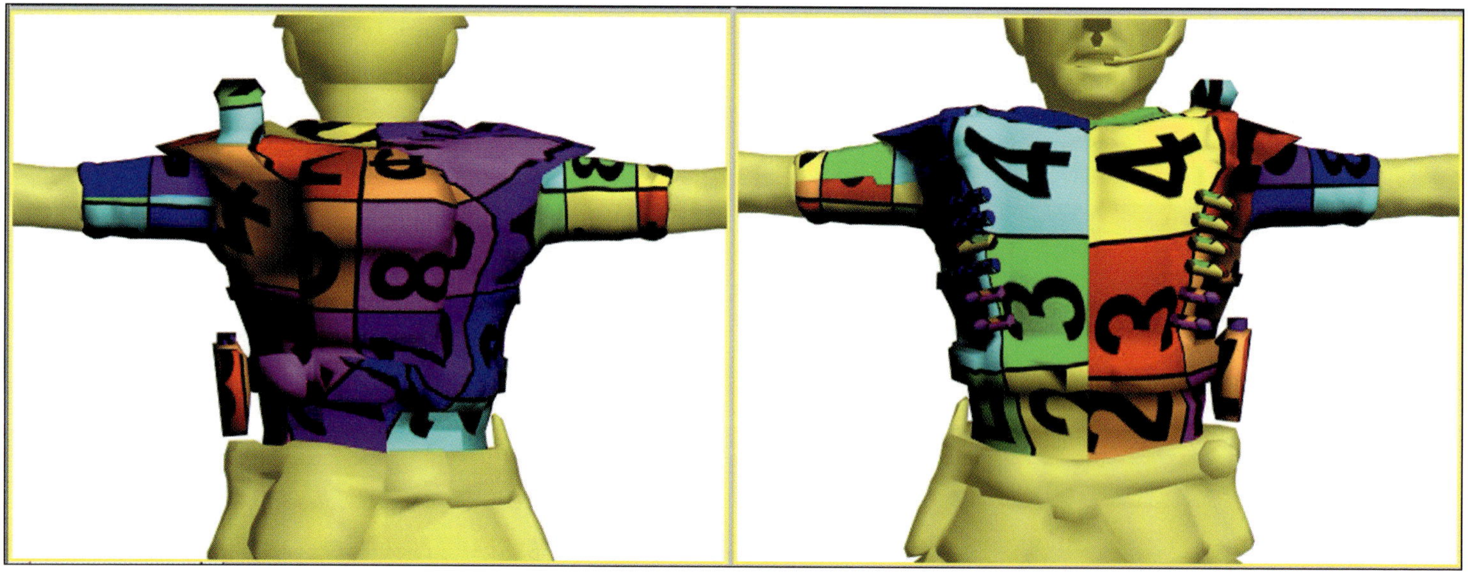

Figure 6.11 After you've fixed several of the mapping problems, the rerendered test mapping looks much better.

10. To fix the stretching on the right arm, reset the UVs using the Reset UVs button and then drag the Unwrap UVW modifier from the left arm and drop it on the right arm. Then select and reapply the mapping for the different selections. The resulting mapping fixes the stretching (see Figure 6.13).
11. Apply the default yellow material to the arms. Select a new sample slot in the Material Editor and name the new material head. Then apply the checkerboard.tif test texture as the map for the Diffuse color, and drag the new material to the head object. After rendering, you can see that the mapping for the front of the head is fine (see Figure 6.14).

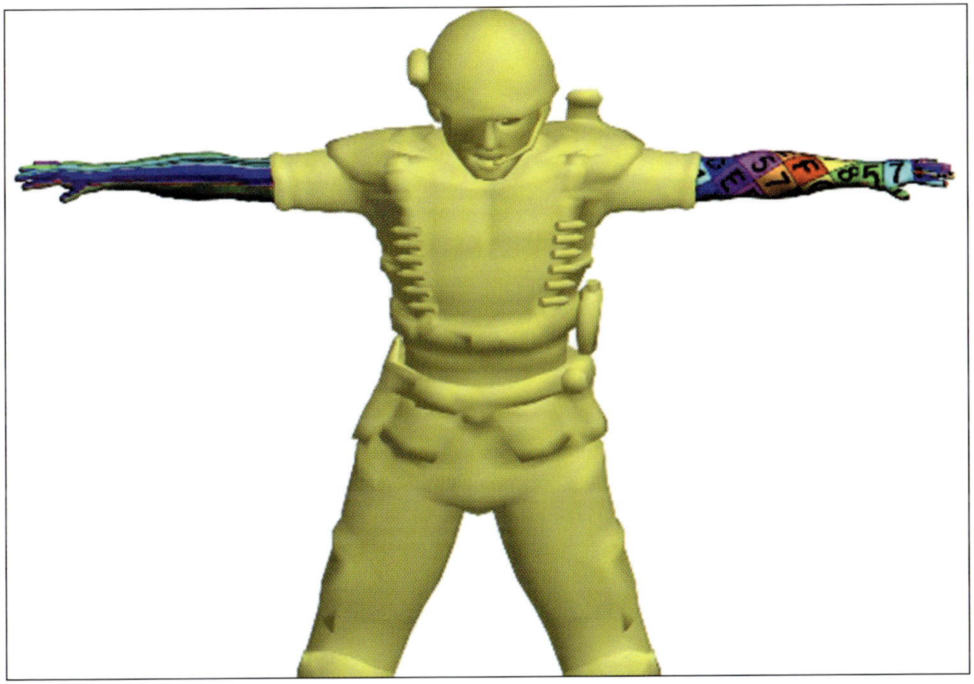

Figure 6.12 The texture mapping for the right arm is stretched and needs to be fixed.

Figure 6.13 Reapplying the UVs fixes the stretching for the right arm.

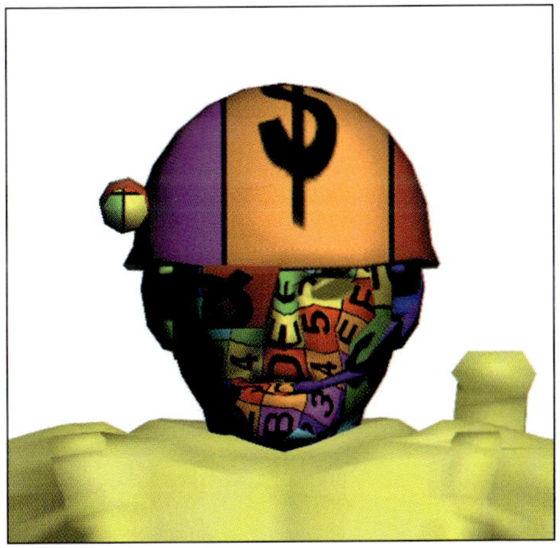

Figure 6.14 The texture mapping for the front of the head is fine.

12. For the back of the head, one polygon that belongs to the helmet is mapped with the neck guard (see Figure 6.15). It is shown in red in the middle of the helmet. To fix this polygon mapping, select the problem face and separate it from the helmet mapping using the Tools, Detach Edge Vertices menu in the Edit UVWs window. Then move the polygon face close to the neck guard. After that, select the edge closest to the neck guard using the Edge subobject mode and choose the Tools, Stitch Selected menu. This attaches the problem face where it should be.
13. Apply the default yellow material to the head. Select a new sample slot in the Material Editor and name the new material eyes. Then apply the checkerboard.tif test texture as the map for the Diffuse color, and drag the new material to the eye objects. After you render, the mapping for the eye is fine (see Figure 6.16). Some portions of the eye are hidden in the shadows and appear dark, but that's okay. With the correct light, the eyes will show up.

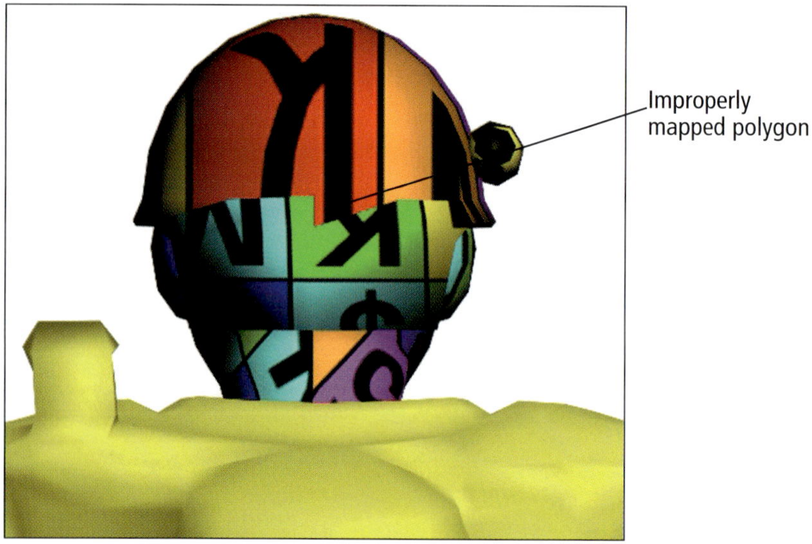

Figure 6.15 One descending face is mapped to the helmet, but it should be part of the neck guard. You can fix this by detaching the polygon and stitching it where it should be.

Figure 6.16 The mapping for the eye looks fine.

14. All the work spent applying test materials to the various body parts can be reused after you've completed the actual textures. Save the file with all the checkerboard textures applied as HICKS-textured.max. You'll reuse this file later in this chapter.

Texturing Hicks

Let's kick this into gear by rendering each of the UV templates from 3ds Max. Then you can load each object's template into Photoshop and begin painting. At the same time, keep 3ds Max open (if you have enough memory) and apply the texture to its object to spot-check how the texture looks on the finished object.

It is helpful to have some images of the Hicks character available for reference. There are plenty of Web sites that have close-up frames of Hicks taken from the movie *Aliens*. Many of them are from different angles.

Rendering Templates

3ds Max includes a feature that renders the UV template to a bitmap that you can open into Photoshop. This is really handy and gives you the chance to draw directly on the template showing all the UV edges.

To render a UV template, select the Tools, Render UV Template command from the Edit UVWs window. This opens the Render UVs dialog box (see Figure 6.17). From this dialog box, you can specify the bitmap's dimensions and the size and colors of the edges and base.

1. Select the torso object and open the Edit UVWs window for each defined set of UVs by clicking on the Edit button. Then select and choose the Tools, Render UV Template command. In the Render UVs dialog box, click on the Render UV Template button. This opens the Render Map window and displays the rendered UV template (see Figure 6.18). I saved the eye and boot templates at 256×256, the arm

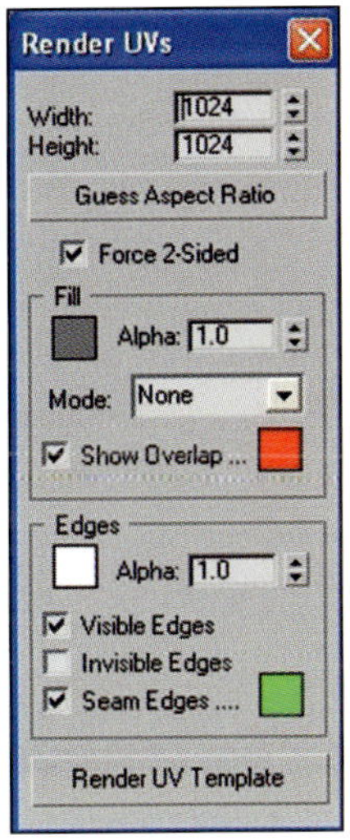

Figure 6.17 You use the Render UVs dialog box to render out the UV templates to be imported into Photoshop.

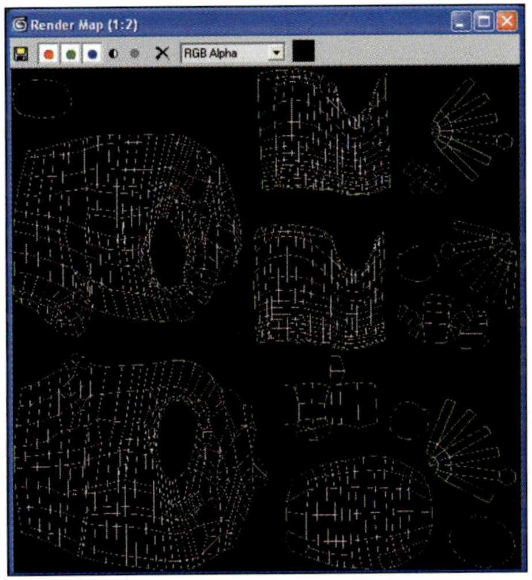

Figure 6.18 The Render Map window shows the UV template for the torso.

templates at 512×512, and the head, torso, and legs at 1024×1024.

Note

The size of the texture images depends on the memory that the game supports. Some games can only handle 256×256-sized textures, but many of the newer systems support larger textures.

2. Repeat the render template process for each object. From the Render Map window, click on the Save button and save each template to a format that you can open within Photoshop.

Opening the UV Templates in Photoshop

The first thing we need to do is open the UV map for the part we want to texture in Photoshop. Then, as you paint the various textures, you can switch over to Max and view the updated texture. The UV and texturing portion of our work is closely related and, in our case, relies on two separate programs. With enough system memory, you can efficiently work with both of these programs open and update back and forth between them as you model, UV, and texture.

Start by opening your UV mapped Hicks model in 3ds Max. This should be the file you saved from Chapter 5, "UV Mapping the Character in 3ds Max," or, if you don't have it, open the HICKS-mapped.max file located on the CD-ROM in the Chapter 5 folder.

1. With the UV mapped version of Hicks loaded in 3ds Max, locate the texture that you want to work on and load it into Photoshop CS2.
2. Open the Layers palette and notice that the template is the background layer. Click on the Create a New Layer button on the bottom of the Layers palette to create a new layer. This is the layer where you'll paint the new texture. Drag Opacity for the layer in the Layers palette down to 50 percent so that the background template shows through the base layer (see Figure 6.19).
3. The texture is now ready to paint. Just remember to disable Visibility for the background layer and reset the opacity value for the base layer to 100% before saving the texture.

With the texture templates loaded in Photoshop, you're ready to begin painting each of the various textures.

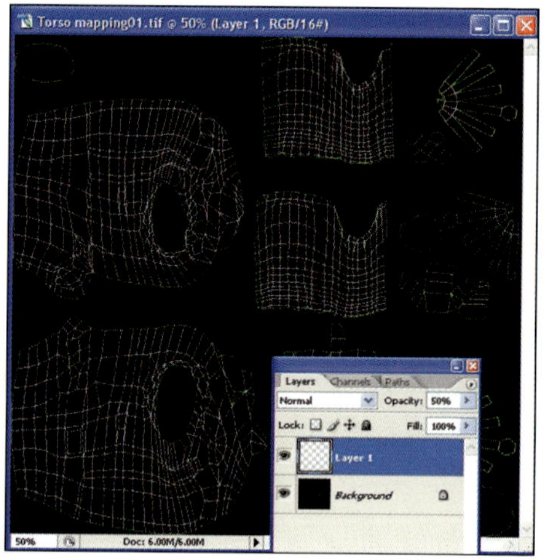

Figure 6.19 With the template on the base, you can paint on the new layer and hide the base when the texture is complete.

Texturing the Head

After you've loaded the UV template into Photoshop, we'll begin painting the texture. We'll start with the head because it has the most detail. Select the loaded head template.

Create a Base Texture

The first step is to create a base texture that covers everything. This base texture should be the most common material for the object, such as a leather texture for the boots or a skin texture for the arms.

1. Fill the entire layer with skin tone color by selecting the color and using the Edit, Fill menu. Then select each item in the UV map and change its base color. Use black for the earphones, camera, and microphone; brownish green for the helmet; and white for the teeth (see Figure 6.20).
2. Apply the Noise filter, about 5 percent monochromatic. This adds some texture to the colors.
3. Make a few adjustments to this base texture, such as clicking Image, Adjust, Hue/Saturation, and desaturate the texture enough so that the colors don't burn a hole in your eyes anymore. A slight Levels adjustment would be good, too, just to sharpen it up and tone it down. At the end, we'll make last-minute adjustments like this to get the texture looking good.

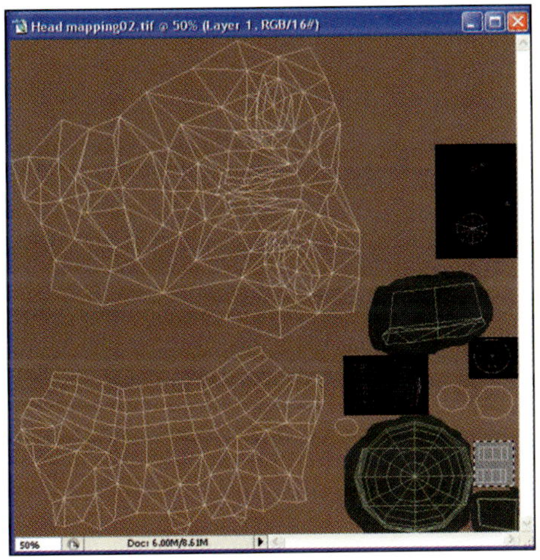

Figure 6.20 The head mapping with all the base colors applied.

Create the Brows

I don't recall mentioning this next technique thus far in this book, but it's a fantastic way to create realistic bump maps in skin and cloth. You can fake the brows that shield the eyes using this technique. You can also use this technique to create muscular folds in the skin. If you're not big into freehand art, like me, you'll appreciate this one to its fullest.

1. Create a new layer above the base layer. Apply an Inner Bevel style to this layer, with settings shown in Figure 6.21. You'll be using this style to bump the texture map for the remainder of this tutorial, so you should save the style in the Styles palette for quick retrieval. The most important part of the bevel here is the Highlight Mode's color—change it from that hideous pure white to a dark greenish brown. Then change the Blend Mode to Linear Burn. The highlights and shadows should be dull and subtle; otherwise, your bumps will look like silly streaks of paint.

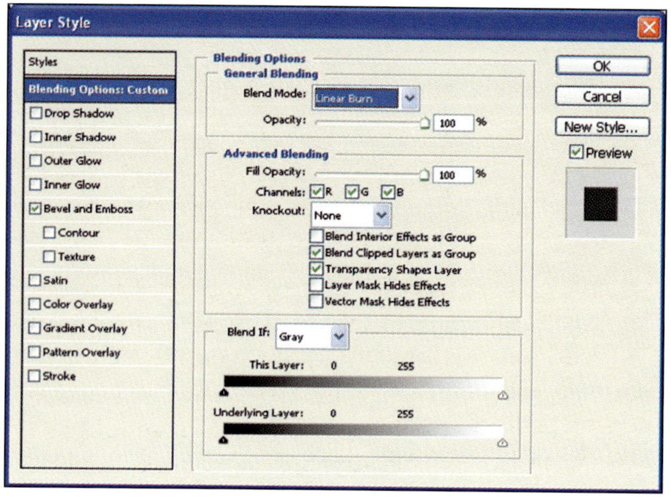

Figure 6.21 Create this Inner Bevel style and store it in the Styles palette for quick retrieval. We'll use this for bumping the surface.

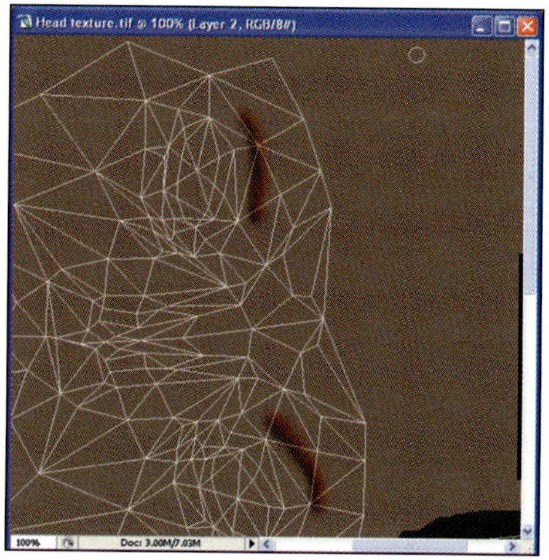

Figure 6.22 Use the Clone Stamp tool to brush in a brow on the effects layer.

2. You should now have a blank layer with an Inner Bevel style applied to it, located on top of the base layer. Click on the Clone Stamp tool, and change that tool's flow rate to about 10 percent. Pick out a brush size, such as Soft Round 21 pixels. Here's the trick: Select the base layer and Alt+click on an area of skin, away from the eyes. Doing so samples that area. Then select the blank layer with the style on it. Use gentle strokes to shape the brow as I have done in Figure 6.22. Totally cool, yes? The surface seems to raise magically! You can always adjust the effects of this by going back into the style for that layer and adding more depth, larger size, and so on. Plus, if you totally screw it up, just Ctrl+A that layer and delete the pixel contents to start anew.

Tip

When doing almost any texturing operation like dodging, burning, or even painting, remember to turn the settings for those tools way, way down, like less than 10 percent. This way, there won't be dramatic changes that look totally goofy.

I really hope I opened up a world of possibilities for you with this technique. You can use it to create muscle peaks and valleys on the legs, arms, and body. The thing is, you really need to be subtle about it, or your character will look like he got the #?@$?! beat out of him! Anyway, when you're finished with one brow, merge it down to the base layer. Hicks looks a little meaner now, doesn't he?

Texture the Neck with Beard Stubble

The sketch of Hicks demonstrates that his beard including the underside of his neck is coarse and thick, as if a beard could sprout at any time. Accomplish this look by preselecting the bearded area on a new layer and then painting in the stubble with a pattern brush.

1. Use the Lasso tool to circle the facial area just under the nose and around the chin. Then select the Subtract from Selection option in the toolbar and drag over the mouth area. Finally, select the front of the neck area with the Add to Selection option. Figure 6.23 shows the selected area where the beard stubble will be applied.
2. Select the Scattered Dry Brush Small Tip brush from the Wet Media set of brushes. Set Flow to about 50 percent, and drag in slow steady strokes that follow the way the beard flows outward from the moustache and downward along the neckline (see Figure 6.24).

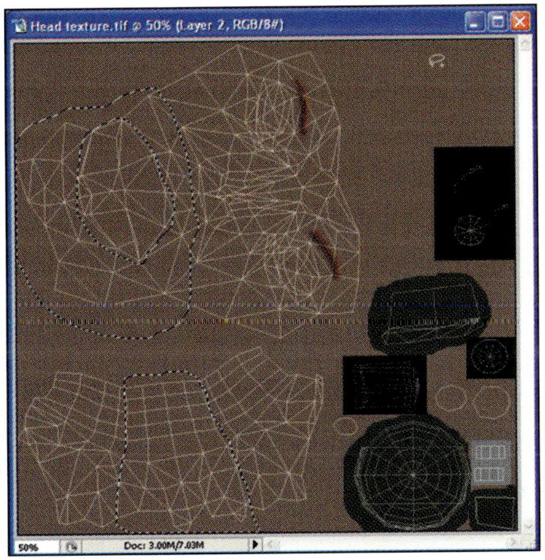

Figure 6.23 Select the area where the beard stubble is located.

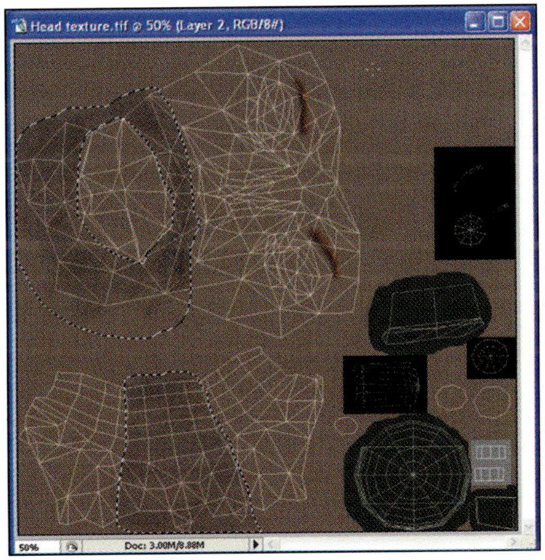

Figure 6.24 Draw in beard stubble with a scattered pattern brush.

Last Touches

Before leaving the head, there are plenty of last-minute touches that we can add to the texture. Any little details that we can add will help the character feel more real.

1. In the base layer, we quickly added base colors to the various items, but a solid base for the helmet eyepiece won't work. Select the eyepiece and fill it with a black color that is mostly transparent. Opacity set at 30 percent should let the eye be visible through the glass.
2. The neck guard on the back of the helmet is a good place to add a patterned camouflage look. Select the camo.jpg image from the Chapter 6 folder on the CD and fill the neck guard with this pattern in the base layer (see Figure 6.25).
3. Select a red color and draw in two circles with some crosshairs in the center of the eyepiece for a targeting device (see Figure 6.26).

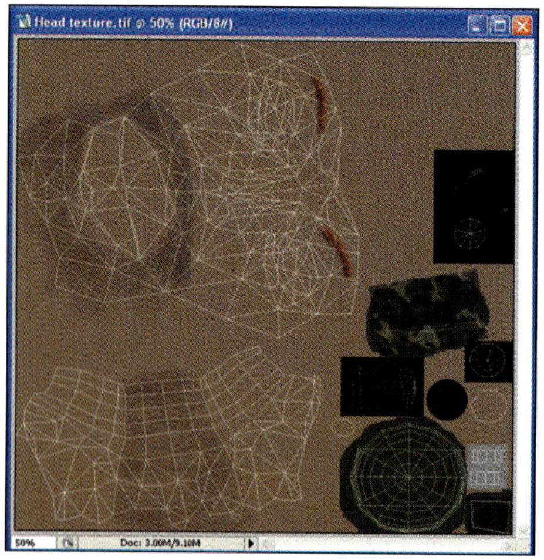

Figure 6.25 Adding a camouflage pattern to the back of the neck guard.

4. Add some thin vertical lines to the teeth to separate the row of teeth into individual teeth (see Figure 6.27).
5. Select all the remaining layers, and merge them into the base layer. Then turn off the visibility on the background layer and increase the opacity of the base layer to 100%. This shows the layer in its final form. From here, save the file as a native PSD so that you can revisit the texture later if you need to. You should also save the texture as a file that you can easily load into Max. I like to use the TIF format.

There's not too much going on here. When you're finished with this step, use the Dodge and Burn tools to touch up the edges and center of the neck area, as with anything else you do. Always take your time putting finishing touches to your work. Nothing's really ever just 1-2-3, you know? If you notice that I explain something but the results seem much better than what I explain, that's because I took a few extra minutes to polish it off, adjust the levels, and so forth.

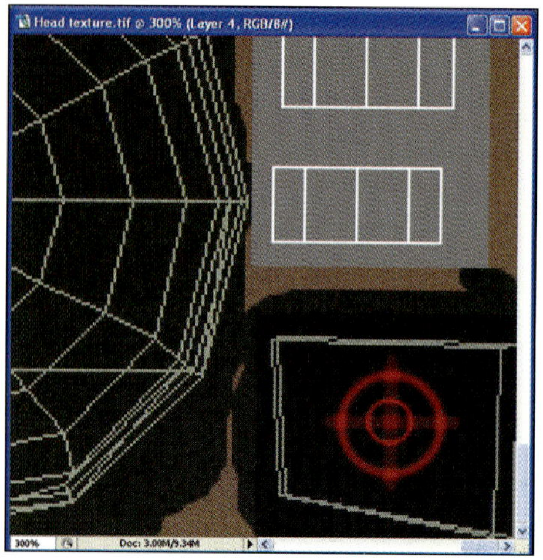

Figure 6.26 Draw in a red targeting set of crosshairs in the helmet eyepiece.

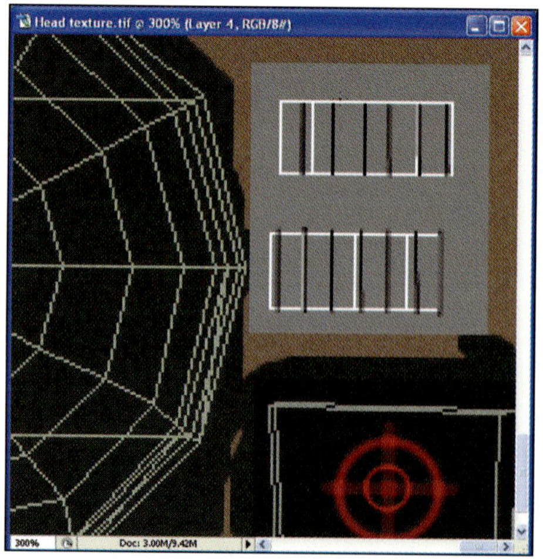

Figure 6.27 Thin black lines separate the individual teeth.

Create a Bump Map

1. Now let's create a displacement map so that we can selectively bump the surface of the individual sections of Hicks' body. Press Ctrl+A to select the entire Base layer, and then press Ctrl+C to copy it. Go to the Channels palette, create a new channel, and paste it with Ctrl+V. Adjust Levels to make the pattern a bit brighter and crisper.

2. Now go back to the base layer. According to the UV layout, for the head, you'll want to apply a bump map to the face details only, so select the Lasso tool to select the face parts. To this selection, apply Filter, Render, Lighting Effects, using the new Alpha 1 channel that you created as a displacement map. I used a Directional light type, at a slight angle pointing from top-right to bottom-left. Play around with this filter to get desired results. We're trying to achieve a pitted, scaly skin look.
3. Choose the inverted selection using the Select, Inverse menu, and fill the inverted selection with white (see Figure 6.28). Then save this image as the head bump map to be applied to the head's bump map channel.

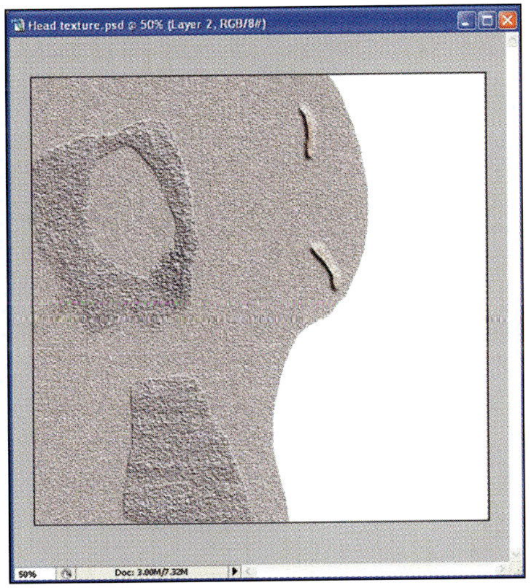

Figure 6.28 Render the Base layer using its copy as a bump map.

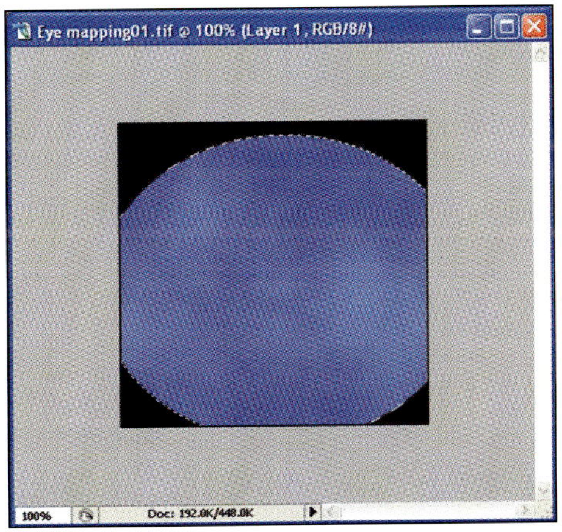

Figure 6.29 Start making the eyes by filling an elliptical selection with a Clouds mix of blue.

Texturing the Eyes

This is cool step, because the eyes really make Hicks look alive. I think having shiny, blue eyes would work quite well, so let me show you how I've accomplished this.

1. Load the eye mapping template, and create a new layer. Using the Elliptical Marquee tool, create an elliptical shape and fill it with the Clouds filter, using two bluish colors of your choice (see Figure 6.29). The eye you're making now should be huge—when finished, we'll scale it down and position it in the proper location.
2. Create a new layer on top of the blue eye layer. Make another elliptical selection, but this time in the circular shape of an eye pupil. Fill this with black, and then apply an Inner Bevel style to this layer (see Figure 6.30).
3. Merge the pupil layer to the eye's layer (Ctrl+E). Then Ctrl+click this layer to reload the eye selection, and start a new layer. With the eye-shaped selection on a new layer, apply a

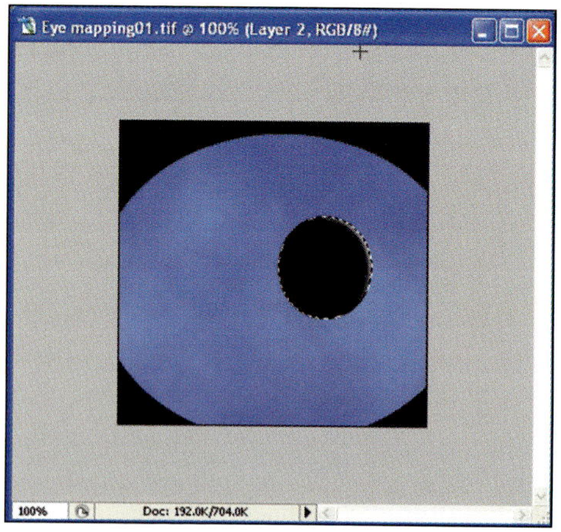

Figure 6.30 Create an eye pupil on another layer and apply an Inner Bevel to it.

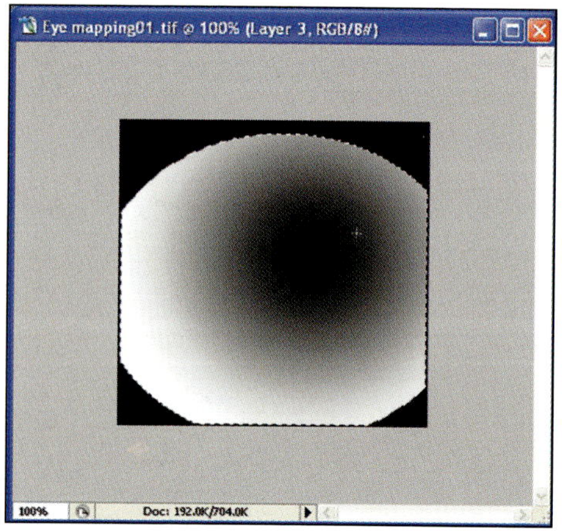

Figure 6.31 Fill the same eye shape with a white-to-black Radial Gradient on another layer.

white-to-black Radial Gradient (see Figure 6.31). We're going to use this to simulate the curvature of the 3D eyeball.

4. Change this gradient layer's blending mode from Normal to Color Dodge in the Layers palette. Notice that the gradient makes a cool lighting effect on the eyeball layer below it (see Figure 6.32). Now the eyeball looks shiny and 3D. You can merge this layer with the eyeball layer so it's complete.
5. You can inset the eyeball into the texture map by applying a slight Outer Bevel style. Then scale and position your eye according to the UV map—at first this might be a best-guess thing (see Figure 6.33). After the eye is in approximate position, duplicate it to the other side. Just remember to click Edit, Transform, Flip Horizontal to the second eyeball so that the lighting effects on it are mirrored.

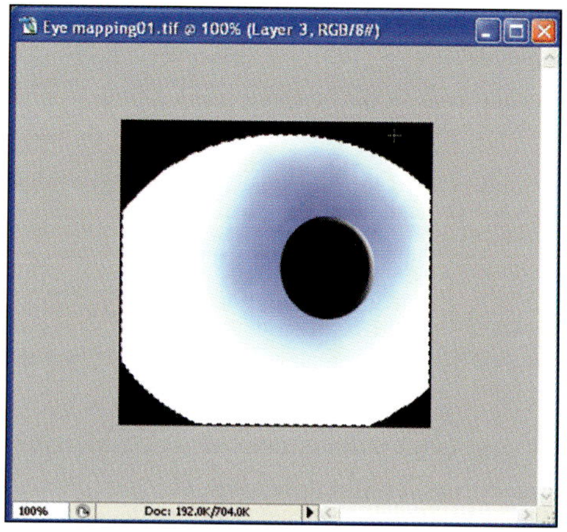

Figure 6.32 Change the gradient layer's blending mode to Color Dodge.

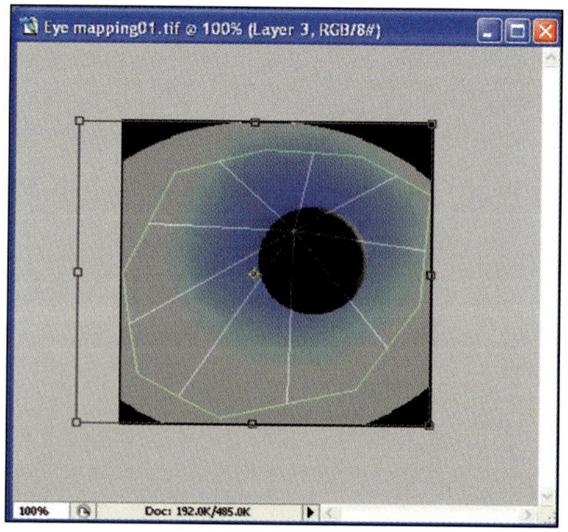

Figure 6.33 Scale and position the eye on the UV map.

6. When you're satisfied with the position and scale of the eyes, go ahead and merge them down permanently to the base layer. However, don't merge them with the background layer that shows the UV lines. You need to hide the background layer and turn up the opacity of the base layer before you save the final texture so that the lines don't appear in the texture. Then save the file as a PSD and TIF file.

Texturing the Torso, Arms, Legs, and Boots

There's not too much rocket science involved in texturing the limbs and body. When I showed you how to do the brow with an effects layer, you saw how easy and effective it was to dynamically raise the surface in a few brushstrokes. That's what we'll do here. However, because our Hicks mesh is detailed as it is, we don't have to do too much in the way of muscle definition.

We'll start with the torso by loading its UV map and defining its base colors, and then we'll add some detail and move onto the legs and boots. All of these parts are clothed and can be textured quickly.

1. Load the torso UV mapping image into Photoshop and add a new layer. This new layer will be the base layer holding all the background colors and textures for the items. Fill the entire layer with a dark green color, which is the most common color for the torso. Then decrease the layer opacity value so that the underlying UVs are still visible.

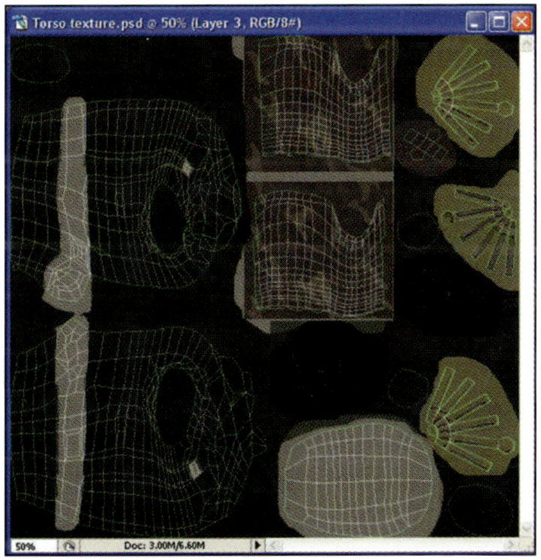

Figure 6.34 The base colors are filled in for all the torso parts.

2. Use the Lasso tool to select each of the parts and fill them with a different background color, including the camouflage pattern for the arm sleeves, dark green for the backpack, black for the shoulder light and the canteen, silver for the canteen cap, and gold for the bullets (see Figure 6.34).
3. Add more details to the jacket, such as brown for the belt and black for the strap that holds the bullets (see Figure 6.35).

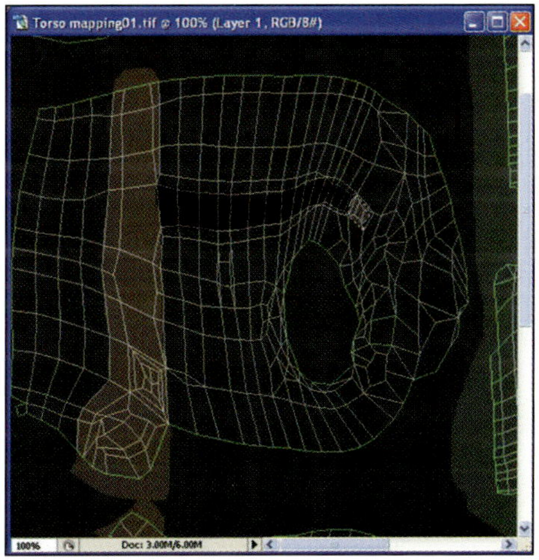

Figure 6.35 More colors define the bullet straps and the belt around the midsection.

4. Select the background layer, and with the Magic Wand, select the interior of all the bullet objects. Then switch to Layer 1 while maintaining the selection, and apply the Filter, Artistic, Plastic Wrap filter to the bullet selections (see Figure 6.36).
5. To add some texture to the jacket and arm sleeves that looks like leather, select just the cloth items and apply the Filter, Sketch, Reticulation filter. Set the Opacity to 100% for the base layer and hide the Background layer (see Figure 6.37). Then save the texture file as a PSD and a TIF file.
6. Load the legs UV mapping image into Photoshop and add a new layer. Fill the entire layer with a dark green color, but make the green color different from the torso for some variety. Then decrease the layer opacity value so that the underlying UVs are visible.
7. Use the Lasso tool to select and color each of the parts, including black for the shin guards and flashlight, white for the first aid kit, and red for the end of the flashlight. Select all the cloth portions, and apply the Reticulation filter to give it some texture (see Figure 6.38).

Figure 6.36 The Plastic Wrap filter adds a chrome look to the bullets.

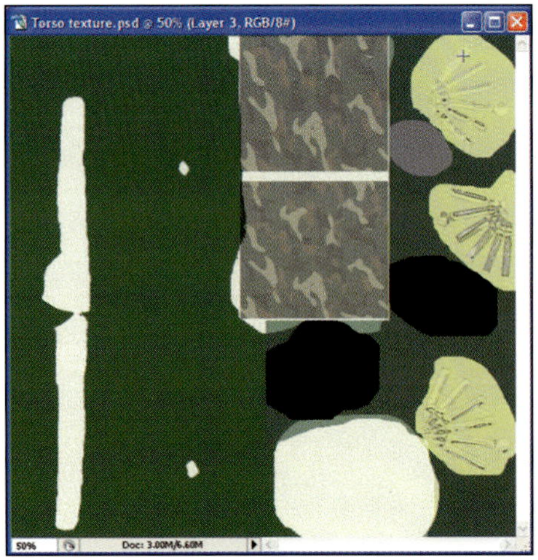

Figure 6.37 The Reticulation filter adds a leathery look to the jacket and backpack.

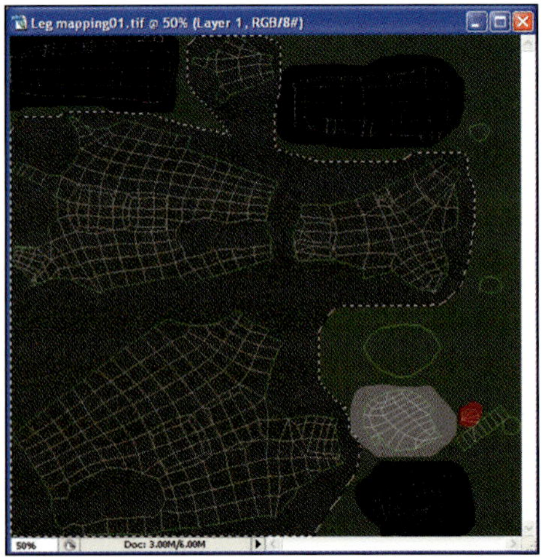

Figure 6.38 The base colors are filled in for all the various leg parts, and some texture is added.

8. Zoom in and add a red cross to the first aid kit by selecting a section with the Rectangular Marquee and filling the selection with red (see Figure 6.39). Use the Free Transform tool to rotate the cross to align with the mapping template.
9. Open the UV templates for both the left and right boots and fill the new layer with black. When you're done, select a circular brush and add several silver eyelets on either side of the boot's midline. Then paint in some laces using a dark brown brush. Finally, copy the laces to the opposite boot, and save both textures (see Figure 6.40).
10. Hide the background layer for the torso texture and both boot textures, reset the base layer's opacity value, and save each of these images as native PSD and TIF textures.

There really isn't much to teach here. Just start small, and keep going back and forth between your texture and 3ds Max to see if you like your progress or want to change something. The great thing about effects layers is that you can always erase your work without disturbing the base texture underneath. You might have noticed that my texture map is starting to have a much more realistic feel to it than the base layer originally contained. This is because when I did

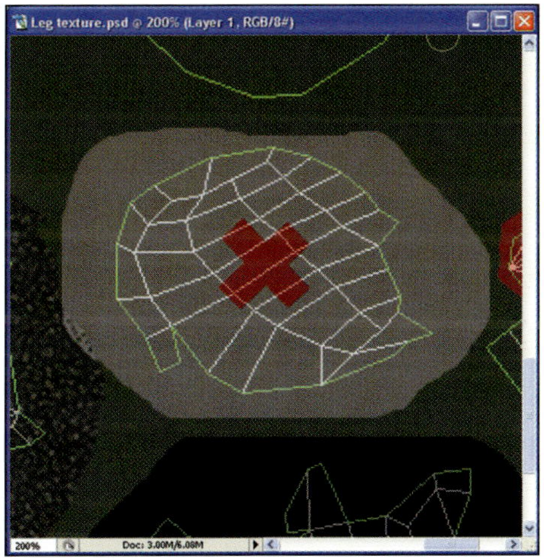

Figure 6.39 The first aid kit is easy to identify with the red cross.

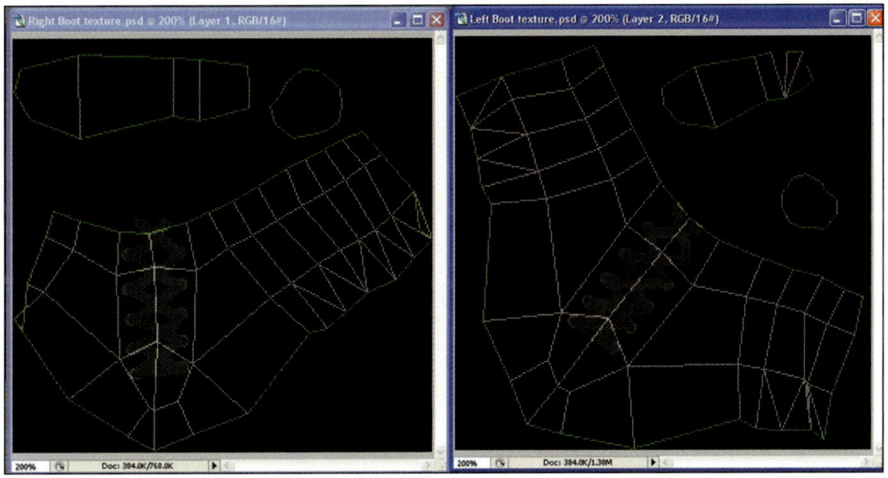

Figure 6.40 Add laces and eyelets to the boots, and color the background black.

all the muscles and whatnot with the Clone Stamp tool, I had that tool's Align option *unchecked*, so although I went over the map, the texture I was cloning from the base layer was becoming completely uneven, almost massaging it to what it looks like now. Should I have had the Align option checked, the original base texture would probably have looked the same, and it would have made it very time consuming cloning without constantly running into areas I didn't want cloned to the effects layer.

Texturing the Arms and Hands

The arms and hands aren't much to talk about. There's plenty of mesh definition, so the base texture nearly suffices. The only thing I did was to highlight the areas where the fingerless glove are. Also, remember to pull the skin color from the face so that the skin tone matches.

1. Open the UV templates for both arms. Add a new layer to each file, copy the skin color from the head texture image, and fill both arm textures with this color.
2. Add Noise to texture, with about 5 percent monochromatic (see Figure 6.41).
3. Zoom in on each hand, and lasso the areas of the hand that are covered by the gloves, with holes at each end. Then fill these areas with a black color, and apply the Reticulation filter (see Figure 6.42).
4. Hide the background layer, reset the base layer's opacity, and save the file as a PSD and a TIF file.

Cleaning Up

After all is said and done, it's usually necessary to make final adjustments to the map. I find that almost every time I texture, my skins have way too much color definition. Take care of this using Image, Adjust, Hue/Saturation, and desaturate the entire image until it looks a little washed. Adjusting Levels and Color Balance is good, too.

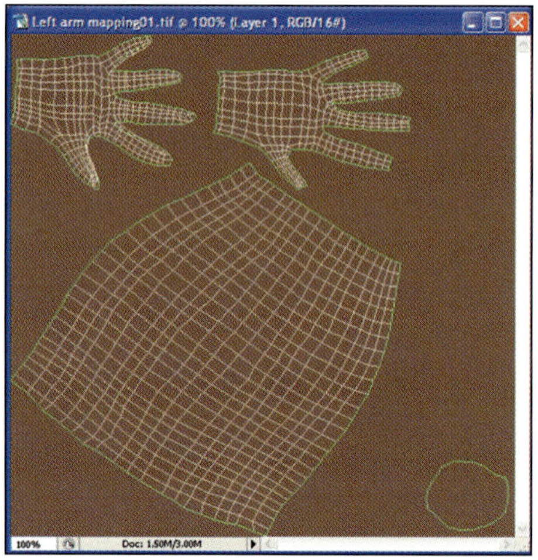

Figure 6.41 The arms and hands are filled with the same skin tone used for the face.

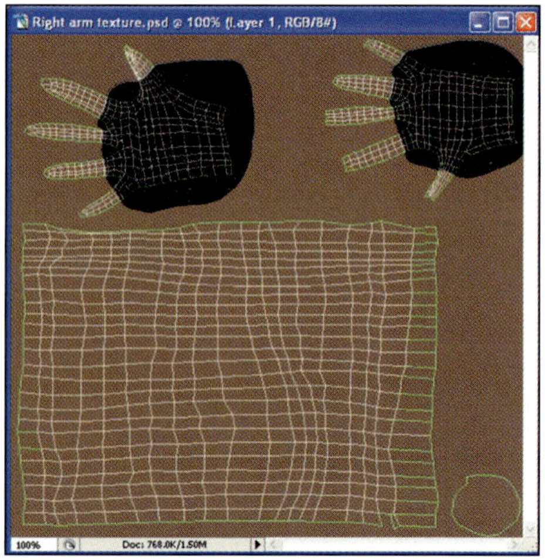

Figure 6.42 Each of the hand gloves is selected and filled with black.

Preparing the Map for 3ds Max

When you're finished with your texture, you need to resize it properly so that the game engine can handle it. For Torque, the texture needs to be 512×512 pixels or smaller, and saved as a PNG file. After you've saved the texture, you can load it in Max. Other game engines, such as *Half-Life* and *Unreal*, require you to save the maps as palettized BMP and PCX files.

To save the texture properly, first save the entire image file as is, with the UV layer on top and a single, merged base layer on the bottom, as a PSD file. This way you can come back to it and make modifications. Next, delete the UV layer entirely. Then click Image, Image Size, and set the dimensions to 512×512 pixels, with Resolution set at 512. Also, set the resampling option to Bilinear to help avoid a border that gets created otherwise. Most games these days use 256×256 bitmaps, but I hate that. We're at the end of those days, and I demand higher resolutions! Anyway, with the texture map properly resized, click File, Save As, and save the image as a PNG file. The PNG file format is one of the best formats you can use for games. It is supported by the Torque game engine.

Applying Textures in 3ds Max

After you've sized all the textures and you're ready to apply them to the Hicks character, you'll need to open the mapped Hicks Max file that includes the UV mappings. Then you can use the Material Editor to create a material for each part. Because earlier we created a material for each part and applied a checkerboard texture to the various parts, at this point we only need to replace the checkerboard with the correct texture and view it in Max.

1. Open the HICKS-textured.max file from the Chapter 6 folder on the CD-ROM. This file is the one that has all the test checkerboard textures applied to it. With this file, you'll only need to replace the checkerboard texture with the actual textures we just painted.
2. Open the Material Editor and select the first defined material for the legs. Click on the texture mapping button for the diffuse color to open the settings for the applied texture. Then click on the button that has the defined texture and select the Leg texture.tif file. Then drag the material to the leg object in the viewport to assign this material to the corresponding part.
3. Repeat step 2 for all the remaining parts. For the head, remember to apply the bump map also. Open the Maps rollout in the Material Editor and click on the button for the bump map. Then select the Bitmap option in the Material/Map Browser and select the bump map texture. Figure 6.43 shows the completed textures on the model in 3ds Max.

Figure 6.43 The completed texture maps applied to Hicks in 3ds Max.

Baking Textures in 3ds Max

The Hicks character is looking good, but there are currently too many textures to carry around in the game engine. We can fix this by baking the textures into the model. That will free up a lot of memory as we go through the animation process in the coming chapters.

Each vertex holds information about where it is located in space, but it can also hold color information using vertex colors. Baking textures is the process of taking the color information for each vertex and attaching it to the vertices. This inserts (or bakes) the texture information into the model.

Some game engines like using baked textures and others don't like them at all. For this example, we'll show you how to bake textures in 3ds Max and use the baked textures while we animate the character.

All kinds of information can be baked into a model, including lighting effects, colors, bumps, shadows, and normal maps. The interface for baking textures in 3ds Max is the Render to Texture dialog box. This dialog box lets you specify the type of map to create, the objects to bake, and how the baked textures are applied to the model.

Before baking the textures, we need to collapse the stack for each object. When you apply modifiers to objects, they are stacked in the Modify panel in a list that you can revisit, so if you apply a modifier to deform a character and later you want to remove it without affecting the underlying character, you can simply select it in the Modify panel and remove it. The problem is that when you try to change a modifier that affects a higher modifier in the stack, you can mess up the order of thing. For example, if you model a character using the mesh commands, apply an Unwrap UVW modifier to map the character, and then try to change the mesh object again, Max reports that your making changes to the mesh will mess up the mapping (see Figure 6.44). We can get around this problem by collapsing the stack, but doing so makes it so that we can't revisit the mapping anymore, but at this point, the mapping is set. Collapsing the stack is fine because the textures are in good shape. It will also simplify the mesh and make it cleaner as we move forward with the animations.

Use the next set of steps to bake the textures for the various parts using a complete map. This map selection will include lighting effects, highlights, and diffuse colors.

1. Select the torso object and open the Modify panel. Then right-click on the top modifier in the stack and select the Collapse All menu. A warning dialog box appears asking if you really want to do this. Click the Yes button, and all the modifiers are reduced to the base Editable Poly object.

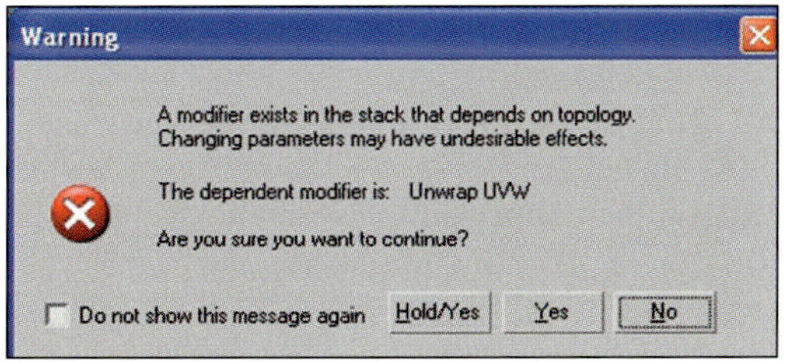

Figure 6.44 A warning dialog box appears when you try to make a change to a modifier below the stack.

2. Repeat the stack, collapsing all the other parts.
3. Select all the objects in the character, and open the Render to Texture dialog box. Each of the parts is listed in the Objects to Bake section. In the Mapping Coordinates section, select the Use Existing Channel option to use the mapping that we spent all this time doing. Then, in the Output section, click on the Add button, select the CompleteMap option, and select the Diffuse Color as the Target Map Slot. Then click the Render button to begin the baking process.
4. Each of the maps is rendered to Max's Render Frame window and saved in the specified path. These maps include all the lighting, shadows, and highlights of the rendered scene (see Figures 6.45 through Figure 6.49).

Figure 6.45 The baked torso texture rendered in 3ds Max.

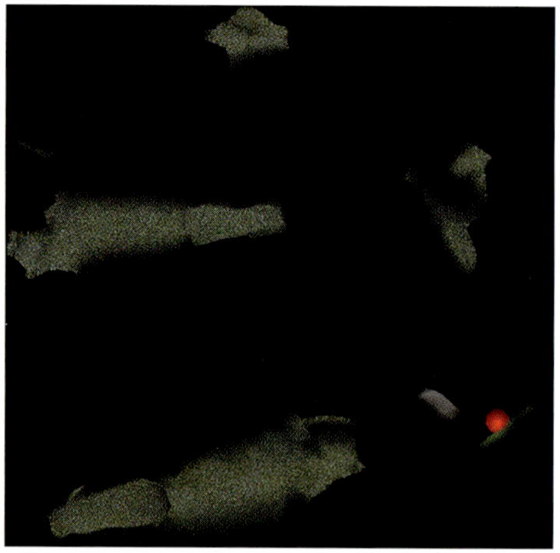

Figure 6.46 The baked leg texture rendered in 3ds Max.

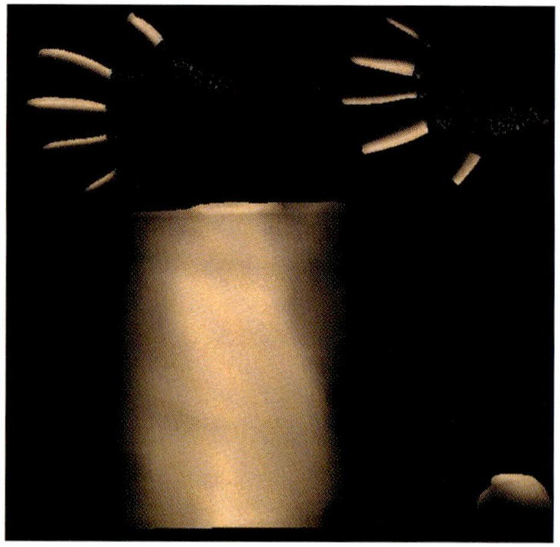

Figure 6.47 The baked arm and hand texture rendered in 3ds Max.

Figure 6.48 The baked head texture rendered in 3ds Max, including a bump map.

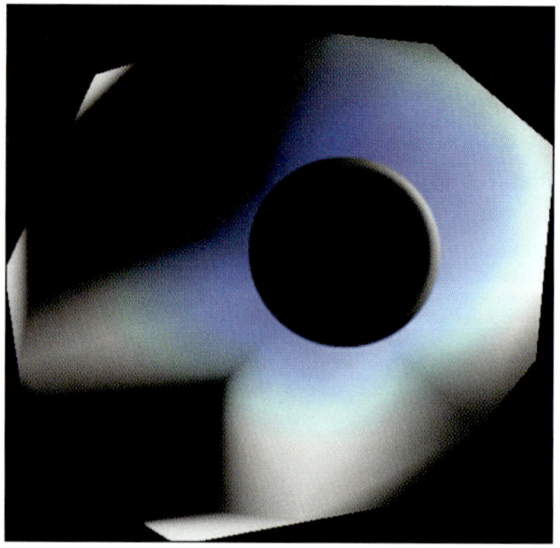

Figure 6.49 The baked eye texture rendered in 3ds Max.

Normal Maps

A recent development that has begun to appear in games such as *Unreal Tournament* and *Half-Life 2* is normal maps. These maps make it possible to add the lighting details from a high-resolution model onto a lower-resolution model using a special type of map called a normal map.

To create a normal map in 3ds Max, you need to prepare a high-resolution version of your character along with a lower-resolution character. You place the high-resolution model on top of the lower-resolution model, and you use the Projection modifier to map the vertices between the two models.

With the Projection modifier in place, you can use the Render to Texture dialog box to choose the normal map type to render. Then you can place this normal map in the bump map channel for the material on the object.

Summary

This chapter discussed how to texture a character in Photoshop CS2 using the UV templates as a background. We started by testing the mapping for each part by applying a checkerboard texture to it. This allowed us to make any changes to the mapping before moving to the texturing phase. We then built each texture by adding new layers to the existing file and filling the layer with a background color. Then, using the various Photoshop tools, we added details to the texture. At the end of the chapter, we reapplied the finished textures to the model and baked the textures onto the model. In the next chapter, we'll add a prebuilt skeleton rig to the character so that we can animate it easily.

Anyone who has never made a mistake has never tried anything new.
—*Albert Einstein*

Chapter 7

Rigging a Character with Biped in 3ds Max

With the character textured and looking good, you can start the animation process. The easiest way to animate the Hicks character is to add a structure of bones underneath the skin mesh. Then you can animate him by simply moving the bones into position, causing the skin mesh to deform along with the underlying bones. In this chapter, you will

- Start to add a biped to the scene
- Position the biped within the center of the skin mesh and move and scale all the bones to align with the skin mesh
- Apply the Skin modifier to the skin mesh and select all the bones to use to control the mesh
- Adjust the Skin modifier's envelopes for each bone to determine which skin vertices move with each bone
- Set the character in a default root pose

By installing a bones and skeletal weighting system, you ensure that the mesh will deform properly during animations. Any 3D video game's character that is capable of performing any type of movement contains a bones structure—invisible to the game world—that resides inside of and is attached to the mesh. The bones can consist of anything from a set of inverse kinematically linked primitive objects, like boxes, to a special Biped object that comes with a modifiable joint system. After you design and place a skeletal system, you can animate the bones. Then, after you create an animation sequence, the Torque exporter can export the sequence. In the game, the sequence will drive the bones system, which in turn animates the character mesh.

When you're finished with your mesh, the animated bones take care of the rest. It's up to you, however, to design animation sequences that the game engine can call during gameplay. For instance, if the user presses the Run Forward key, the Torque engine calls the player_forward.dsq animation, and the mesh deforms accordingly. (That is, the left and right leg bones move in a running motion.) For every action that is required of your character in a game, you must develop a sequence that drives it. Thankfully, however, the Torque engine and many others come with default character animations that you can use to drive the skeleton you create. (See the "Adding and Attaching a Biped" section that follows.)

Note

In many games, you can blend animation sequences, as is the case when a character is running and firing a weapon at the same time.

How 3ds Max Works with Characters

3ds Max includes a unique set of features for handling characters. This set of features is collectively called Character Studio. These features used to be available as a separate set of plug-ins, but they have recently been added to Max's base package. The key component of these features is a predefined bipedal skeleton system (called a biped in 3ds Max) that you can modify to your character's shape, attach to your character, vertex weigh, and animate. (Of course, you could set up your own skeletal system from scratch, but why bother when someone else has already done it for you?) In fact, this set of features also contains many predefined basic animations that you can apply to your characters. Here's a short list of the main steps you'll take to get the Hicks model running, so to speak:

Caution

Not all game engines will work with Max's biped objects. Some only accept bones. Check with your game engine documentation before using the biped features.

1. **Install the biped.** This involves adding and modifying a bipedal bones system, which starts off as a template of sorts. The biped is positioned and scaled to the inside of the limbs of the mesh, and finally attached using the Skin modifier. After you've attached the biped, you can deform the mesh around the bones by grabbing them and moving them around.
2. **Weight the skin.** This is the process of defining the envelopes of influence that the bones have over the neighboring vertices. Put simply, there is a 1:1 bone-to-mesh ratio for deformation. The bones apply themselves directly to the vertices of the mesh. In some cases, however, you must further define preferences that the bones themselves have for moving certain vertices over others. This is called *weighting*, and it's fun but somewhat tedious. If you don't weight certain areas

correctly, like where the upper arm meets the forearm, the movements will look weird, such as seeing the forearm bulge instead of the bicep.

3. **Animate the bones.** When the skeletal weighting is satisfactory, the next step is to generate individual animation sequences for the bones to follow. You can use presets in Character Studio, or you can define your own. Animation of bones is subject for an entire book, literally, so for now we'll use the default Torque sequences.
4. **Export the mesh/animation.** The last steps are to export the mesh (and the individual animations that drive the skeletal system) to the game engine of your choice using that engine's proprietary Max exporter plug-in. In this case, you'll dump out just the mesh with a biped object installed to the Torque engine, without animations. (The game engine's default animations will do the trick and drive the bones of the Hicks model character.) Generally speaking, the game needs a reference mesh—which is just the static, unanimated model—and a series of animation sequences without the mesh that drive the static model. Typically, the static mesh model is referred to as a *reference*.

These first two steps including installing the biped and weighting the skin will be covered in this chapter, and the final two steps of animating the bones and exporting the mesh to the Torque game engine will be covered in Chapter 8, "Character Animation in 3ds Max."

Adding and Attaching a Biped

The first thing you should do before you begin adding a Biped is hide all the objects that you created earlier, except for the Hicks model mesh. Doing so helps unclutter your workspace. To hide all your objects, click on the Display panel, and then choose Hide by Name within the panel's rollout. In the Hide Objects dialog box that pops up, select everything except the Hicks model item, and then click Hide (see Figure 7.1). Use the Display

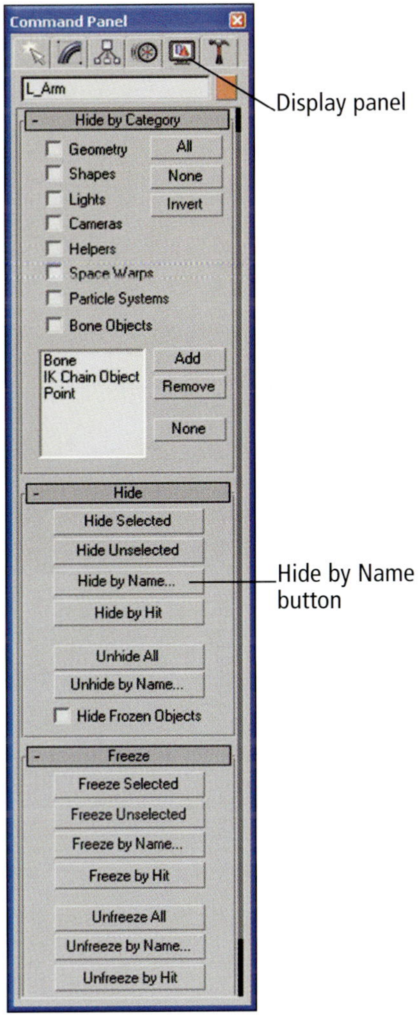

Figure 7.1 Hide everything except the Hicks model mesh using the Display panel.

panel to hide and unhide objects, and to freeze and unfreeze them. (Freezing locks down objects so they can't be manipulated.)

It would be difficult to install the biped in the Hicks model while it's in solid render mode, but it would be helpful to have a visible, see-through shape of him. Click on the Hicks model to select it. Then, at the bottom of the Display panel, check See-Through in the Display Properties section. The solid rendered mesh should turn into a see-through object (see Figure 7.2). Finally, to prevent the Hicks model from being affected while you're adjusting the biped, freeze him in place by choosing Freeze Selected in the Freeze section of the Display panel rollout.

Adding, Adjusting, and Aligning a Biped

Follow these steps to install and position a biped structure that will be used by the animations in the Torque engine to move the Hicks model mesh.

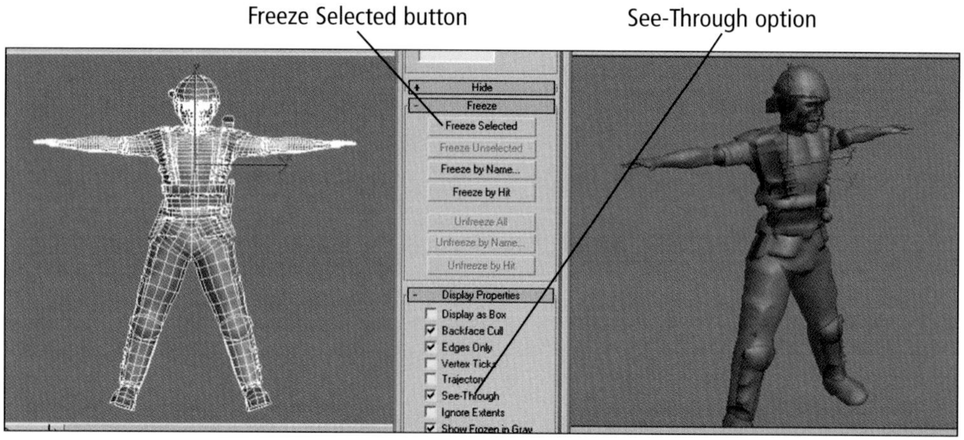

Figure 7.2 Make the Hicks model transparent using the See-Through option; then freeze him.

1. Click on the Create panel, and then click the Systems button. Under the Systems section, click the Biped button. A default parameterized panel rolls out, allowing you to make adjustments to the number of limbs, fingers, toes, and so on that your character will have. For now, leave that section alone, because you can adjust those settings after you create the biped. In the User view, click and drag the cursor to the approximate height of the Hicks model, and release it. In a flash, the new biped skeleton is created (see Figure 7.3).
2. Now change the Spine Links to 3 in the Create panel's Biped rollout. Notice that when you do that, the spinal column bone count of the biped drops automatically, and the entire biped shifts to compensate (see Figure 7.4). Next, change the Fingers to 1 and the Finger Links to 1. Do the same for the toes. Even

though the Hicks model has five fingers, and you could just as well install all five, his hand will be the only thing animating that portion of the general appendage, according to the default animations of the Torque engine. (For other game engines, you might need to utilize these finger bones to articulate the fingers in the mesh.) Finally, change the Height parameter to 1.78m; this will be the approximate height of the Hicks model.

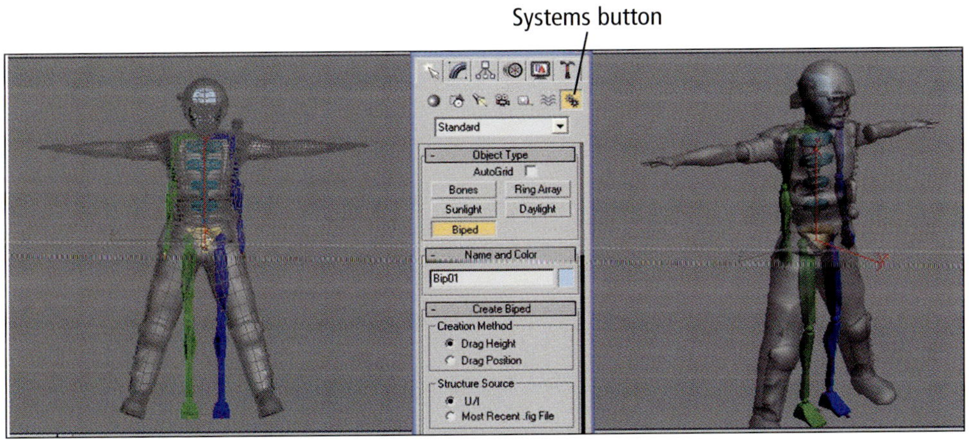

Figure 7.3 Select Biped from the Object Type section of the Create panel, and click and drag to create a biped.

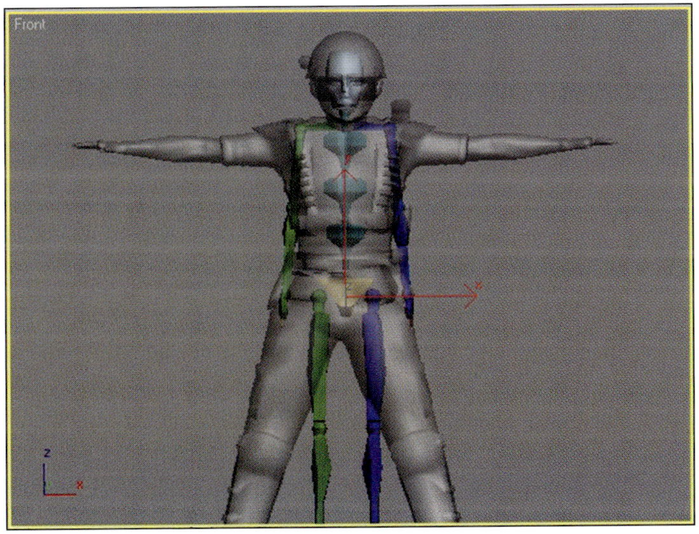

Figure 7.4 Adjust the parameters of the biped to change the bone structure.

Note

You can change the parameters in the Biped rollout to create a nearly infinite amount of skeletal structures that would fit and work with almost any shape mesh. The possible bipedal arrangement has a couple of interesting features. For instance, you can use the Ponytail links to drive the lower jaw of a character, which you can then animate to simulate speech.

Figure 7.5 Enable the Figure Mode button in the Motion panel.

3. Now you must move the biped and rotate it into position. The goal here is to place the biped in the exact center of the Hicks model mesh; then you can adjust the individual limbs to coincide with the Hicks model's joints. To do this, click on the Motion panel, and then click on the Figure Mode button (see Figure 7.5). The Figure Mode button allows you to fine-tune the biped's shape to match the Hicks model's. The Motion panel is also where you can make and modify animations for the biped.

4. Use the Select and Move tool, along with the Left, Top, and User views, to position the biped so that the pelvis is in the approximate location of the Hicks model's pelvis (see Figure 7.6). The pelvic area houses the biped's center of mass (COM), which helps determine the overall balance that the character possesses when in motion. Be sure to align the biped so that it is as centered as possible within the mesh.

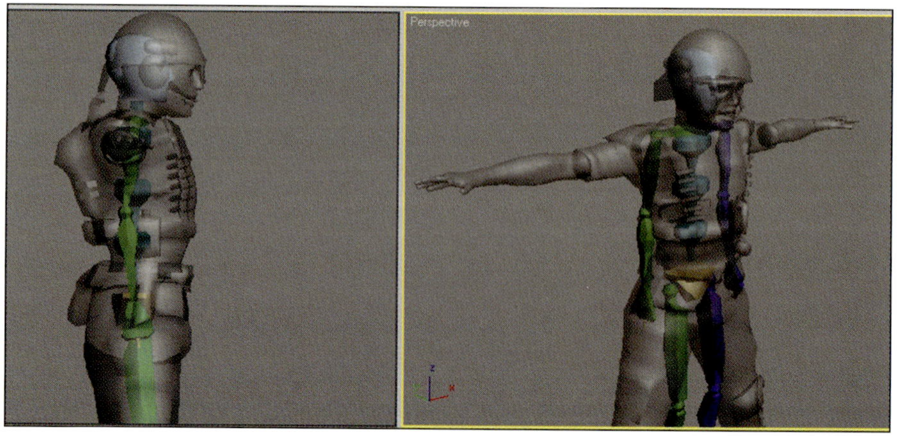

Figure 7.6 Rotate and move the Bip01 object so that the biped pelvis is centered to match Hicks' pelvis.

Note

The COM is a separate element of the biped structure, and not really a bone object. You can position it during animations to change the way a character moves. For instance, when a character transitions from a walk to a sprint, it would be more natural for the COM to shift forward, causing the character to lean forward. If the COM stayed exactly in the center of the pelvis, the character would remain unnaturally erect when going from walking to sprinting.

Matching the Biped Skeleton to the Hicks Model

Now for the fun part (note sarcasm). This next part, where you have to scale, transform, and align all the bones of the biped so that they take on roughly the same shape as the character mesh, is probably one of the most time-consuming and tedious of things to do in the modeling industry. The point of this careful aligning is to make the skin-weighting job (discussed in the next section) much easier. 3ds Max does a fantastic job of making biped alignment a fairly smooth process, but let me warn you now—you must take your time and have patience. This process will become easier with experience.

The bones in the biped have special properties called *envelopes*, which are mechanisms with which the animator makes adjustments so that the bones properly control their nearby vertices. The size of each bone directly corresponds, generally speaking, to the size of the control envelopes after you apply the Skin modifier to the mesh. Therefore, the more precise you are about matching the biped bones to the mesh, the easier the overall weighting process will be. Following are the general steps you need to take to align the biped skeleton to the Hicks model mesh:

1. Switch to a Front view (this displays the front of the model) and click the Min/Max toggle button at the bottom-right corner of the screen. This makes your character take up the entire screen space.
2. Start by swinging the biped's arms up so that they generally match the Hicks model's. Do this by clicking once on the Select and Rotate tool, and then once on the left upper arm, which should become highlighted. Next, click on the Symmetrical button in the Motion panel; the right upper arm of the biped becomes selected. It's best to work symmetrically; that way, everything stays even. Now click and drag on the first yellow concentric circle of the Rotate gizmo, which represents the Z-axis of the bone. As you drag, notice that both arms swing upward (see Figure 7.7). You might have to turn off the Angle Snap Toggle button to position the arms more precisely. The arms should now be somewhat in the same position and shape as the Hicks model's.

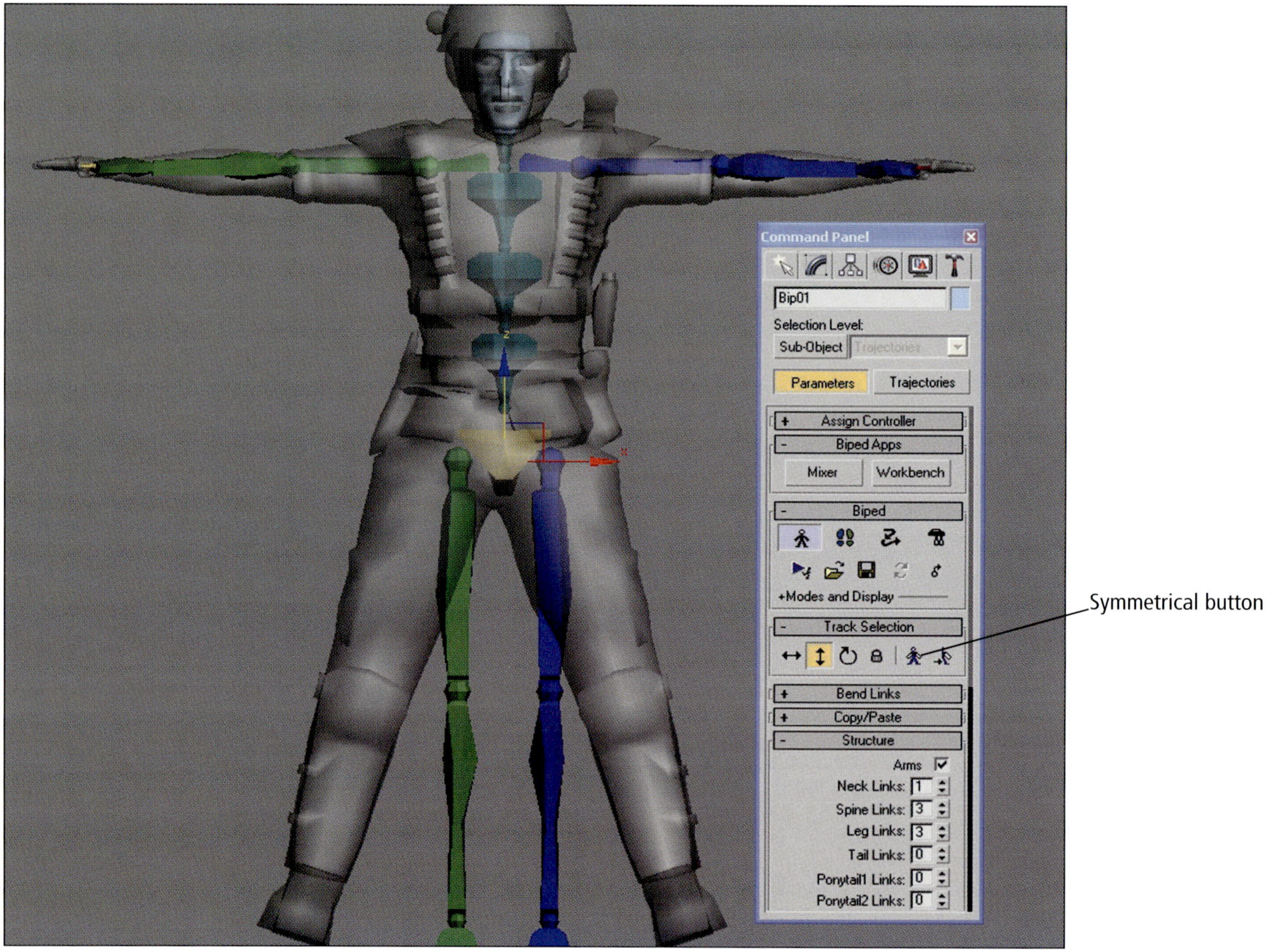

Figure 7.7 With the Symmetrical button enabled, rotate the upper arms so that both are in the same position as the Hicks model's.

Note

The biped object's bone structure works in almost the same way that a human's does. That is, if you try to rotate the forearm back and forth, it only goes toward the body and does not bend backward at the elbow. Also, as you pull forward on the forearm, the upper arm naturally (and not rigidly) follows with it. This process is called *inverse kinematics*. It is a characteristic feature of Character Studio bipeds.

3. Now you need to scale the upper bones of the biped to match the Hicks model's mesh. First click on the Select and Non-Uniform scale button, and then click on one of the clavicle bones. After that, select the Symmetrical button in the Motion panel and scale the bones so that they spread the arms away from the body a bit. This action pushes the upper arm bones out so that they're in better position (see Figure 7.8).
4. Continue scaling the other spine, neck, and head components to fit the mesh. The spine doesn't need to precisely fit the belly of the Hicks model; simply adjust the spine so that the arms drop down and center themselves within the mesh. You can scale the head fairly big and elongated to cover the entire neck and face of the Hicks model.
5. Next, you can stretch the arms and scale them outward. A cool feature of biped is the Rubber Band option, located in the Motion panel. Click on this option; then select the forearms and scale them. Notice that as you scale the forearms toward the palms, the upper arm bones follow in a stretching attitude (see Figure 7.9). You can use the Rubber Band feature only with the arm and leg bones, but it does make your job much easier.

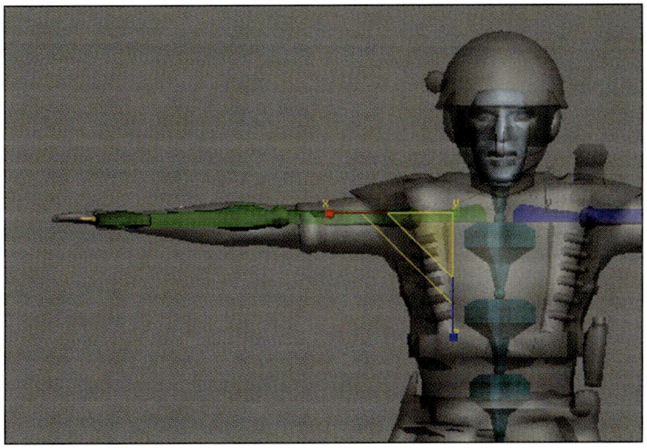

Figure 7.8
Symmetrically scale the clavicles so that they spread the arms away from the body.

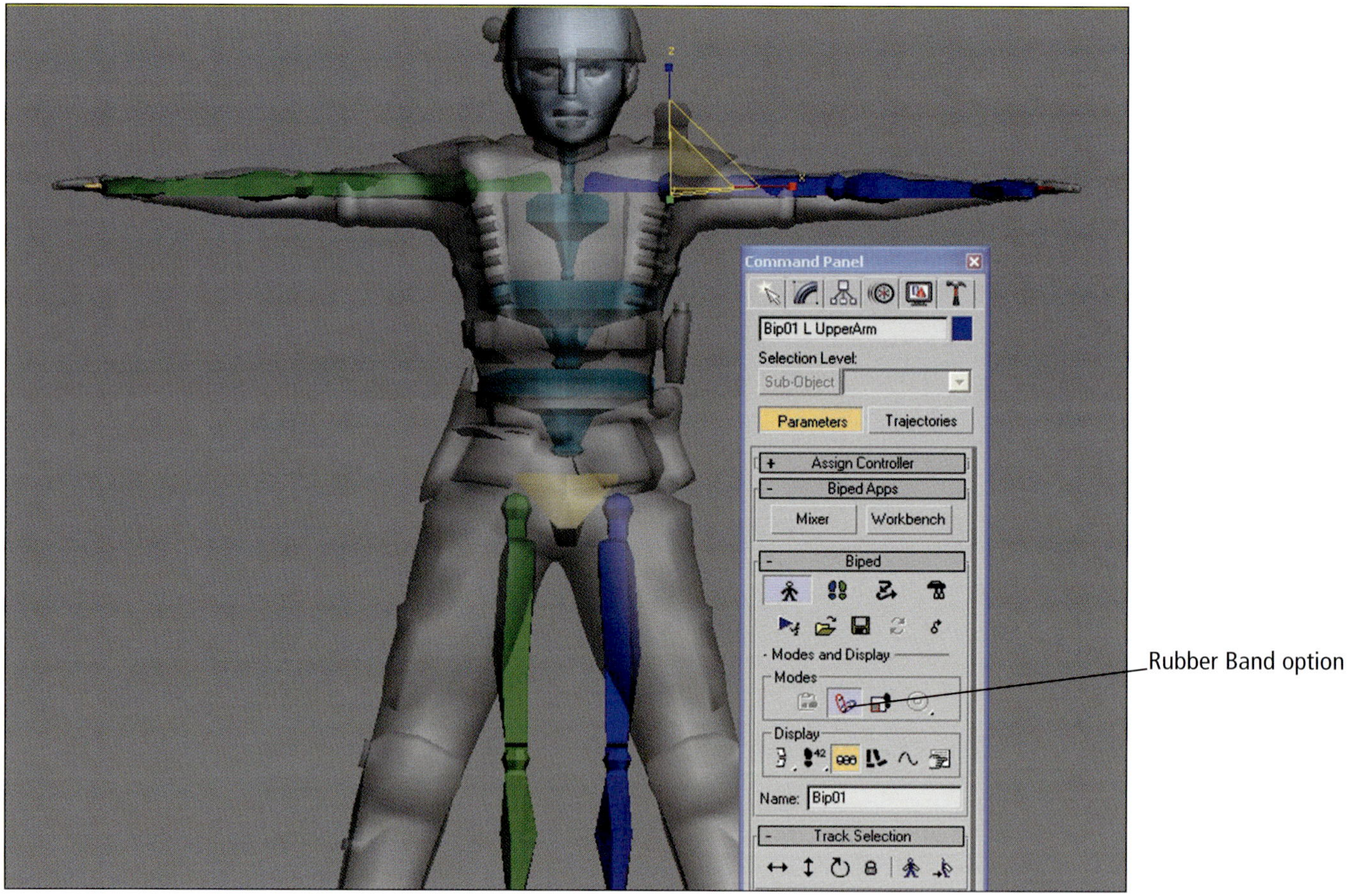

Figure 7.9 Enable the Rubber Band option and symmetrically scale the forearms to match the Hicks model's.

Tip

If you're having trouble conceptualizing the rotation of bones, or if you try to rotate one bone and, annoyingly, another bone moves, mimic the same movements yourself. Just place your arms straight out, palms down, and rotate your forearms backward. Your hands have no choice (unless you're weirdly jointed) but to rotate backward, too.

6. Continue scaling and adjusting the biped's upper arms, forearms, and hands to completely fill the Hicks model. Be sure that the joints generally match up to the joints of the Hicks model mesh. That is, the elbow is where the upper arm and the forearm meet, and the end of the forearm is the wrist, just after the Hicks model's metal cuff. Then switch to the Top viewport and align the arms in this view also.
7. Repeat steps 2 through 6 for the legs (see Figure 7.10).

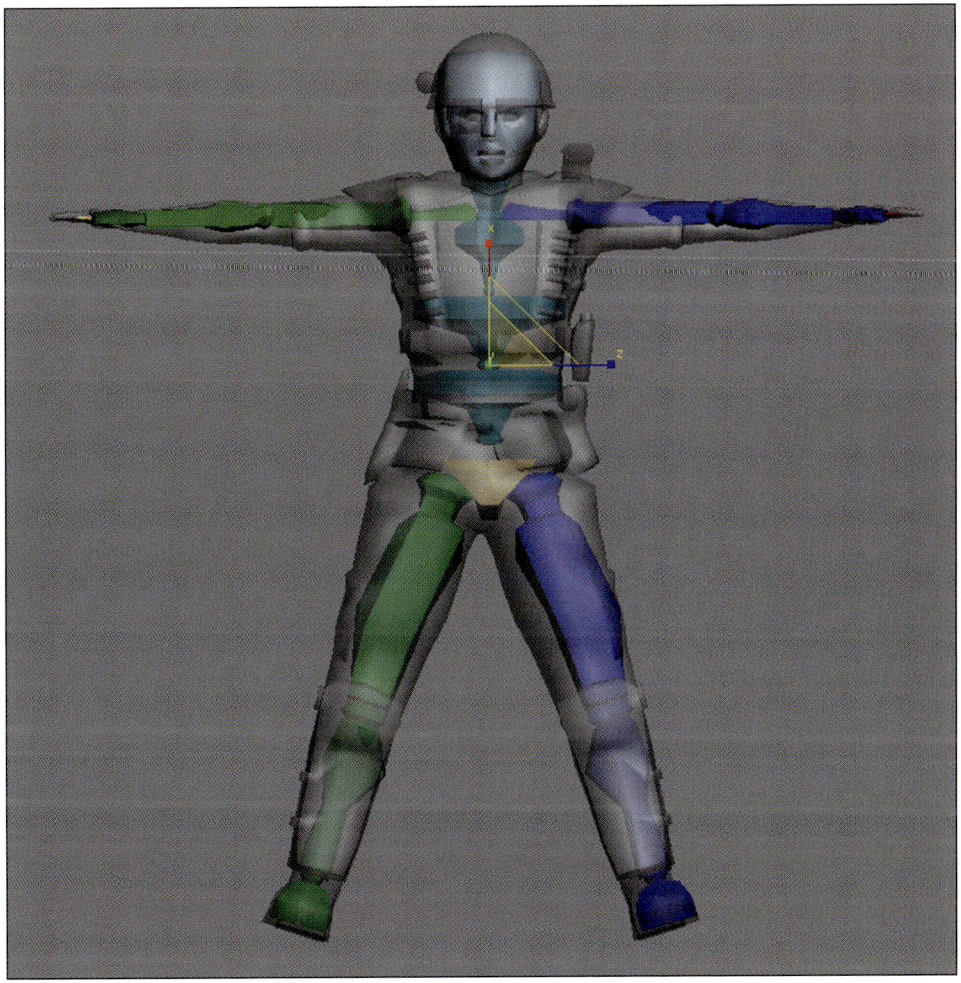

Figure 7.10 Repeat the moving, rotating, and scaling procedure for the legs. Be sure that the joints match up.

8. When the bones are scaled and they match the Hicks model as well as possible, click the Min/Max toggle button to go back to the orthogonal view screens. Select and maximize the Left viewport, and spend some time scaling and aligning the biped from this view. Scale and move all the bones so that the entire biped structure fits as well as possible into the Hicks model mesh (see Figure 7.11). Note that the spine objects don't have to be big; in fact, scaling them to the size of the mesh only makes the weighting envelopes enormous and causes them to hog all the vertices of the Hicks model.

You can now click on the Save Figure button, located in the Motion panel. This saves the current figure of the biped, which you can recall should anything go awry later on. Also, when you're satisfied with the biped, click the Figure Mode button in the Motion panel to exit this mode. After you're out of the figure mode, try clicking the Save button again. It now saves the biped object (that is, the bones structure that you created). Saving these items (FIG and BIP files) is a good idea so that you can recall them later if you accidentally move any of the bones. Saving them also allows you to retrieve the biped for another character (see Figure 7.12).

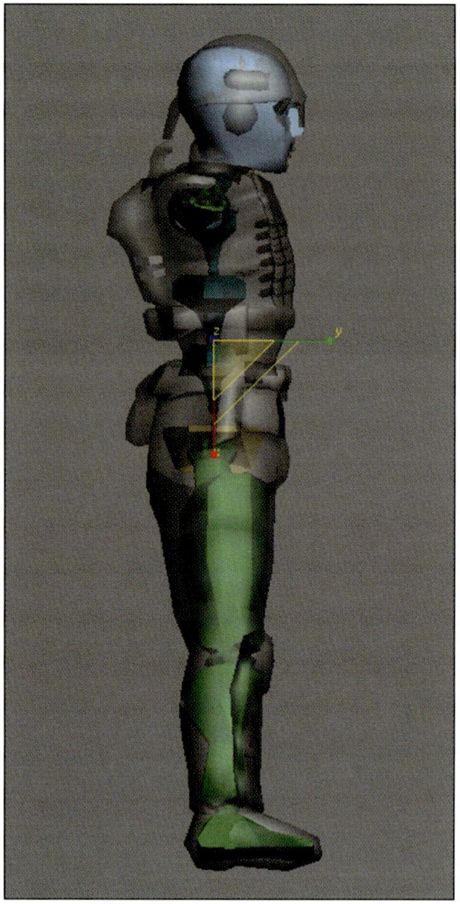

Figure 7.11 Use the other orthogonal views to scale and rotate all the components to match the side profile of the Hicks model's body. Note that you don't have to scale the spine objects to match the Hicks model's body.

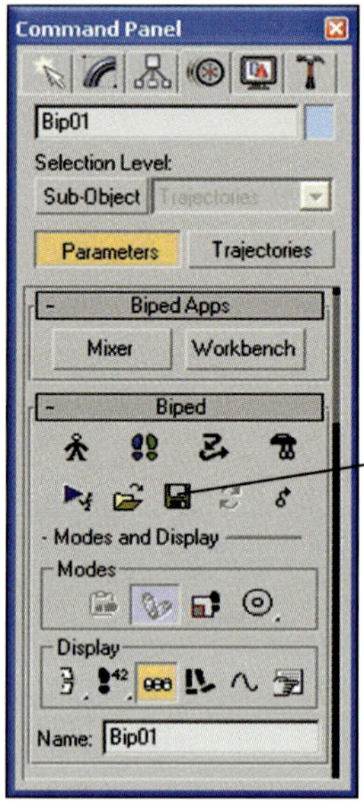

Figure 7.12 Save the biped figure using the Save Biped File button in the Motion panel.

Attaching the Biped to the Hicks Model by Using the Skin Modifier

You must apply the Skin modifier before the biped can drive the mesh of the Hicks model. Before you proceed, change the view of the bones to a more comfortable one by clicking on the Bones button in the Motion panel; a wireframe version of the bones is displayed. Click on the Objects button right next to the wireframe. This turns on and off the 3D representation of the bones (see Figure 7.13). The small + signs between bones represent the joints, giving you a better view of their alignment with the mesh. Hmm, doesn't look like all that work you put in was worth it now, eh?

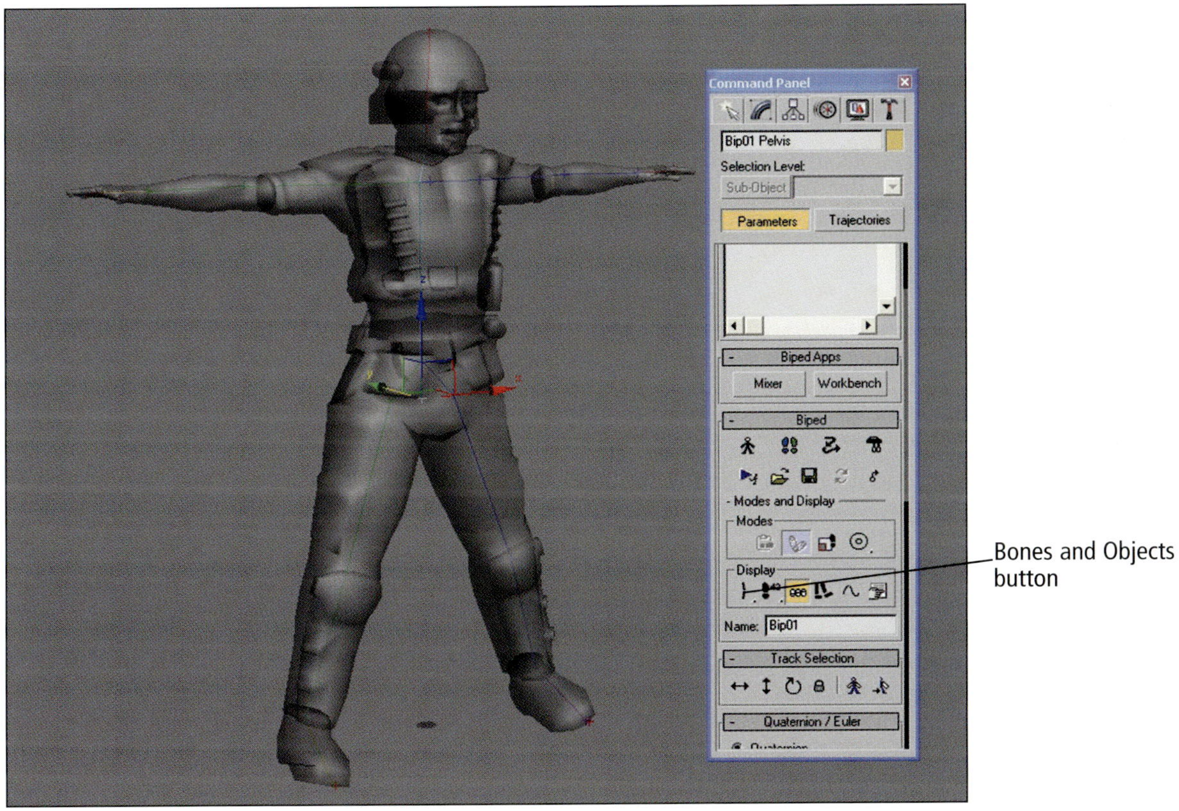

Figure 7.13 In the Display section of the Motion panel, turn on Bones and turn off Objects.

Before you continue, you need to combine all the various body parts into a single skin mesh. Because the skeleton is a single system, the skin also needs to be a single object. To combine all the objects, select a single part such as the torso, click on the Attach List button in the Modify panel, and select all the other body parts. This combines all the parts into a single skin mesh object. You can tell when you're successful because all the parts will have the same object color.

You need to unfreeze the Hicks model and unhide any object that you hid earlier in the chapter. Go to the Display panel and choose both Unhide All and Unfreeze All. The Torque engine uses the Bip01 object as the top level of the hierarchy. All that should be in the scene now are the Bip01 biped structure and the Hicks mesh (see Figure 7.14).

Now select the Hicks model mesh and, in the Modifier panel, apply a Skin modifier. This modifier doesn't look like much, because you haven't added the bones. Click on the plus sign to the left of the Skin modifier to expand the modifier, and then select Envelopes. In the Envelopes rollout, click on the Add button. Doing so displays a Select Bones screen (see Figure 7.15), which allows you to select which bones you want to drive the mesh. For the Torque engine, you need everything except the Bip01 object, Footsteps, all toes, any fingers, and nub objects.

You're excluding the toes and fingers because you'll only really need them to help position the arms. You could have included additional fingers in

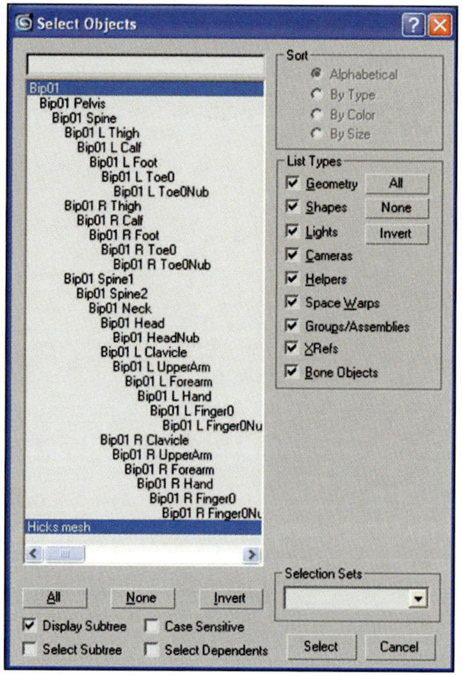

Figure 7.14 In the Select Objects dialog box, only the Bip01 structure and the Hicks mesh exist.

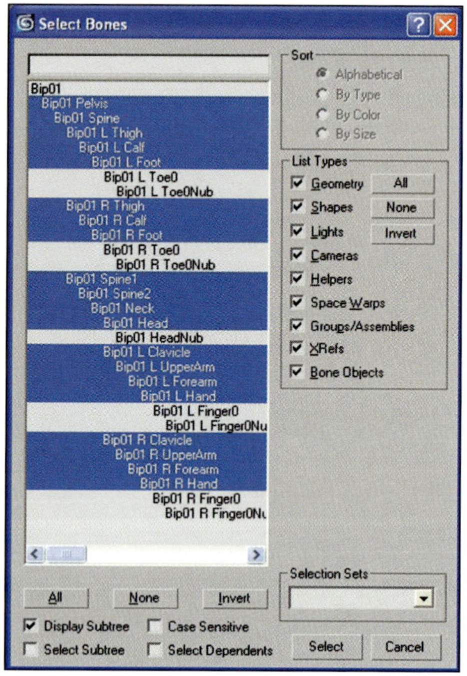

Figure 7.15 Apply the Skin modifier to the Hicks model mesh. Expand the modifier, select Envelopes, and then add all biped objects (except Bip01, Footsteps, toes, any fingers, and nubs) to the Envelopes section.

the original biped object, to curl the fingers of the Hicks model mesh, but the Torque engine's default animations don't use them—the hand bones move both the hands and fingers of the Hicks model. After you've included the proper selection of bones in the Skin modifier, the Hicks model mesh becomes surrounded by wireframe representations of the adjustable skin envelopes (see Figure 7.16).

Weighting the Model

After you've added the bones to the Skin modifier, they're linked to the mesh, and you're free to grab them and move them, which in turn should drive the mesh that surrounds them. However, before you move the bones, you need to be sure that the envelopes of the bones equally surround all vertices of the mesh, so that the mesh moves smoothly at each bone location of the Hicks model's body. Also, stray vertices that weren't included in an envelope stick in 3D space and don't move with the bones, preventing the Hicks model character from working

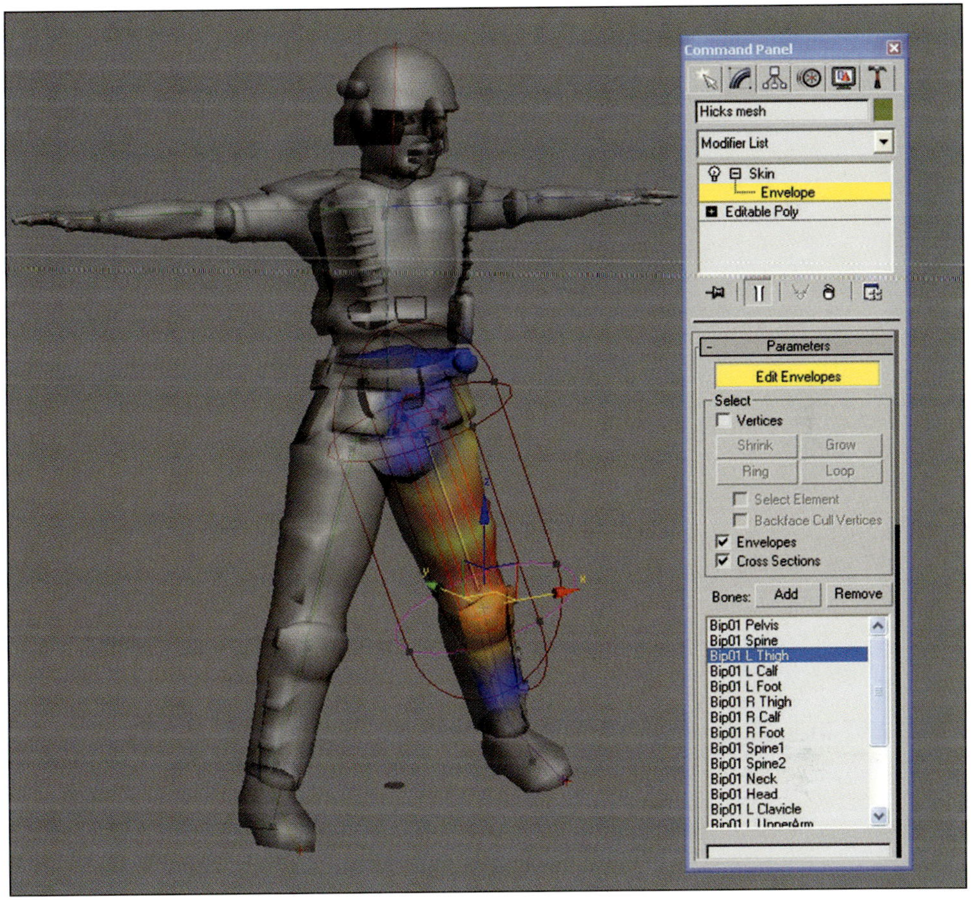

Figure 7.16 The attached biped, displaying the skin envelopes.

properly (or at all) in the game engine. Following are the steps for adjusting the weights (balance of bone usage) of the vertices:

1. To make viewing the weighting much easier, make the mesh solid by going to the Display panel and unchecking the See-Through option in the panel's Display Properties section. Next, in the Display Color section at the top of the Display panel, check the Shaded: Object Color option. This makes the Hicks model mesh a solid color (see Figure 7.17).

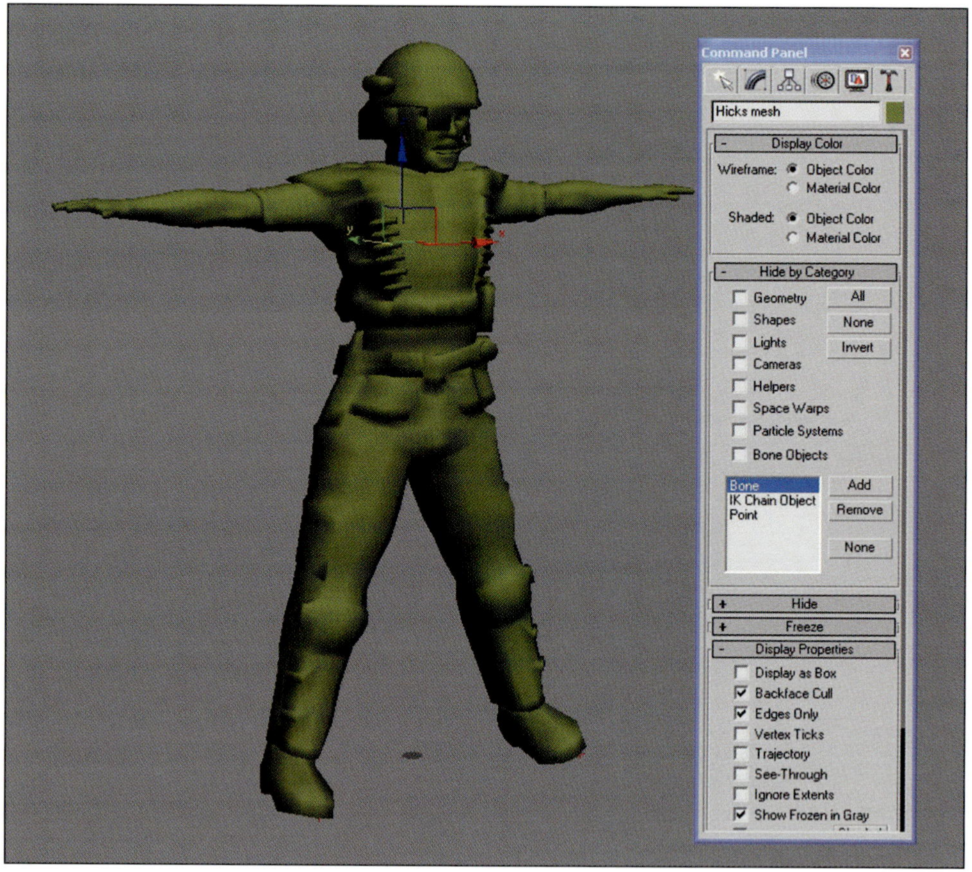

Figure 7.17 Select the Hicks model mesh, and in the Display panel, select Shaded: Object Color. Press F3 to see the flat, shaded Hicks model.

Tip

You can turn off the grid by clicking Views: Show Home Grid in the top menu bar. This makes your workspace even less cluttered.

2. Now go back to the Modifier panel and select Envelope in the Skin modifier. The currently selected bone should display its envelope as varying shades of light yellow (least influenced vertices for that bone) to dark

red (strongly influenced vertices) (see Figure 7.18). The various shades represent the weighting of the skin (mesh) for that particular area. Try selecting different bones from the list to see their influence on the vertices of the mesh. Also, by pressing F3, you can switch back and forth between the solid rendered mode and the wireframe mode that shows the vertices.

3. Click on each bone and look at the weighting around that area. Check for bones that are taking up too much weight on vertices that don't really belong to them. For instance, in my situation, the head is covering vertices that belong to the Hicks model's back (see Figure 7.19). In a case like this, it's necessary to adjust the envelope for this bone so that it covers only the head of the Hicks model.

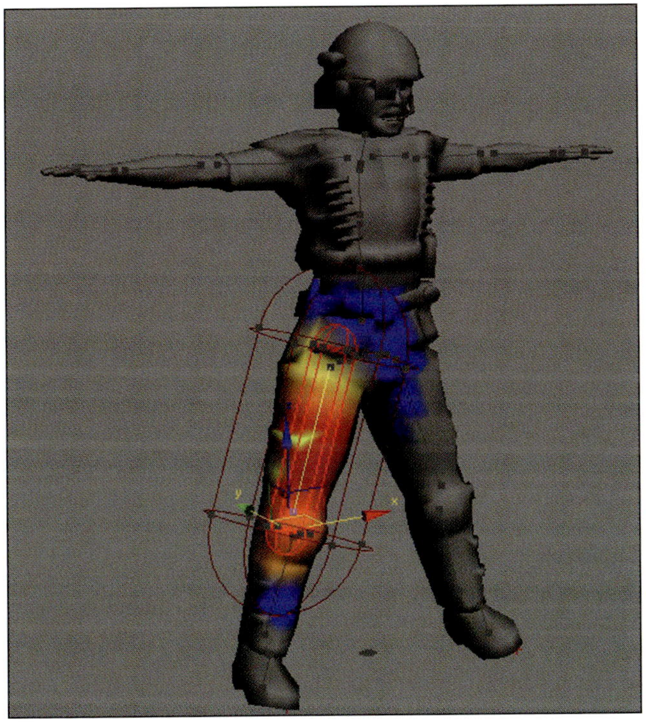

Figure 7.18 By clicking on a bone, you can see various shades of color that indicate the bone's preference to the vertices nearest its area.

Figure 7.19 Notice that the head's envelope encompasses too many vertices, including those from the back. Adjust the head's envelope so that it uses mainly those vertices from the head portion of the mesh.

4. In the Skin modifier's rollout, just below the bone list, is an Envelope Properties section. By changing the Radius value, you can effectively increase or decrease the size of the envelope. Or, you can click on the Move tool and then click on any one of the envelope's control points to move or scale them. In Figure 7.20, I selected the outer envelope points and reduced the Radius value, which effectively occluded the vertices of the back.

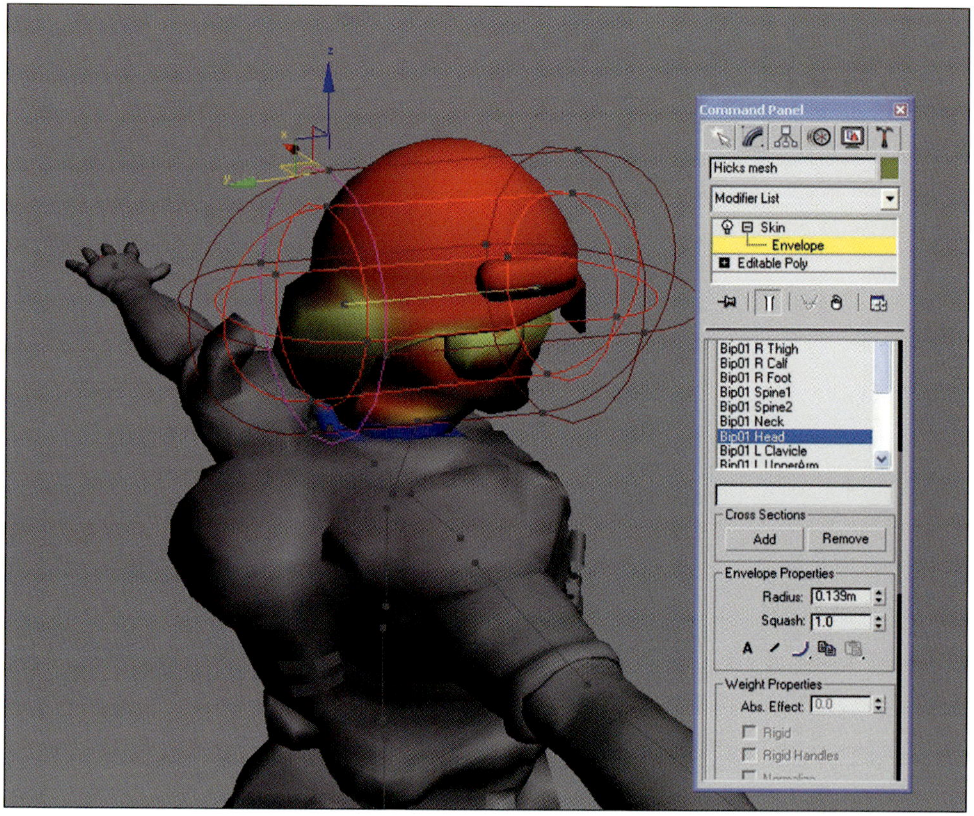

Figure 7.20 The adjusted head's envelope.

5. Sometimes it's hard to see if there are any stray vertices that aren't enclosed by an envelope. Try this: Click on the Skin portion of the Skin modifier to exit envelope mode, click on the Select by Name button at the top of the screen, and then select the hand bone. Use the Move tool to swing the Hicks model's arm forward. Notice in Figure 7.21 the stray vertices that need to be encompassed by the hand's envelope. They seem to stick in place.

6. With the arm still swung outward, I went back to the Envelope portion of the Skin modifier and adjusted the hand's envelope to extend a little further beyond the fingers. In a flash, the stray vertices got sucked back in, becoming part of the hand bone's control (see Figure 7.22). The stray vertices, in this case, are the byproduct of the finger bones not being included in the envelope list.
7. Continue checking the rest of the bones for stray vertices. Pressing F3 to enter wireframe mode is another good way to do this, because the strays will not show up in colored envelopes, but will instead be a blue-colored vertex. Just play around a bit with the bones, and see how the mesh behaves around them. Also, adjusting the envelopes where one bone meets another can improve on the bulge of the mesh when the bones are flexed.

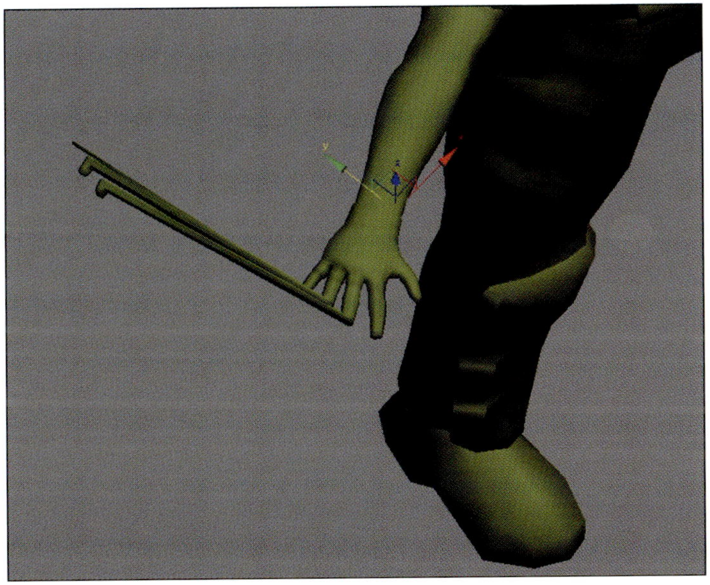

Figure 7.21 By moving certain bones around, you can detect stray vertices that need to be encompassed by the bone's envelope.

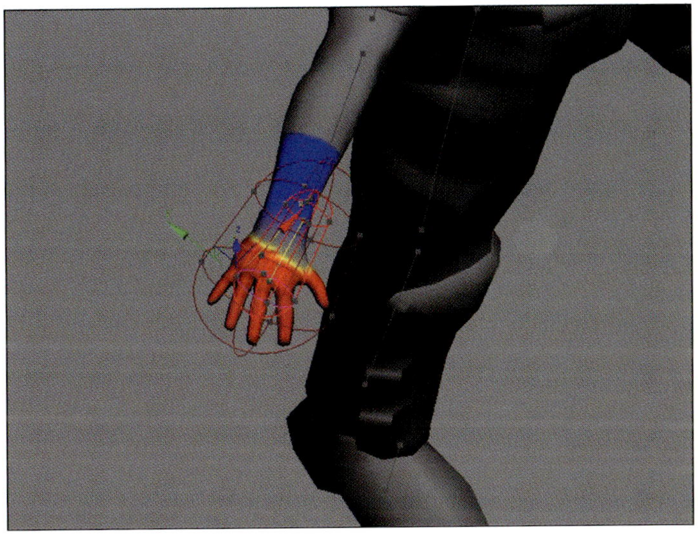

Figure 7.22 By adjusting the hand's envelope near the end, the stray vertices are sucked in to the hand and corrected.

8. Another way to adjust the weighting of the vertices is by using the Paint Weights option in the Skin modifier's envelope rollout. For instance, press F3 to enter wireframe mode, and look at the back area. I'd like to have the pelvis bone take control of this area, because the back doesn't do much else aside from following the pelvis in motion. With the Paint Weights button active, click the ellipse button to bring up the Painter Options screen. Here you can adjust the brush size and strength, along with about a billion other parameters. Change both the Max Strength and Max Size to 0.2; doing so makes the painting brush a small crosshair with not so much strength. Then, with the pelvis bone selected, just click and drag over the back area to paint the weighting onto the vertices (see Figure 7.23). The Paint Weights option is handy if you're positioning bones and notice weird or improper bulges between them. By painting on these affected areas, you'll dynamically see the bulges shift around accordingly.

Tip

When painting weights, you can press the Alt key to remove the weight from the selected vertices.

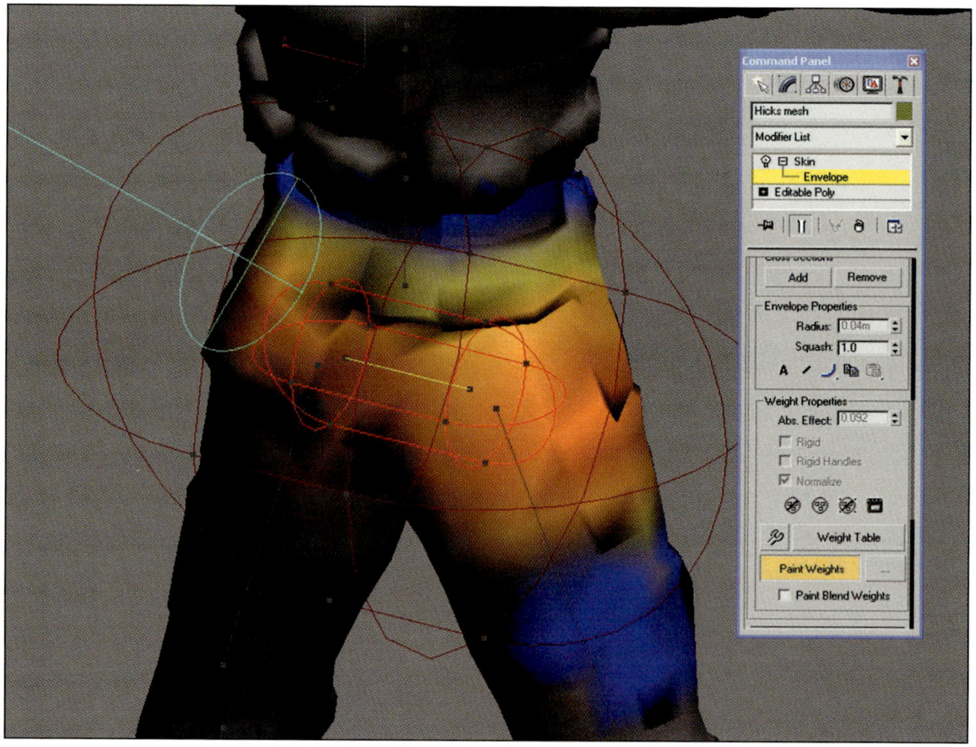

Figure 7.23 Use the Paint Weights option in the Envelope rollout to manually paint the vertices of the tail to be included with the pelvic bone.

9. This feature probably should have been explained earlier, but you can also mirror the skin weights between one-half of the skin to the opposite half. Did you notice that the biped is colored green and blue, with all the green bones on the right and all the blue bones on the left? If you click on the Mirror Mode button, you have access to several buttons that let you copy the bones or weights from the blue side to the green side and vice versa. This way, you only have to set the weights for half of the Hicks character and then use Mirror Mode to copy the weights to the other side. After setting all the vertex weights for the right side of the Hicks character, click on the Mirror Mode button and then click on the Paste Green to Blue Verts button (see Figure 7.24).

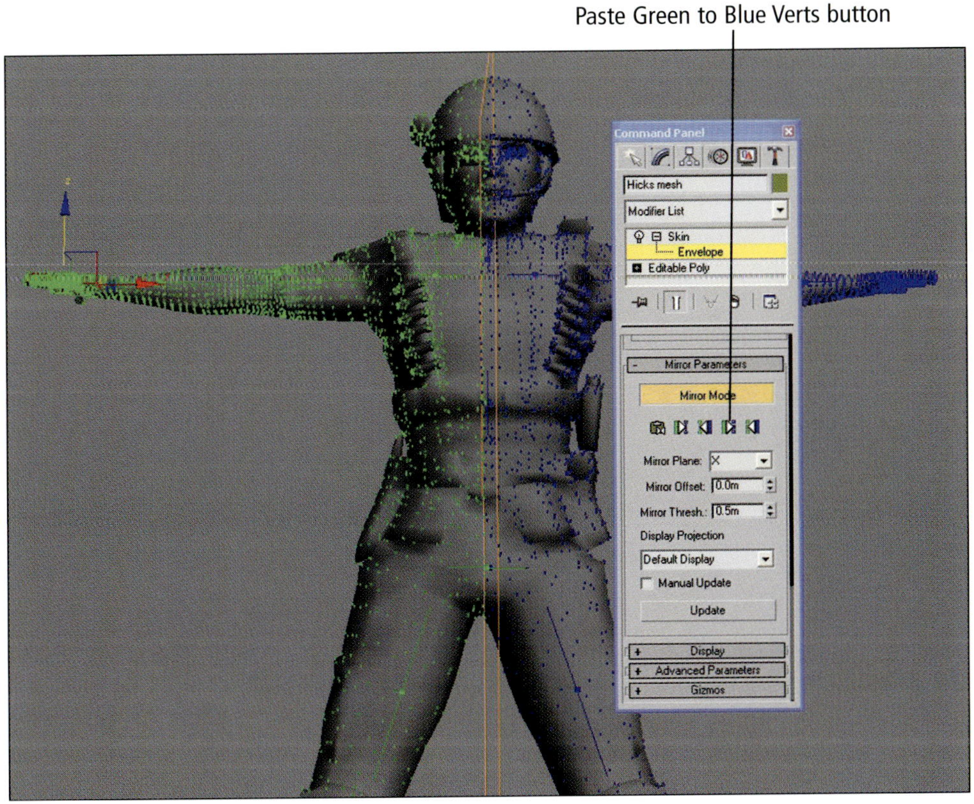

Figure 7.24 Use Mirror Mode to copy all the skin weights on the right side to the left side.

10. One final way to adjust skin weights is with the Weight tool. Just under the Edit Envelopes button is an option that lets you select vertices. When this

option is selected, you can drag over the vertices in the scene. With a selection of vertices, you can use the Weight Tool dialog box (see Figure 7.25) to change the vertex weight by clicking on a button. This dialog box also lets you scale the weights, shrink, grow, ring, and loop the selection of vertices. You can also copy and paste weights between vertices.

Continue adjusting weights all over your model until you're satisfied. Then save your scene as a MAX file.

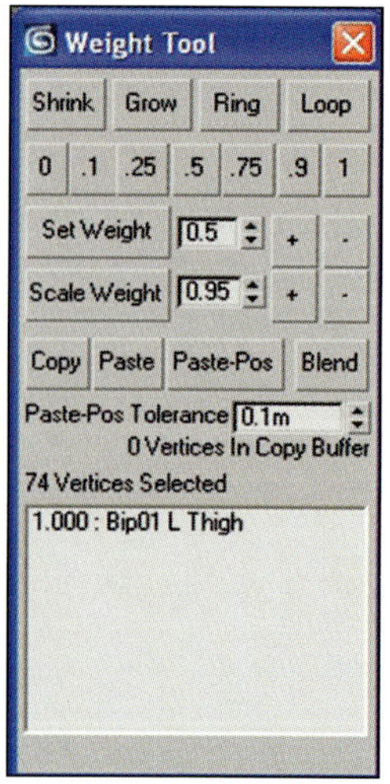

Figure 7.25 The Weight Tool lets you change the weight value using a button click.

Smooth Versus Rigid Binding

Each envelope can be either smoothly or rigidly bound to the selected bone. A smooth binding is the default. This causes all vertices within the envelope to move based on their distance from the joint, which creates a smooth, skin-like blending of skin at joints like the elbow (see Figure 7.26).

A rigid binding, on the other hand, moves all envelope vertices equally with the bone. You can specify that an envelope is rigid by enabling the Rigid option in the Modify panel. Rigid skin is good for certain joints, such as the neck and head or any armor or inflexible clothing that the character is wearing (see Figure 7.27).

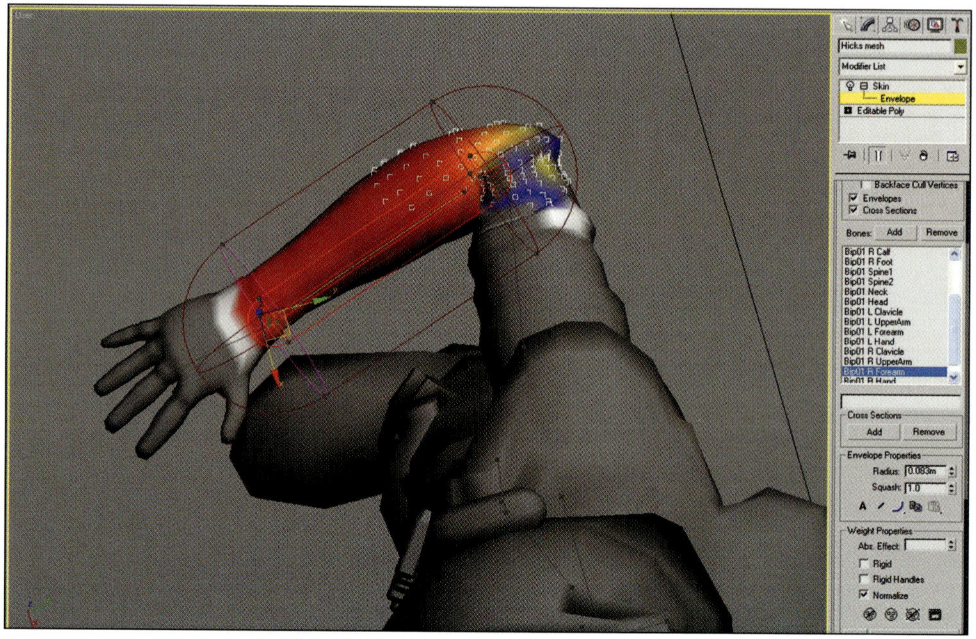

Figure 7.26 Vertices with a smooth skin binding behave like real skin, with good flow at the joints.

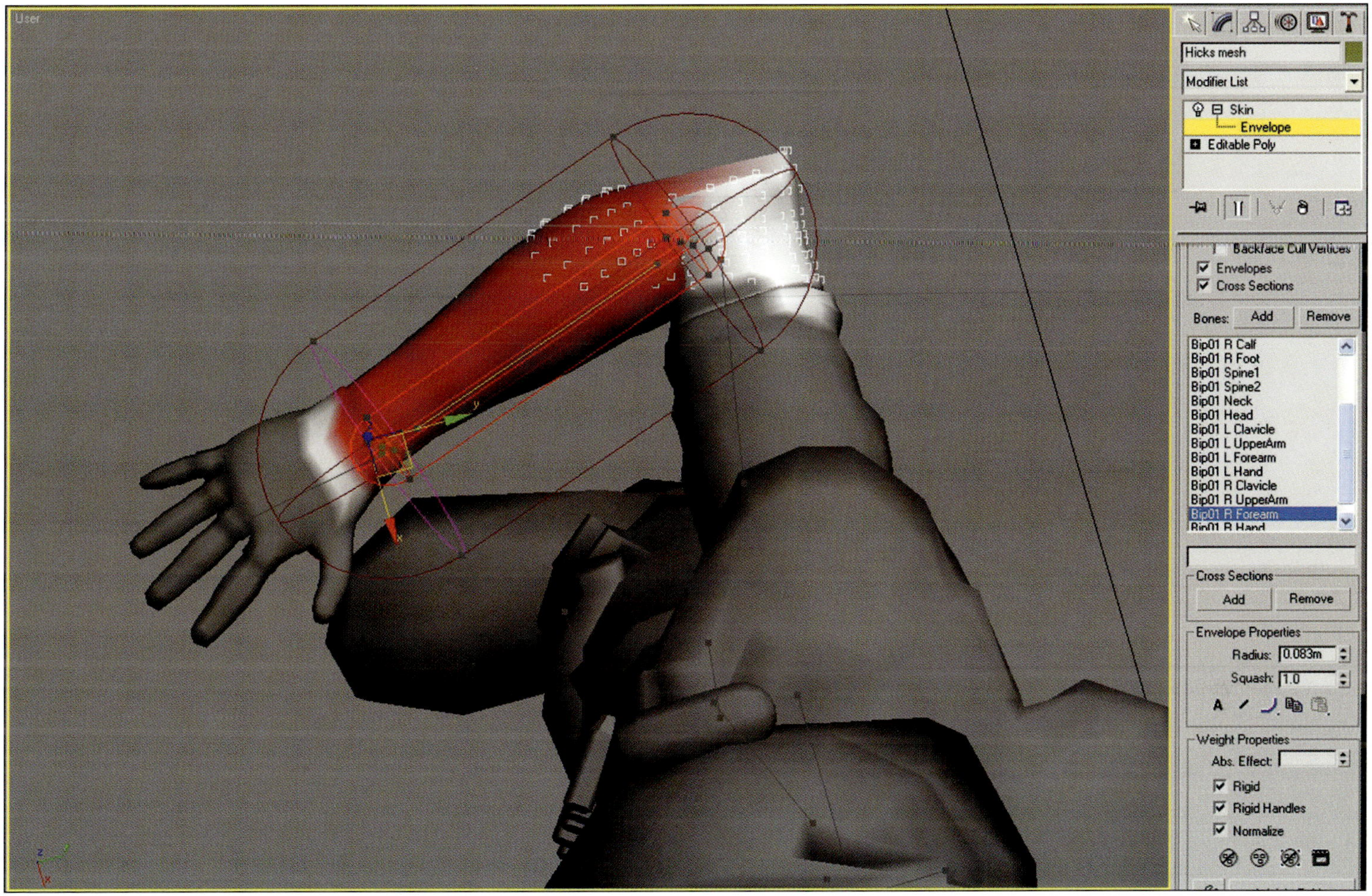

Figure 7.27 Vertices with a rigid skin binding move together with the bone.

Creating a Root Pose

When you export the Hicks model to the Torque engine, he'll need a default pose (unless you want him standing with his arms spread wide). Create a root pose simply by manipulating and moving Hicks' arms and legs so he's in a position of your liking. In Figure 7.28, I modified the biped in the Hicks model's mesh so that he looks like he's leading the troops forward.

Summary

This chapter discussed how to rig your character using 3ds Max's biped feature. Using the prerigged biped, you can quickly add a skeleton to the character that moves just like the actual body moves. After you positioned the biped in place under the Hicks mesh, you learned how to bind the skin mesh using the Skin modifier. The Skin modifier lets you control the envelopes around each bone to determine which vertices move when the bone moves. The chapter concluded by setting Hicks into a root pose. The next chapter moves into animating the Hicks character using the biped skeleton.

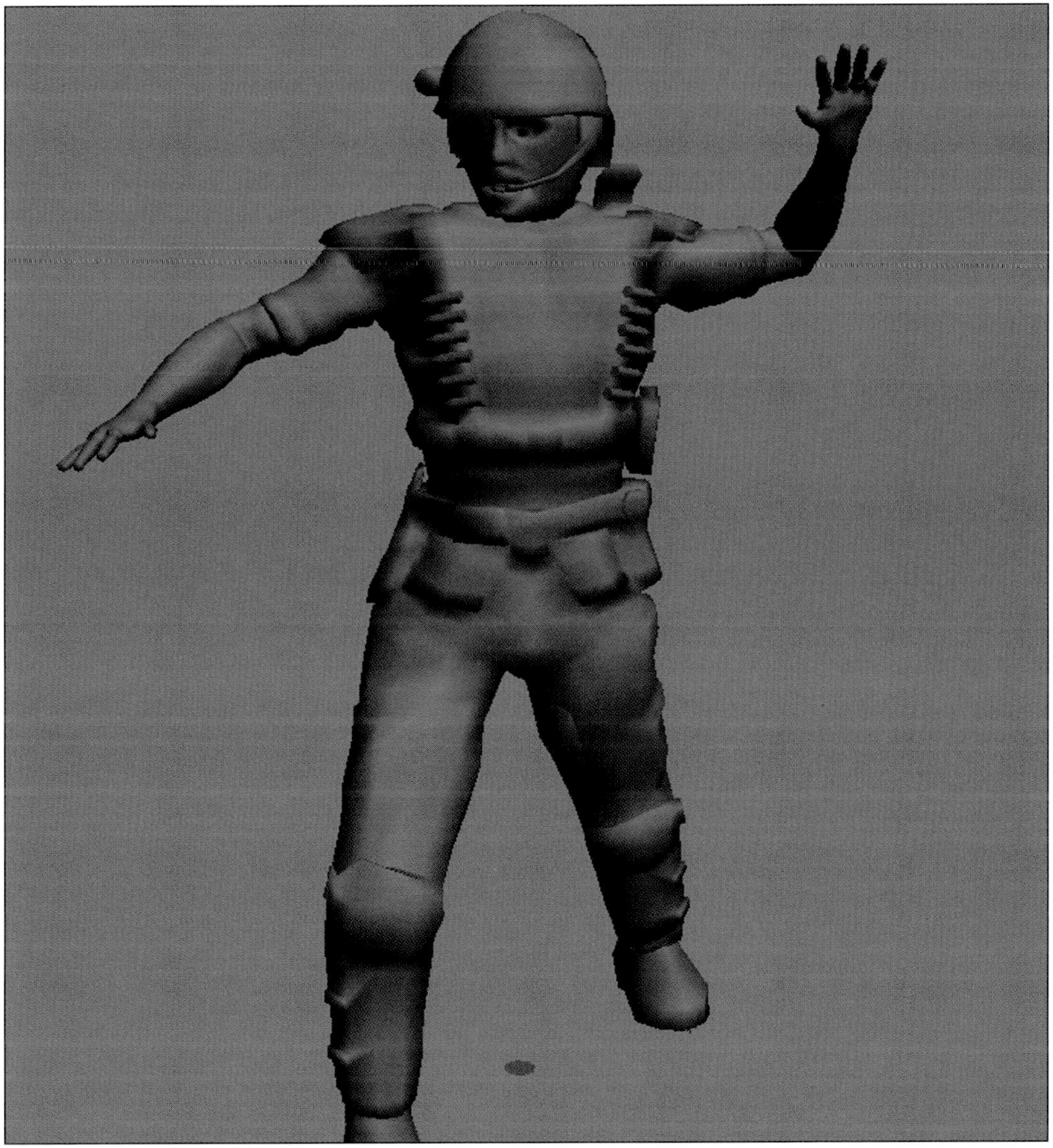

Figure 7.28 Create a root pose by moving the bones of the Hicks model.

Vision is the art of seeing the invisible.
—*Jonathan Swift*

CHAPTER 8

CHARACTER ANIMATION IN 3DS MAX

Character animation is a complex topic that could fill volumes on its own, but it would be a waste to go to all the trouble of building a character without being able to animate it a little. 3ds Max includes many different features for animating characters, and we'll cover a few of them. We'll also look at attaching dummy objects to the character mesh and preparing to export the character to the game engine.

In this chapter, you will

- Learn the basics of animating with keyframes
- Make a walk and run cycle using biped's footstep feature
- Animate facial expression using morph targets
- Add and link dummy nodes to the scene that the game engine can use to attach weapons and interact with other scene objects
- Export the character to the game engine

Animating with Keyframes

You can think of keyframes as the beginning and ending points of an animation. You can break down all motions into a series of simple motions that can be represented by keyframes. For example, think of a character jumping to dodge a swinging ninja's sword. The beginning pose has the character crouching ready to jump, and the end pose has the character raised up off the ground (and hopefully away from the attacking ninja's sword) with legs extended.

If you know these two character positions, you simply need to define and set a keyframe for each pose and define the number of frames in between, which is the time that it takes the character to complete the motion. With these two positions defined, Max is smart enough to figure out all the positions in between these two end positions and voilà, animation.

For many simple character animations, such as a waiting cycle or a ready-to-fight sequence, keyframe animation is easy to use. If you create keyframes from one pose to another and then another keyframe that returns the character to the first pose, you can loop the animation sequence to create a seamless motion.

1. Select the Hicks character and move and rotate his bones to create an initial pose (see Figure 8.1). This pose is a simple standing-still pose.
2. The time slider is already set on frame 1 by default. Open the Select by Name dialog box and select the entire biped structure. You need to select the biped structure because the keys are set for the bones and not for the mesh skin. The bones control the skin, so you need to apply the keys to the bones.
3. Click the Auto Key button at the bottom of the interface. This button automatically records keys for all changes made to a character for the given frame. Then select and move the Hicks character up and back down to the same spot to set a key for frame 1. You can see the key mark in the time slider when you set a key.

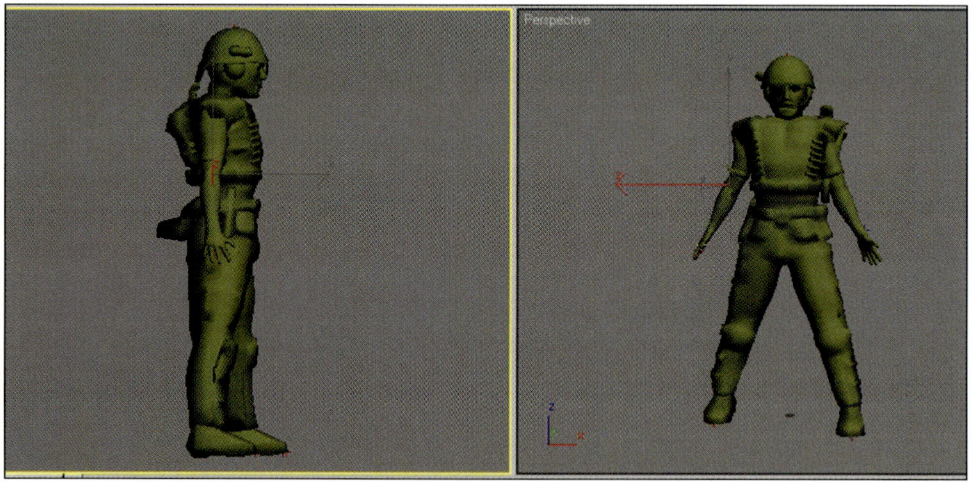

Figure 8.1 The Hicks character is standing still waiting for some action.

4. Drag the time slider to frame 10. Then move and rotate the bones to create a secondary pose (see Figure 8.2). The new key is added automatically after you move the bones.

Caution

Be careful when using Auto Key, because it sets a key for all changes, including changes to the interface. If you're not sure if Auto Key will record changes, turn it off before you make the change.

5. Drag the time slider back and forth between frame 1 and frame 10 to see the resulting motion. Pretty cool, eh? And easy to do. Keyframe animations are great for simple motions, but they can quickly become overworked for complex motions.

6. Reselect all the biped objects, and with the Shift key held down, drag the gray key on the time slider at frame 1 to frame 20. This copies the first key to frame 20. Now if you drag the time slider between frames 1 to 20, the character moves into its fighting pose and then back to its waiting pose. This animation loop helps prevent skips or jumps in the animation.

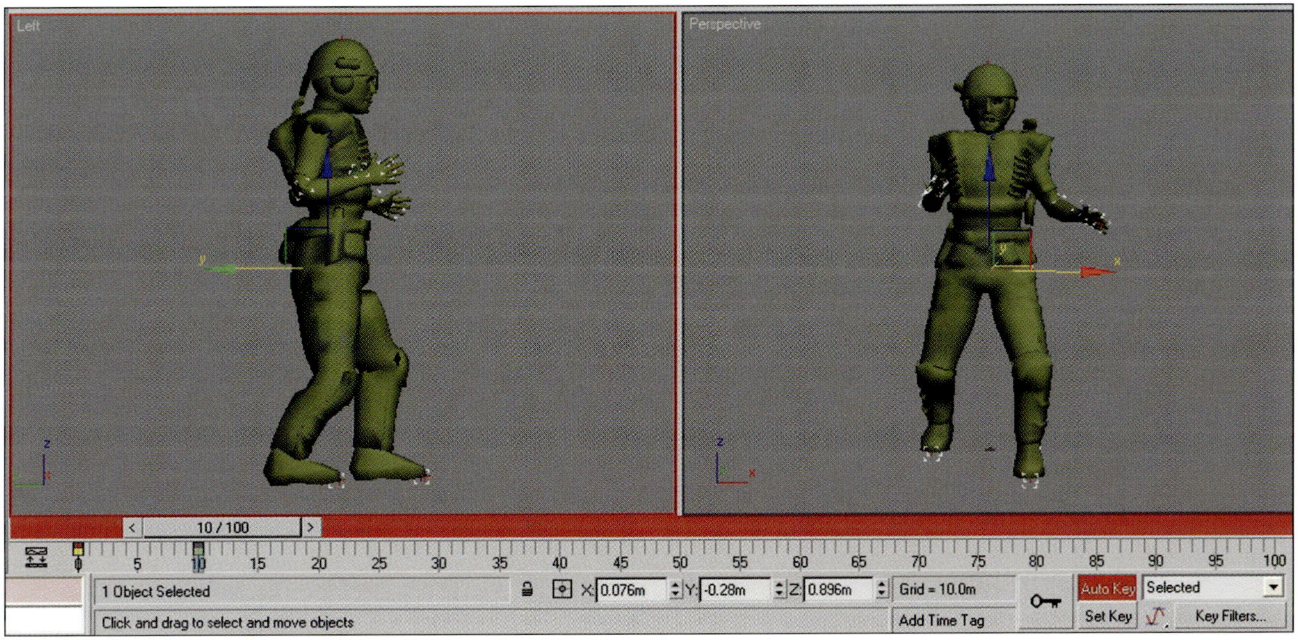

Figure 8.2 The Hicks character is now ready for some action.

7. Before moving on, save the animation sequence using the File, Save Animation menu. This opens the Save XML Animation File dialog box, where you can save the animation sequence (see Figure 8.3). Be sure to save only frames 1 through 20. You should also save the Max file because some game engines require that animation sequences are loaded as Max files. Saving the animation sequence separate from the Max files lets you revisit and blend the animation at a later time or apply the animation to another character.

Now that you have a "ready to fight" animation sequence, you'll want to create several more animation sequences, including one for ducking, dodging, and firing a weapon. There should be a separate animated sequence for each action that the game player can do.

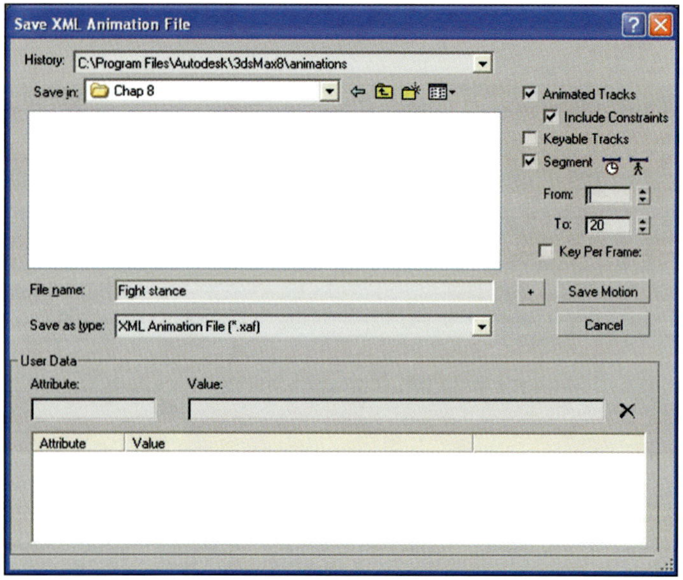

Figure 8.3 The Save XML Animation File dialog box lets you save animation sequences where you can recall them at a later time.

1. With the "ready to fight" animation sequence still open, drag the time slider to frame 1 and choose the Character, Set Skin Pose menu. This defines the standing pose as the default pose. You can recall this default pose at any time using the Character, Assume Skin Pose menu.
2. Drag the time slider to frame 10, click the Auto Key button, and move the biped bones to position Hicks in a firing position by rotating his head, positioning his arms, and setting him in a sideways stance (see Figure 8.4).
3. Drag the time slider to frame 20 and select the Character, Assume Skin Pose menu. This causes the character to return to his default pose. Because the default pose at frame 1 is the same as the one at frame 20, the animation sequence loops between the two poses.
4. Save the file as HICKS-keyframe-firing.max, and save the animation sequence using the File, Save Animation menu.

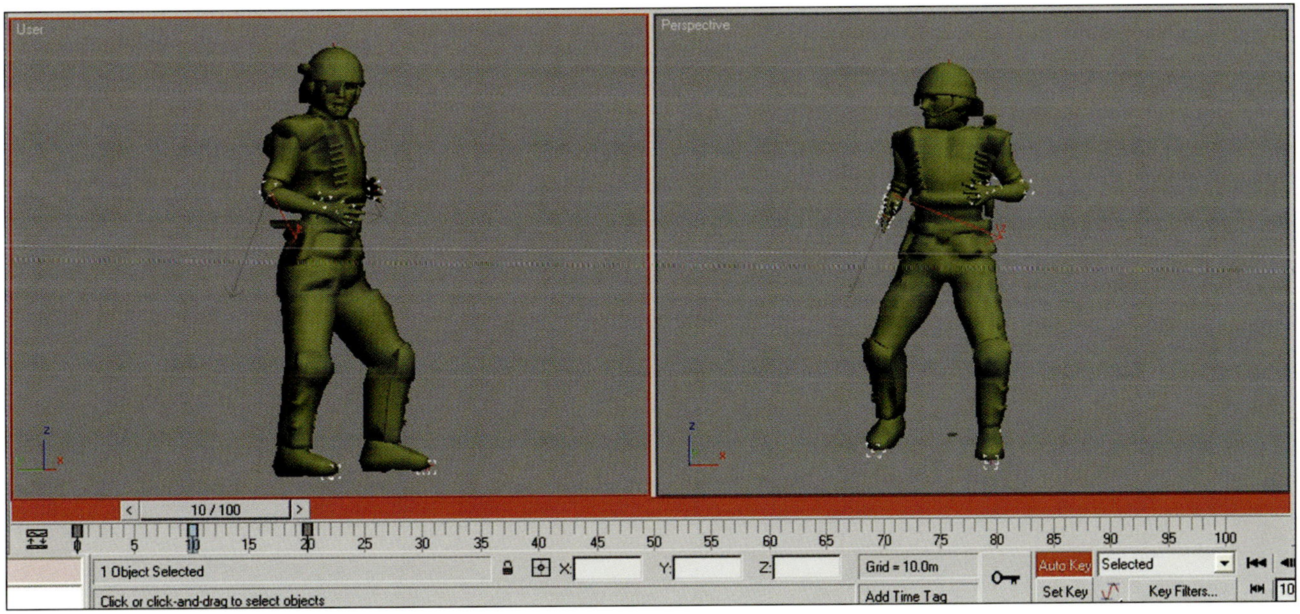

Figure 8.4 The Hicks character in a firing position, allowing space for his weapon.

Before moving on to walk and run cycles, we'll create one more standing animation sequence for having the character duck to avoid a shot. We can create this sequence using the same steps that we used previously for the firing stance.

1. With the "firing" animation sequence still open, drag the time slider to frame 1 and choose the Character, Assume Skin Pose menu. This sets the first frame of the character sequence.

Note

When the Character, Assume Skin Pose menu is selected, only the selected bones are returned to the set skin pose. To return the entire character to the default skin pose, select all the bones in the biped. You can also select to return only a single bone to its default.

2. Drag the time slider to frame 10, click the Auto Key button, and move the biped bones to position Hicks in a dodging position by rotating his legs and arms and moving the entire biped downward (see Figure 8.5).

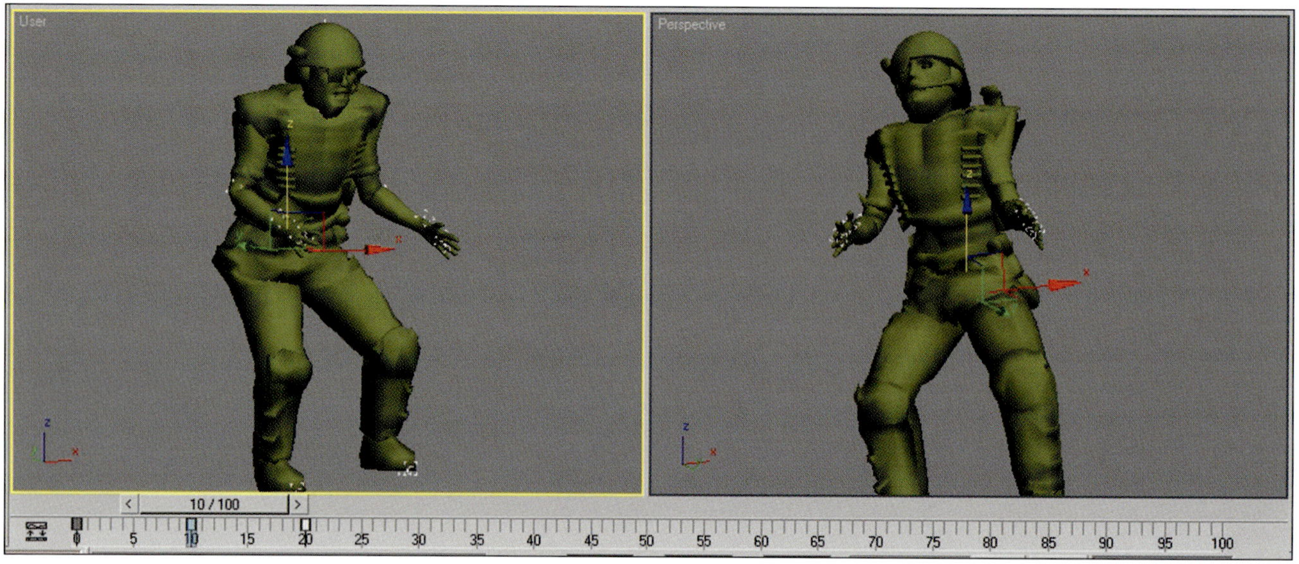

Figure 8.5 The Hicks character in a dodging position.

3. Drag the time slider to frame 20, and select the Character, Assume Skin Pose menu. This causes Hicks to return to his default pose. Because the default pose at frame 1 is the same as the one at frame 20, the animation sequence loops between the two poses.
4. Save the file as HICKS-keyframe-dodge.max, and save the animation sequence using the File, Save Animation menu.

Creating Walk and Run Cycles with Biped

Now that you have a feel for keyframe animation, it's time to get a little more complex. A simple walk cycle seems easy enough—just put one foot in front of the other—but you need to remember to swing the opposite arm, and there's a lot of secondary motion involved in a walk cycle that makes the walk believable, like swinging of the hips and raising and lowering of the shoulders.

Another key benefit to using Max's biped is that it understands all these complex secondary motions and can reproduce them while walking, running, and jumping using preset controls.

To make a biped follow a walk cycle, you need to define the number of steps that you want to take and then click within the scene to place the right and left footprints that the character will follow. The biped then knows all the motions to include to animate the character following the footsteps.

1. Select the Hicks character and open the Motion panel. Click the Load File button, and open the Hicks biped.bip file that you saved in Chapter 7. This loads a fresh copy of the biped without keys.
2. Click the Footsteps Mode button, and then click the Create Multiple Footsteps button to open a dialog box where you can specify the number of footsteps to take. Select to take eight steps and to start with the right foot. Then click the OK button to close the dialog box. The footprints are added to the scene in front of the Hicks character (see Figure 8.6).
3. Click on the Create Keys for Inactive Footsteps button to have Max calculate all the keys necessary to create the walking motion. This causes Hicks to snap to the default footsteps directly underneath him at frame 1. Drag the time slider to see Hicks walk calmly from footstep to footstep (see Figure 8.7).

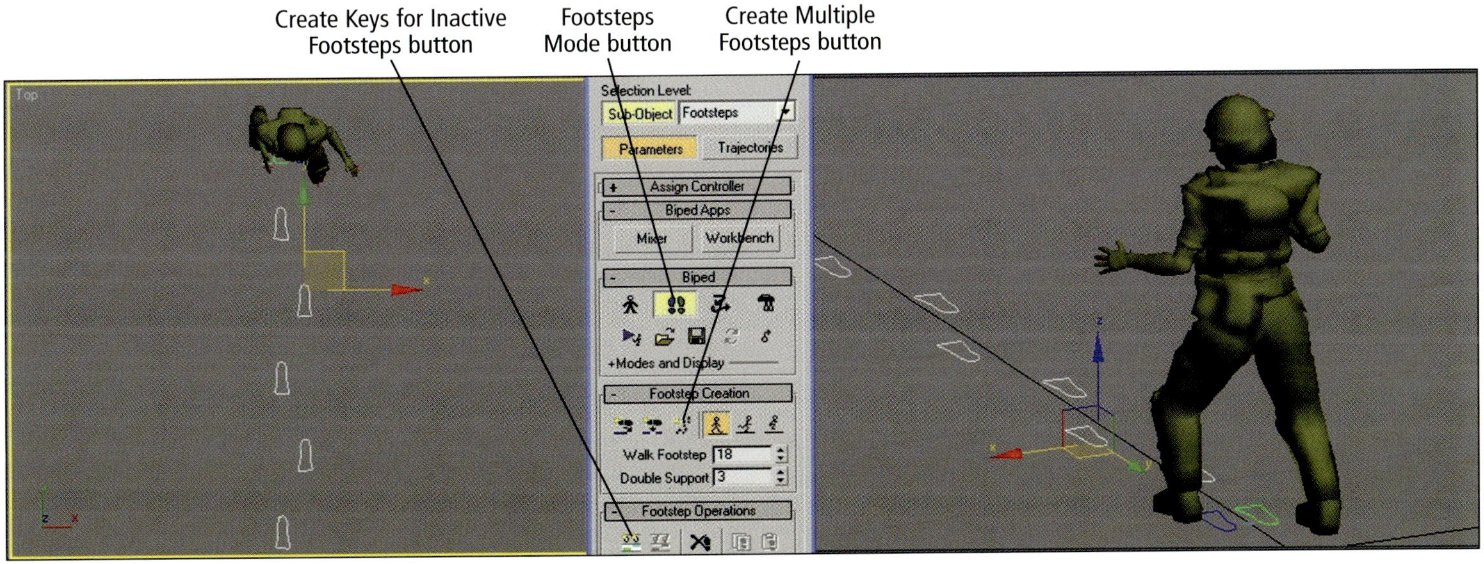

Figure 8.6 Footsteps are added to the scene directly in front of the Hicks character.

Figure 8.7 After you calculate the keys, Hicks follows the footsteps with all the necessary motions.

If you want to change the direction that Hicks walks, just rotate the footsteps, and the biped makes the adjustments to follow the changed footsteps. You also have options to make the biped run and jump.

To make the biped run, you need to activate the Run button in the Footstep mode. With this button active, the Walk Settings dialog box changes to a Run dialog box (see Figure 8.8).

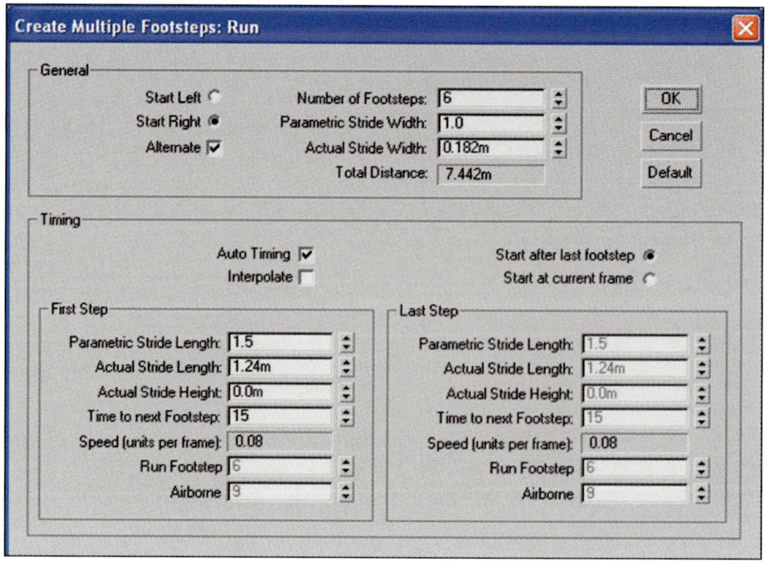

Figure 8.8 The Run Settings dialog box lets you define the number of footsteps and the stride width and height for each step.

When you enable the Run button (or the Jump button), the biped changes the way it moves to match the footprints. For the run mode, the strides are longer and the body attains a higher vertical height between steps.

1. Select the Hicks character and open the Motion panel. Click the Load File button, and open the Hicks biped.bip file that you saved in Chapter 7. This loads a fresh copy of the biped without keys.
2. Click the Footsteps Mode button, and then select the Run button. After that, click the Create Multiple Footsteps button to open a dialog box where you can specify the number of footsteps to take. Select to take eight steps and to start with the right foot. Then click the OK button to close the dialog box. The footprints are added to the scene in front of the Hicks character (see Figure 8.9).
3. Click on the Create Keys for Inactive Footsteps button to have Max calculate all the keys necessary to create the running motion. This causes Hicks to snap to the default footsteps directly underneath him at frame 1. Drag the time slider to see Hicks run hectically.

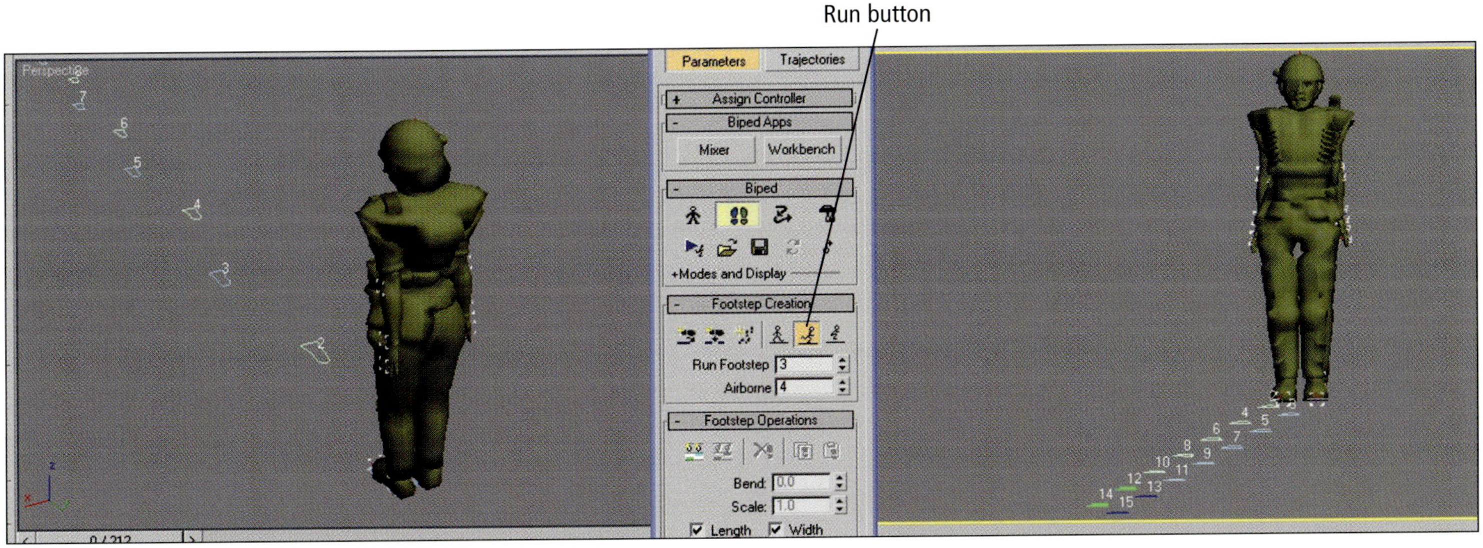

Figure 8.9 Footsteps for the run cycle are added to the scene directly in front of the Hicks character.

4. If you look closely at Hicks in the previous figure, you'll notice that his arms are tucked in too close to its body. To fix this, we need to spread his arms away from the body for each key. Select his upper arm bone and click the Symmetrical button. Then rotate his arm away from his body slightly. After that, select both forearm bones and bend them slightly. This puts Hicks in a much better position to run (see Figure 8.10).

Creating Facial Expressions with Morph Targets

Full-body motion is one thing, but creating facial animation is another bag of worms altogether. Facial animations are created by making several morph targets of the various expressions and blending between them to create the animated effect.

You can create morph targets in 3ds Max using the Morpher modifier. It's best to select the object that you want to morph, such as the head, and make several copies of it. Then select each copy of the head and deform the mesh to create a new expression. You can select each of these new expressions and save them in different channels (see Figure 8.11). Then you can create a whole new repertoire of expressions by combining different percentages of each morph target.

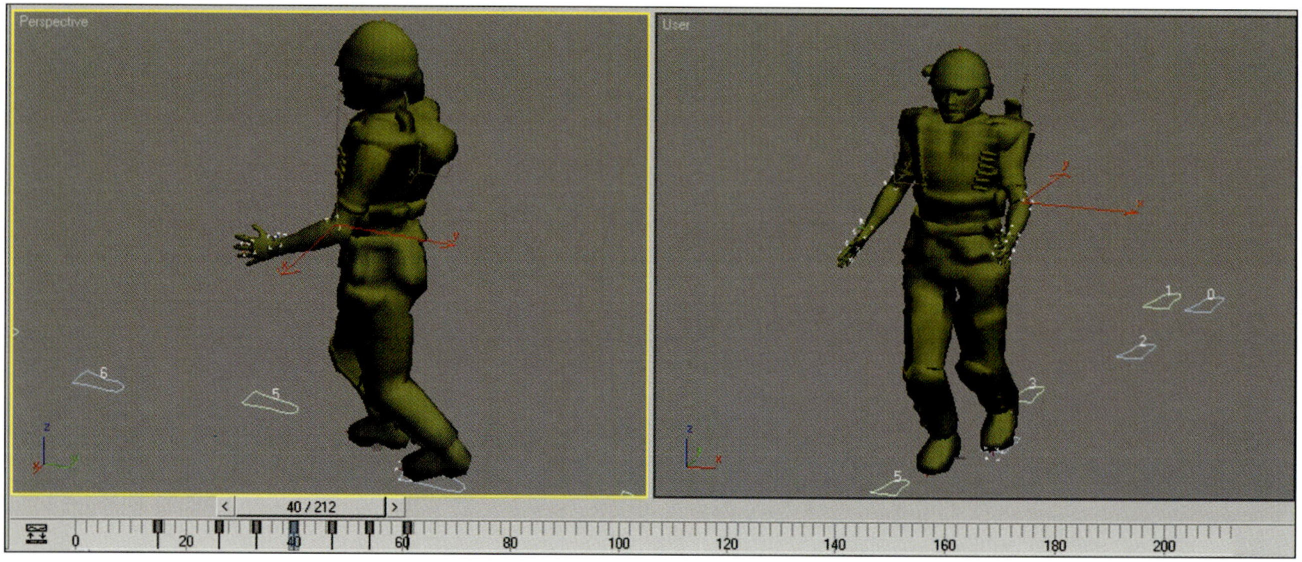

Figure 8.10 Even when biped footsteps are in place, you can revisit the character and change his positions.

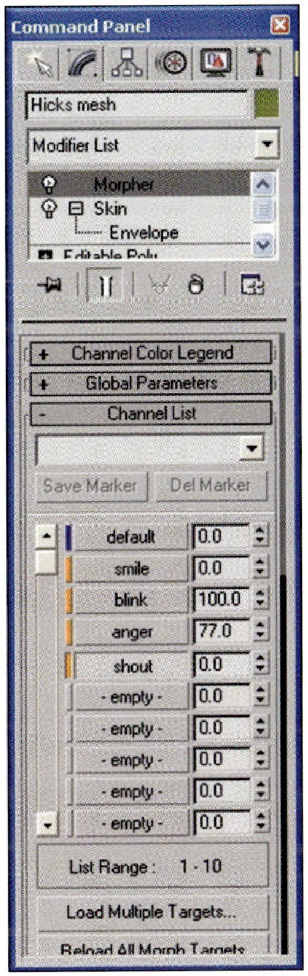

Figure 8.11 You can use morph targets to create different facial expressions. Then you can combine these expressions to create new looks.

1. Select and open the Max file with the textured Hicks character. Then select and delete all body parts except for the head object.
2. Select and drag the head object with the Shift key held down to create two more cloned copies of the head object (see Figure 8.12).
3. Use the mesh deformation tools to alter the expression of the face for the first cloned object to have a slight smile. You can accomplish this easily by selecting the vertices at the edge of the mouth and moving them upward (see Figure 8.13). Be careful as you move the vertices, because extreme repositioning throws off your mapped textures.
4. Use the mesh deformation tools to alter the expression of the face for the second cloned object to have a shouting expression. You can do this by selecting the vertices at the top and bottom edges of the mouth and moving them upward and downward (see Figure 8.14).
5. Select the original head object, and apply the Morpher modifier to it. Click on the first empty channel button, click the Pick Object from Scene button, and then select the smile expression. The name of this object is added to the channel button. Repeat for the shout expression. For each expression, type a name that describes the expression, such as "smile" or "shout."
6. With the original head selected, click on the Auto Key button, and drag the time slider to frame 10. Then drag the smile channel value to 100. After that, drag the time slider to frame 20, and change the smile channel value to 0 and the shout channel value to 100. This causes the face to morph over 20 frames between the various expressions (see Figure 8.15).
7. Save the Max file to be imported into the game engine.

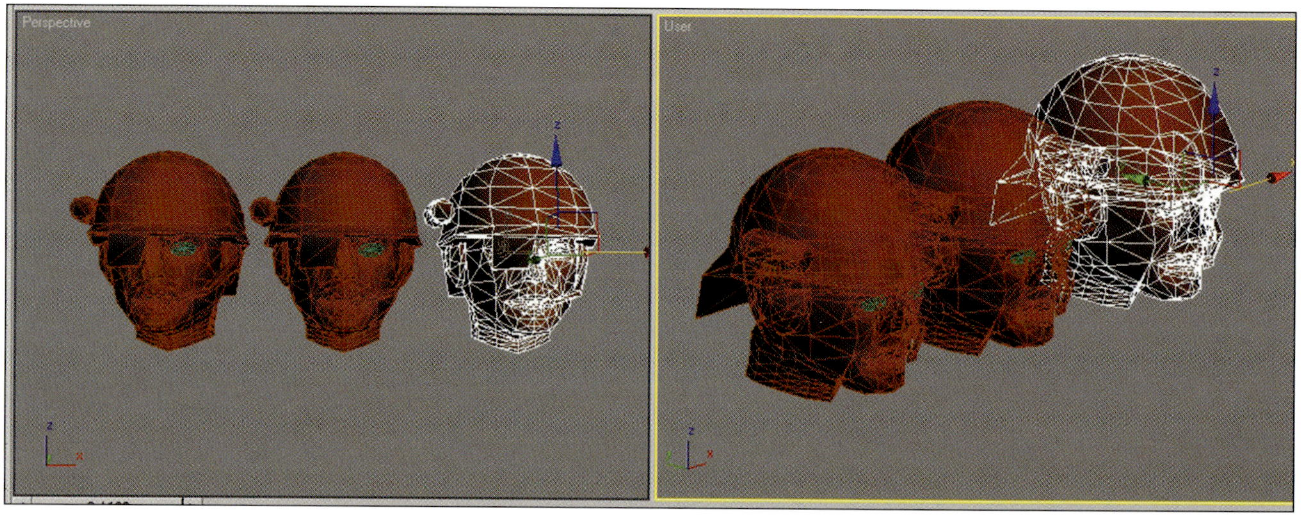

Figure 8.12
Cloned copies of the head let you create morph targets for different expressions.

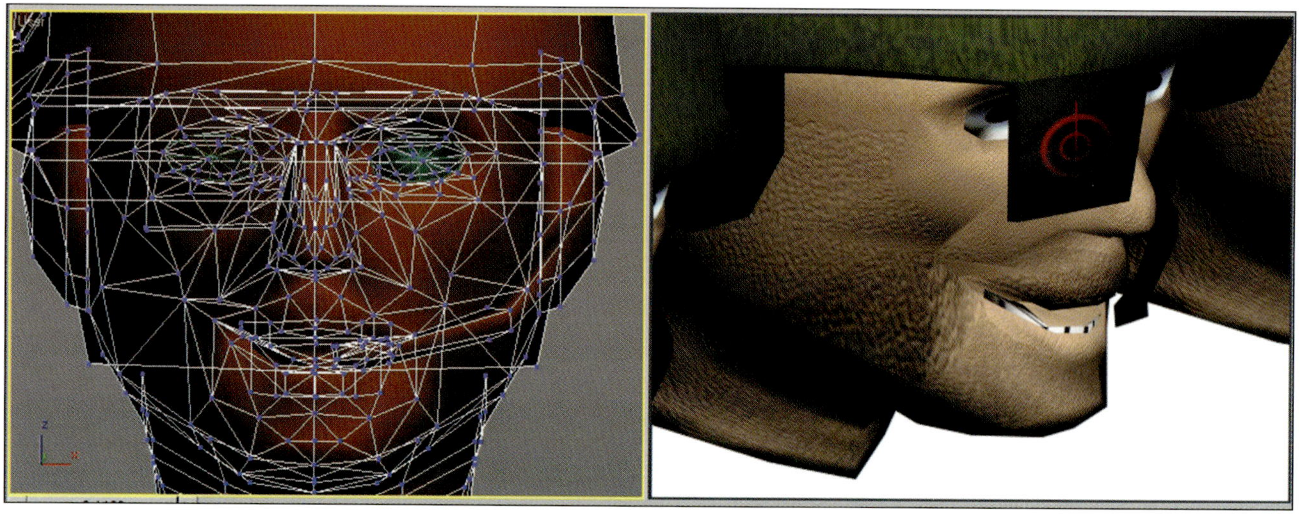

Figure 8.13
The first cloned face is deformed into a smile expression.

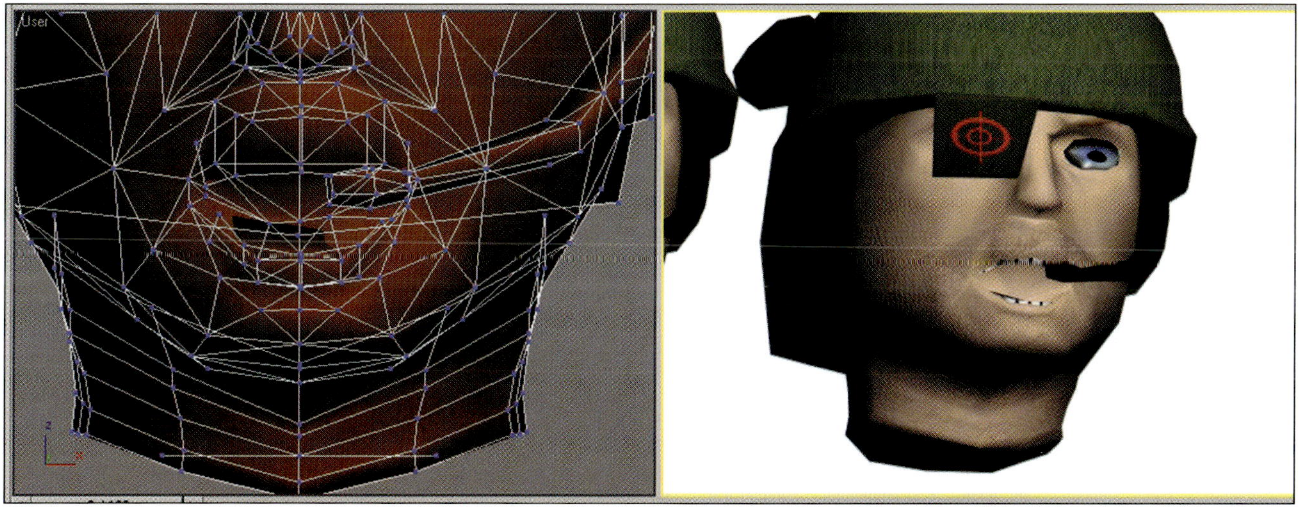

Figure 8.14
The second cloned face is deformed into a shouting expression.

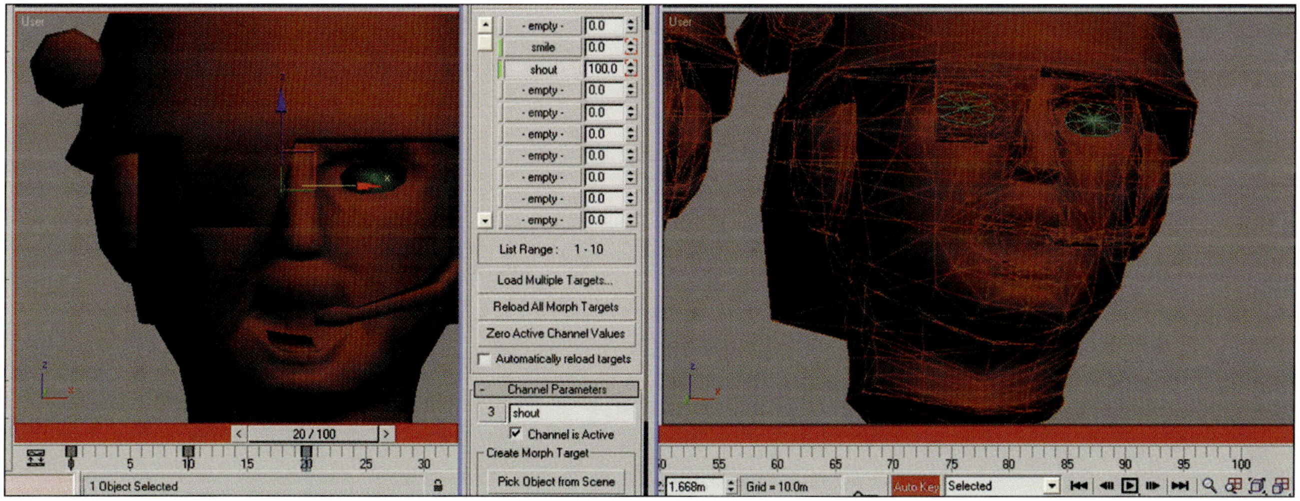

Figure 8.15
Using morph targets, you can set the face to morph between several different expressions.

Adding and Manipulating Dummy Nodes

You need to create several dummy objects to represent those critical game hooks. *Dummies* are simply inert boxes that you create, label, and link to specific parts of the character's body so that the game engine knows where to place items like weapons, backpacks, and so on. Some common ones for Torque are

- A mounting location called Mount0. This is the primary weapon-mounting location on all characters. For the Hicks model, it will be on the hand of your choice. It's required on all character models.
- Secondary mounting locations, called Mount#, where # is a successive number 1, 2, and so on. These locations represent other mounting areas, so that the Hicks model can attach items like backpacks, other weapons, and vehicles. Mount1 and Mount2 are required dummies to be located just outside of the Hicks model's back.
- A dummy called Eye. This is located and oriented directly in front of the character's face. Eye represents the camera through which the player sees the game world when playing the game, using the character model as his own player mesh. For bots (nonplayer characters), this might not be required. Consult your game engine's requirements.
- A dummy called Cam. This is the camera-mounting location, which can represent several things. For instance, when a player switches to a flying mode, in which he is no longer manipulating a character mesh (such as in post mortem, which is when you fly around the game world undetected until you respawn), the camera uses Cam to see the world. Some programmers use Cam to circle around a player who has been killed, as is the case in *Unreal.* For the Torque engine, this dummy is attached to another dummy called Unlink.
- Detail objects, called Detail#, where # defines the level of detail (LOD). Each model must have at least one detail dummy to represent the base polygon count of the character's mesh. LOD is critical for character meshes, because having a game full of 3,000+ characters walking around at all distances would be a complete waste of polygons. (See the "LODs" section ahead for details on creating, er, details.)
- Vehicle dummies, such as Ski0 and Ski1—which are located near the character's calves—enabling the character to mount or sit in a vehicle.
- The character can also have Light# dummies to allow for a lighting source for special situations like self-illumination.

Some games and their engines require additional mount and sprite locations, such as an ExplodePoint location for the programmers to hook a death explosion sequence onto. It's up to you to let the programmers know what will be attaching where, and what it will be called.

For now, your Hicks model really only needs the Detail2, Mount0, Mount1, Mount2, Eye, Cam, Ski0, and Ski1 dummy objects, plus another one called Unlink (for death camera purposes). Here's what to do:

1. In the Create tab of the Command Panel, click on the Helpers button. (It looks like a tape measure.)
2. In the Object Type section, click the Dummy button.
3. In an Orthogonal view, click and drag to create a small dummy box (see Figure 8.16), and position it in one of the Hicks model's hands, just in front of the palm and between the thumb and first finger. This is where the Hicks model will hold the weapon.
4. Type Mount0 in the field in the Name and Color section.

Note

The size of the dummy is irrelevant. The Torque engine simply looks for a dummy object with the name Mount0 for a weapon-mounting location, and references the dummy's axes for the weapon's location and alignment.

5. You need to align the axes of the Mount0 dummy. In this case, however, the Y-axis must point in the direction that you want the weapon to point. To begin, click on the Hierarchy tab in the Command Panel; then click the Affect Pivot Only button.
6. Use the Select and Rotate tool to rotate the axis so that the Y-axis points toward the Hicks model's fingers (see Figure 8.17). Use the Angle Snap tool, located at the bottom of the

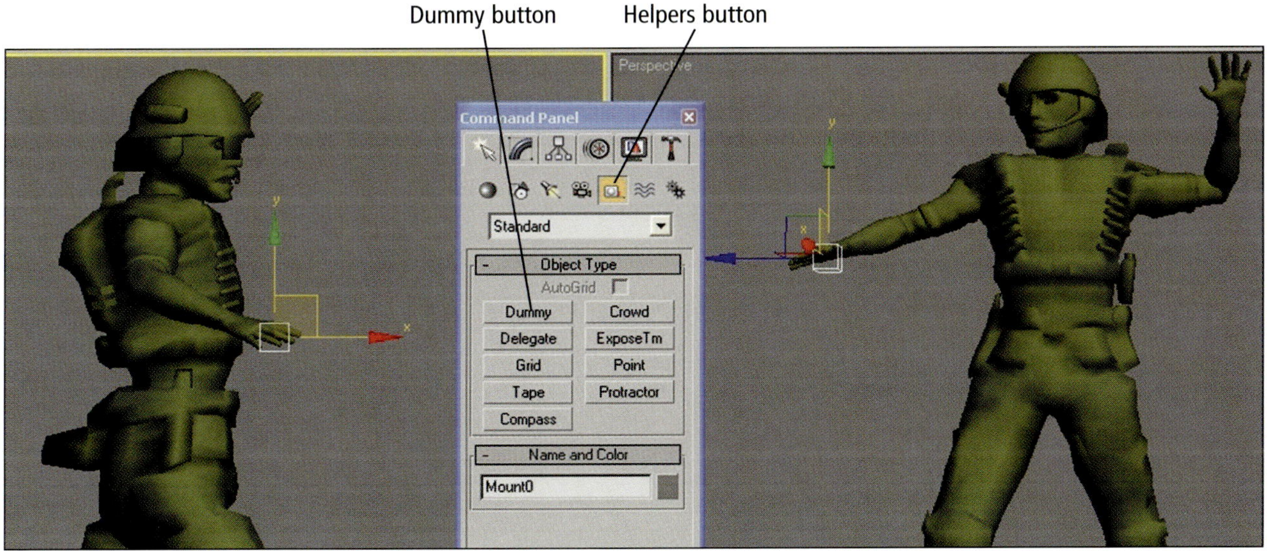

Figure 8.16 Create a dummy object named Mount0, and position it in the Hicks model's hand. This represents the mounting location for weapons.

screen, to constrain this rotation in degree increments. With the Y-axis pointing forward, the weapon's grip mounts to it and faces in the same direction.

7. Create and position three more dummies: Eye, Cam, and Detail2. You should place Eye and Cam right between the Hicks model's eyes and a few inches ahead of them, respectively. Place the Detail2 dummy at the center of the character's pelvis, where the character's center of mass is located.
8. Align the pivot point so that the Y-axes for both the Eye and Cam dummies are pointing forward, with the Z-axes pointing up.
9. Create and position two dummies: Mount1 and Mount2. Position both of these at the Hicks model's back, between the shoulders.
10. Create and position another two dummies: Ski0 and Ski1. Locate the first behind the left calf bone, and locate the second in the same location behind the right calf. Position the Y-axes so that both dummies face forward.
11. Create another dummy called Unlink. Position it on the floor between the Hicks model's feet (see Figure 8.18).
12. Create a final dummy called Bounds that is sized to the bounding box of the character. This box is used to tell if another object comes in contact with the character (see Figure 8.19).

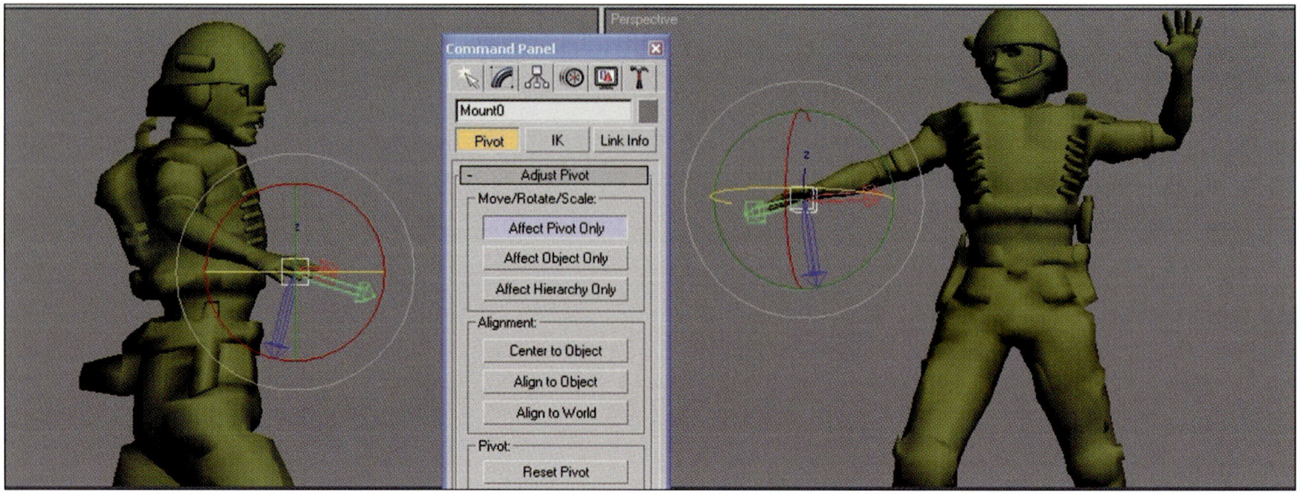

Figure 8.17 Align the pivot point (axes) of the dummy object so that the Y-axis points in the direction that the weapon should point.

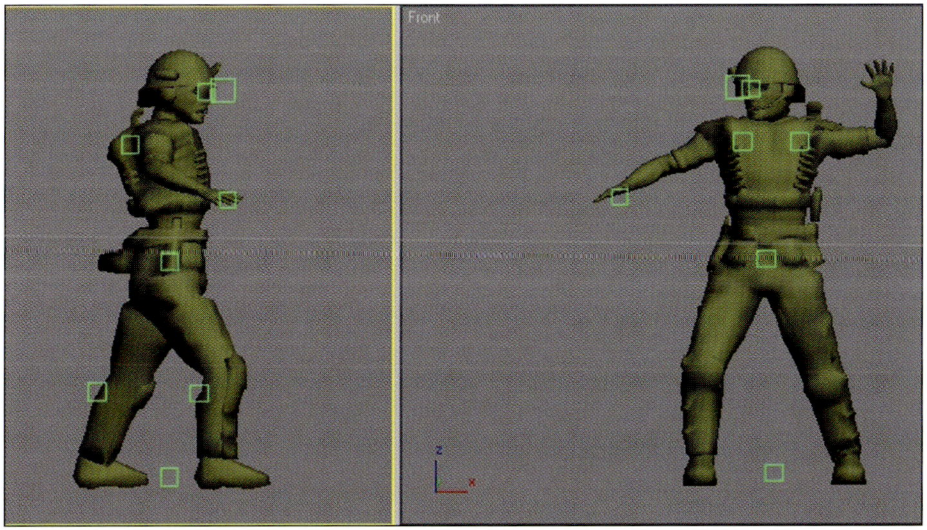

Figure 8.18 The Hicks character with all the game engine dummy objects added.

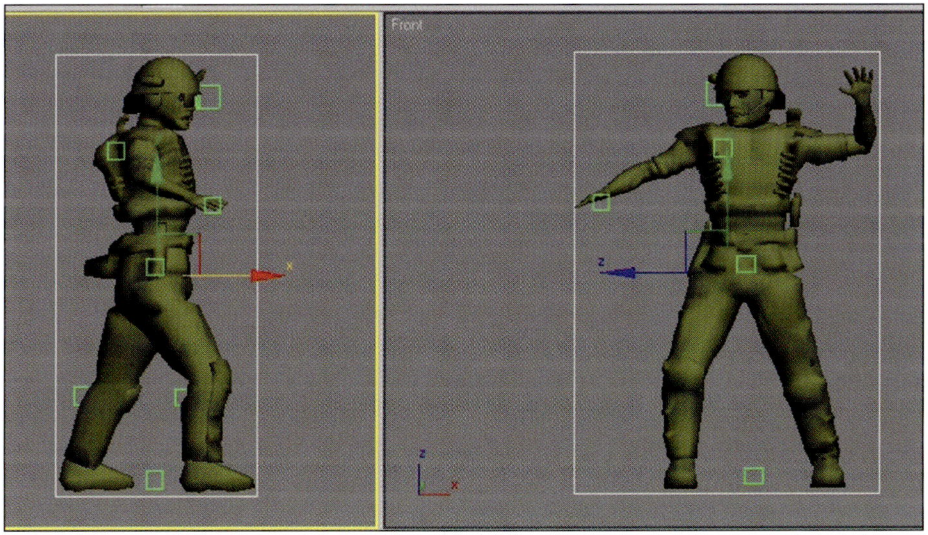

Figure 8.19 The final dummy object is a bounding box named Bounds.

Linking the Nodes

Now that you've created all the basic nodes required to make the Hicks model work in Torque, you need to link them to the proper locations in the Schematic view. You open the Schematic View window using the Graph Editors, New Schematic View. This window is great for linking objects, because every object is represented by a simple labeled rectangle called a *node*, and links between objects are simple lines. To link between two nodes, click the Connect button and drag from the child object to its parent.

Open the Schematic view and link each node as follows:

- Link the Detail2 dummy to the Bip01 node (at the top of the hierarchy).
- Link the Mount0 dummy to the Bip01 Right Hand.
- Link the Mount1 and Mount2 dummies to Bip01 Spine2.
- Link the Eye dummy to the Bip01 Head.
- Link the Unlink dummy to the Bip01 node. Then you must link the Cam dummy to the Unlink dummy.
- Link the Ski0 and Ski1 dummies to the Bip01 Left Calf and Right Calf, respectively.

Finally, link the Bounds (bounding box) to the Bip01 node (at the top of the hierarchy). Figure 8.20 shows the exploded schematic view you should have.

LODs

Here's the last thing you can do to optimize the mesh in the game. The LODs for the Hicks model represent the varying mesh densities that the character will have in relation to the distances of the other players. It's important to have these LODs, because it would bog down the game engine to unnecessarily process a 3,000-polygon model that a player can't see from afar. I'll show you how to make two LODs.

1. In the Schematic view, you should have the Detail2 and Hicks mesh objects; they currently should not be linked to anything. Just link the Detail2 dummy object to the Bip01 object (the root of the biped). This represents the lowest level of detail—the higher the number, the higher the detail. Of course, these are just reference markers for the game engine to use.
2. With the Detail2 object still selected, you need to create another dummy object representing the highest level of detail. The easiest way to do this is by clicking Edit, Clone on the top menu bar. In the Clone Options dialog box, make sure Copy is checked. For the name, type in detail64 and click OK. The number is arbitrary, but it's good to keep the trailing number large, so you know that the larger the number, the higher the mesh density will be. Now look back to the Schematic view, and notice that the new detail marker has been added and attached to the Bip01 object, because it is a clone.

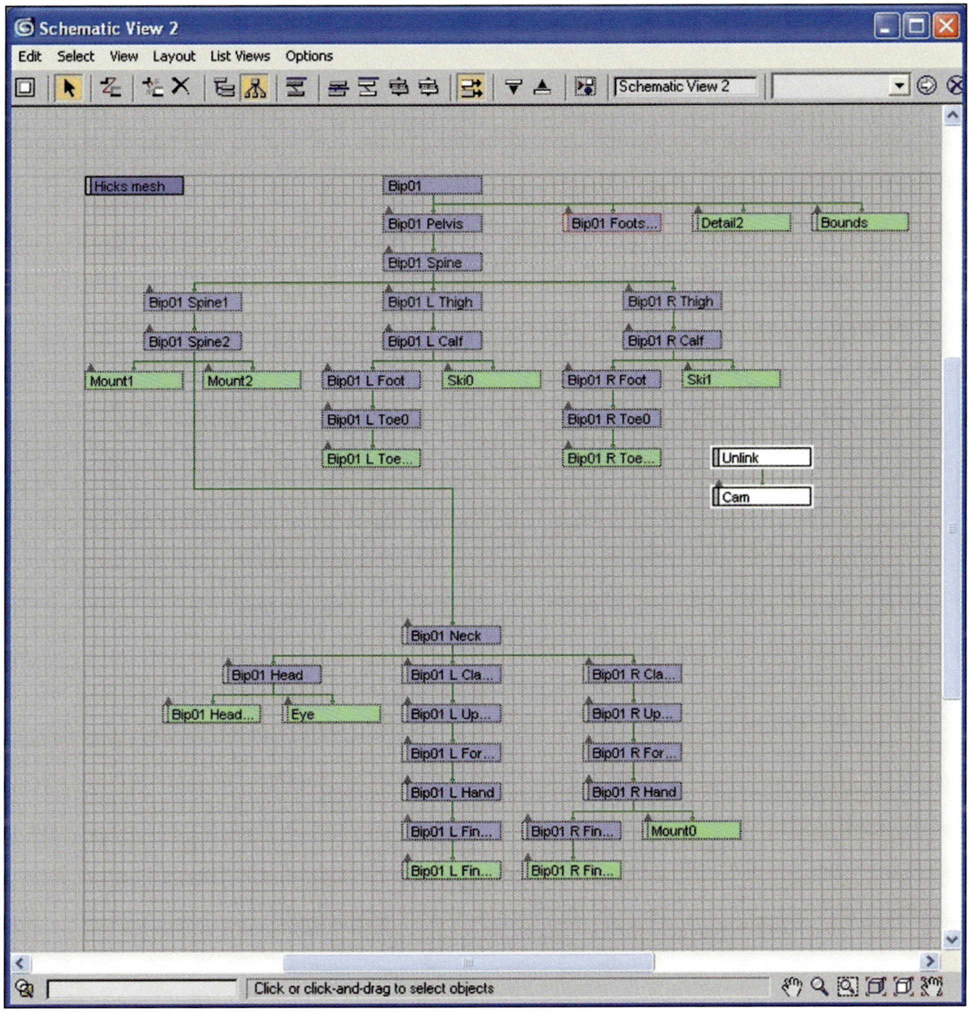

Figure 8.20 The properly attached nodes to the biped.

3. With the detail markers in place, you need to create a single LOD mesh using the MultiRes modifier. First select the Hicks mesh object in the Schematic view; then create a clone of the mesh. Just click Edit, Clone, and name the new copy Hicks model64. This represents the highest LOD.
4. Finally, reselect the Hicks mesh object. Then, in the Modifier panel, apply a MutliRes modifier to this mesh. In the MultiRes rollout, click Generate. Change the Vert Percent parameter to 50.0, which reduces the polygon count to 50 percent of the original mesh, or in this case, about 1500 faces. That's not bad, considering there's not much loss in detail. This represents the lowest LOD that other players will see from afar. You should now have two Hicks model meshes in your scene (Hicks mesh and Hicks model64) that are referenced, by the Torque engine, by the detail dummy markers Detail2 and Detail64, respectively.

Exporting and Viewing the Hicks Model in Torque

You can export the character to the Torque game engine using the DTS Exporter utility, which you can find in the Utilities panel after you install the plug-in. Go to the exporter and select Whole Shape. Make the name player.dts, and save the file to the \RealmWars\rw\data\shapes\player\ area instead. Be sure to have your player.cfg file in the same directory, along with the 3ds max MAX file and the Hicks modelSkin.png skin file. The difference in exporting this time is that you need to create the DTS object in the existing\player\ folder. Navigate to that folder, and you'll see more than 30 different DSQ files, which are Torque's animation sequence files. These were also generated using the DTS Exporter utility. These files will animate the Hicks model's bones structure during gameplay.

The exporter might take a while, because there is a lot to process. Remember to look at the dump.dmp file if anything goes wrong, or if an animation sequence does not work properly. Sometimes when a certain animation sequence won't work, you need to adjust the CFG file and include or exclude node or bone labels.

After you've loaded the model using the realmwars.exe show utility, click on the Thread Control button. This loads a Thread Control panel that you can use to view the different animation sequences being applied to the bones in the Hicks model. Make sure that the animations work, or you'll have problems using the Hicks model during the game!

Last Note on Other Game Engines

You're probably wondering about using the Hicks model in other games. Most of the information about creating meshes, skinning them, and setting them up for use in the Torque engine apply to other games like *Half-Life*, *Quake*, and *Unreal*. All that's really necessary is to obtain the 3ds Max plug-ins for those games so that you can export your models and change the naming of an object or two, add a dummy, and so on. I decided to avoid getting into any detail on those engines, because getting permissions to use plug-ins, screen shots, and so on from companies like that is *very* difficult, not to mention time-consuming. GarageGames was kind enough to allow me to use Torque, an excellent 3D game engine. Coupled with the fact that Torque is so affordable ($100), what could be better? Remember, for that small price, you're not just getting a game, but an entire game engine whose code you can modify to create your own game, including your own personalized graphics. Anyway, for other game engines, just get on the Web and download the SDK (software development kit) for whatever you want to develop. I'm sure the kits (not the engines) will be free of charge.

See Appendix B, "Related Web Sites and Links," for information on popular game engine sites. The SDKs are usually free for download and contain the plug-ins and instructions necessary to get you rockin' and rollin'.

Summary

This chapter discussed some of the basic animation features available in 3ds Max for animating characters, including keyframe animation and biped's footsteps mode. The last part of the chapter covered preparing the character to be exported to a game engine by placing and linking dummy objects to identify certain locations to the game engine.

I don't paint things. I only paint the difference between things.
—*Henri Matisse*

Appendix A

3ds Max 8 and Photoshop CS2 Keyboard Shortcuts

Appendix A represents the majority of keyboard shortcuts I use with 3ds Max 8 and Photoshop CS2. You should know these shortcuts by heart not only because they are the most common functions, but also because they will speed up your work tremendously. The point-and-click technique of selecting menu options is analogous to the hunt-and-peck method of typing. Time is of the essence when modeling or texturing.

Note that many of these shortcuts have the same mapping to previous versions of Max and Photoshop.

3ds Max 8 Keyboard Shortcuts

Modeling is more complicated than texturing because you're working with *both* hands much more frequently than just using the mouse. I've found that remapping some of 3ds Max's shortcuts to suit my left hand for some basic, common operations works much better than using Autodesk's default settings. The following section describes my recommendation for this remapping.

Remapping Commonly Used Max Shortcuts

Over the years, I've worked with several modeling/animation programs and have found that with each, I've had to remap the program's default shortcuts to the ones described in Table A.1, making my work go even faster. Modeling is an intense multitasking scenario making frequent use of *both* hands on a near-constant basis. Newer peripherals, such as the SpacePilot from Logitech (see http://www.3dconnexion.com), are available that attempt to consolidate many common functions onto themselves so that you have to use only one hand. This may be invaluable to those with any type of disability on one limb.

To remap a key in Max, click Customize, Customize User Interface, and select the item you want to remap. Click in the Hotkey text box and then enter the shortcut you want to use. (You also can map just about any key and key combinations using Ctrl, Alt, and Shift.) Then click the Assign button to map the new shortcut. When you're finished mapping your keyboard to your liking, be sure to click Save and save the layout to file. This way, you can always reload your user interface preferences in case they are accidentally reset.

Tip

Customize User Interface has another tab representing a page called Quad. In this section, you can design unique keyboard mapping environments and save them for scenarios such as modeling, animating, and so forth. This way, you can enter single keyboard shortcuts that will instantly set up entire custom environments and mappings the way you want them.

Table A.1 lists my frequently used keyboard shortcuts, starting with Max's defaults, and then the remapped keys the way I like them.

Again, these are keys I press repeatedly with my left fingers. Notice that the shortcuts in Table A.1 are mostly located on the *left* side of the keyboard. If you set up your keyboard mapping this way, you can position your left fingers at a resting position with your ring, middle, and index fingers over the Z, X, and C keys respectively. You'll be modeling most of the time, and these keys (in conjunction with the mouse) will help you to quickly move, rotate, and scale objects and their vertices with ease and use

Table A.1 My Frequently Used 3ds Max Shortcuts

Action	Default Shortcut	Remapped Shortcut
Move	(none)	Z
Rotate	(none)	X
Scale	(none)	C
Restrict to X-axis	F5	A
Restrict to Y-axis	F6	S
Restrict to Z-axis	F7	D
Pan view	Ctrl+P	Spacebar
Arc rotate	Ctrl+R	V
Undo	Ctrl+Z	(same)
Redo	Shift+Z	(same)
Angle snap toggle	A	F
Material Editor	M	(same)
Left viewport	L	Q
Front viewport	F	W
Top viewport	T	E
Perspective viewport	P	R

your thumb to tap the spacebar to pan view the area on which you are operating. (You can also pan the view by holding down the middle mouse button and dragging.) Use the A, S, and D keys to constrain axial movement when modeling.

Photoshop CS2 Keyboard Shortcuts

Table A.2 represents shortcuts in Photoshop that I use frequently. I recommend becoming proficient with these to make your work go quicker. If you want to map your own shortcuts in Photoshop, click Edit, Keyboard Shortcuts, and select the command you want to remap.

Table A.2 My Frequently Used Photoshop Shortcuts

Action	Shortcut
Copy	Ctrl+C
Cut	Ctrl+X
Deselect	Ctrl+D
Fill with foreground color	Alt+Backspace
Hand tool	Spacebar, with most other tools
Merge layer down	Ctrl+E
Move tool	Ctrl, with most other tools
New canvas	Ctrl+N
New canvas with previous settings	Ctrl+Alt+N
Nudge object/selection left	←
Nudge object/selection right	→
Nudge object/selection up	↑
Nudge object/selection down	↓
Paste	Ctrl+V
Quick mask	Q
Repeat filter	Ctrl+F
Select all	Ctrl+A
Select layer opacity	Ctrl+click on layer
Step backward	Ctrl+Alt+Z
Step forward	Ctrl+Shift+Z
Toggle cursor shape	Caps Lock
Toggle grid	Ctrl+Alt+'
Toggle snap	Ctrl+;
Undo	Ctrl+Z

Painting is easy when you don't know how, but very difficult when you do.
—*Edgar Degas*

Appendix B

Related Web Sites and Links

Here is a listing of a number of my favorite sites, many of which are dedicated to modeling and texturing, and others to game mods, hardware, and software resources. Of course, a billion other texturing sites exist, but visit this handful, and I guarantee that you will find links to a plethora of other useful sites.

Mods, Modeling, and Game Engine Sites

After visiting these sites, you'll open a ton of doors to many other sites that offer modeling and texturing tutorials and links for patches, model and texture files, plug-ins, and software development kits.

GarageGames

(http://www.garagegames.com)

Home of independent games and game makers, this site has developed the Torque engine, one of the most popular and affordable 3D game engines on the market ($100). This is a great site for finding work with independent game developers and being able to contribute to the overall development of the Torque engine.

iDDevNet

(http://www.iddevnet.com/doom3/downloads.php)

This is the ultimate resource for id's *DOOM 3* software development kit (SDK), containing links to Max and Maya model importers and exporters, tutorials, and other helpful information regarding the *DOOM 3* engine.

Polycount

(http://www.planethalflife.com/polycount/)

This is a huge site offering tons of character and weapon models and their skins for download. You'll also find great modding info and accessories for games like *Half-Life*, *Unreal Tournament*, *Jedi Knight*, and *Quake*. This is also a great source for modding news and forums.

Quake3bits

(http://www.quake3bits.com/)

Here you'll find maps, models, textures, and tutorials for anything *Quake/DOOM 3* related. This site has good information for incorporating your models and textures into *DOOM 3*.

Steam Powered

(http://www.steampowered.com/)

This is the official Valve Web site supporting Steam products, particularly *Half-Life 2*. Find links and other sources to downloadable patches and other *Half-Life* files here. This replaces the original *Half-Life* Web site.

Texturing Sites

The following sites have given me lots of tutorials and inspiration for my texturing tutorials. They also provided information on texturing specifications for many popular video games.

Digital Art

(http://digitalart.org/)

This is an astounding site dedicated to the serious digital artist. It's geared more toward the freehand painter type, but you can find great examples of digital texture ability here. This is a site that you'll definitely want to join. Check out the sci-fi images too; they inspired some of my alien skin textures.

Undulation

(http://www.planetunreal.com/undulation/)

You'll find lots of grueling, sinister, malicious, and twisted textures here.

UnrealFiles

(http://www.unrealfiles.com/)

UnrealFiles features a good selection of utilities and skins and an excellent link list to other sites related to *Unreal*, *Quake*, and *Half-Life*.

Unrealized

(http://www.unrealized.com/)

You have to see this site! It's packed with great tutorials, expert advice, level-design articles, scripting tutorials, you name it.

Graphics Software

The sites that follow are the sources of all the software used in this book, plus additional vendors of well-known 2D and 3D graphics programs.

Adobe Systems Incorporated

(http://www.adobe.com/)

This is the site for Adobe, creators of Photoshop CS2 ($650), the best texture-creation and image-editing program in the world. From this site, you can download trial versions of their software, along with plug-ins and documentation.

Autodesk

(http://www.autodesk.com)

This is the official Web site of 3ds Max 8 ($3,500) and other Autodesk products. Find patches, demo downloads, and software tutorials here, too. Max is the most popular modeling and animation program used by video game development companies.

Autodesk now also owns Maya 7. Maya 7 is one of the leading 3D modeling and animation software packages available, competing with 3ds Max. The full version of Maya 7 costs about $2,000. The free version of Maya 7, called the Personal Learning Edition (PLE) is also available for download here.

Avid Technology

(http://www.softimage.com/home/)

Avid Technology is the maker of SoftImage|XSI, another leader of 3D modeling and animation software for games. Avid offers several packages, including the Essentials version, which costs $2,000, and a free downloadable Mod Tools 4.2 package for creating 3D game content.

Blender Foundation

(http://www.blender3d.org/cms/Home.2.0.html)

Blender 3D is a free, open source 3D modeling and animation package capable of producing quality game content used by many artists in the modding community.

Caligari Corporation

(http://www.caligari.com/)

Caligari Corporation created trueSpace and gameSpace, which have an outstanding modeling interface with support for UV mapping, animation, and texturing. gameSpace ($300) is affordable game-specific software available for purchase here.

chUmbaLum sOft

(http://www.swissquake.ch/chumbalum-soft/)

chUmbaLum sOft offers another free 3D modeling package, MilkShape 3D, for video game use. MilkShape 3D is similar to Blender and is used frequently by the modding community.

Corel Corporation

(http://www.corel.com/)

Corel Corporation is the creator of Paint Shop Pro X, an inexpensive (just $100) alternative to Photoshop. Corel acquired Jasc Software, the original creator of Paint Shop Pro, in 2004. Corel also owns Painter 10, an excellent program for traditional artists for the creation of hand-painted textures.

Newtek

(http://www.newtek.com/)

Creators of LightWave 3D, a runner-up 3D modeling and animation package with an affordable price tag ($800).

Pixologic

(http://pixologic.com/home/home.shtml)

Pixologic is the maker of ZBrush 2 ($500), an inexpensive yet excellent modeling, editing, and 3D painting program capable of creating high-quality game models and materials.

Graphics-Related Hardware

Here are some sites I highly recommend for purchasing hardware that is 2D and 3D digital-art specific. If you take your CGI seriously, you should also have some of these helpful design tools. The most important product to purchase here is one of the ATI or NVIDIA video cards, because they allow your computer to properly display graphics software and game imagery at high resolutions and speeds.

3Dconnexion

(http://www.3dconnexion.com/)

Owned by LogiTech, 3Dconnexion makes the SpacePilot, SpaceBall, and SpaceMouse devices that give you freedom to do much of the modeling, animation, and texturing work with one hand. The SpacePilot costs $500 but can greatly decrease your production time by isolating many repetitive graphics functions at your fingertips.

ATI Technologies

(http://www.ati.com/)

ATI Technologies is the producer of the Radeon series of video cards. The Radeon card is one of the top-of-the-line graphics components you should have in your system to stay ahead in the gaming industry.

NVIDIA Corporation

(http://www.nvidia.com)

NVIDIA Corporation is another video card producer that makes the GeForce line of number-one selling video chips. It's an absolute must to have at least a GeForce 2 chip in your computer system, because it allows you to take advantage of the latest Direct Draw capabilities implemented in most 3D video games and software.

Wacom Technology

(http://www.wacom.com/)

Wacom Technology is the producer of the most popular graphics tablets, enabling you to more naturally create and edit textures in conjunction with Photoshop. An Intuos 4×5 tablet costs only $220 but lets you draw in pen-and-paper style instead of using a mouse.

General Gaming Sites

These links will guide you to some popular gaming forums where you can meet other developers, download gaming files, and feel generally right at home in your gaming.

Gamasutra

(http://www.gamasutra.com/)

Gamasutra is the absolute fulcrum where game designers and developers meet to share their wisdom and resources. Membership is free.

GameDev.Net

(http://www.gamedev.net/)

This is the best place on the Internet to learn about game development. This site pulls together thousands of game programming and design articles, forums, and files, and it is frequented by well over 250,000 game developers each year.

Game Developers Conference

(http://www.gdconf.com/)

This site is the online home of the Game Developers Conference, held every year—usually in March—in downtown San Jose, California. Use this site to register and to get information about airfare and hotels. (Warning: Every hotel room will be snatched up, so make your reservations early!) The conference kicks off with a few days of interactive workshops in every area of game development, followed by presentations by leading game-related companies of their latest and greatest stuff. If you can get yourself out there, I guarantee you'll love it.

Game Developer Magazine

(http://www.gdmag.com/homepage.htm)

I started buying *Game Developer* magazine back in 1994. Now I can't imagine not having a regular subscription. Each issue covers every aspect of the game-development world, keeping you up to date with professional tips, tricks, insights, innovations, and resources.

Game Development Search Engine

(http://www.gdse.com)

The Game Development search engine has compiled links to every game-related hardware and software manufacturer. This site will point you in every gaming direction imaginable—graphic design, programming, forums, you name it.

Creativity takes courage.
—*Henri Matisse*

INDEX

E

J–K

L

M

N

O

P

Q–R

T

U

V

W–X

Y–Z

THOMSON

One Force. One Solution.

For Your Game Development and Animation Needs!

Charles River Media has joined forces with Thomson Corporation to provide you with even more of the quality guides you have come to trust.

Game Programming Gems 6
ISBN: 1-58450-450-1 ▪ $69.95

AI Game Programming Wisdom 3
ISBN: 1-58450-457-9 ▪ $69.95

Basic Game Design and Creation for Fun & Learning
ISBN: 1-58450-446-3 ▪ $39.95

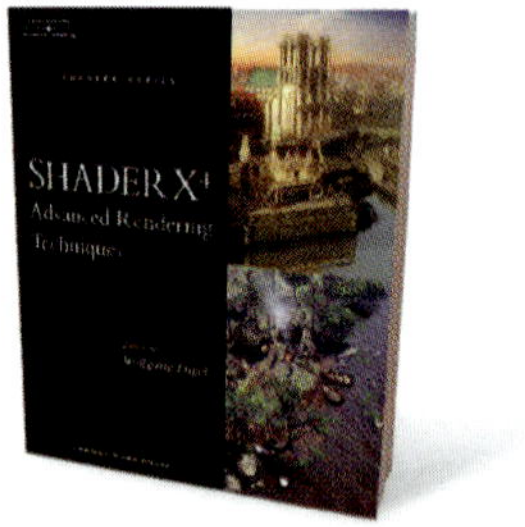

Shader X^4: Advanced Rendering Techniques
ISBN: 1-58450-425-0 ▪ $59.95

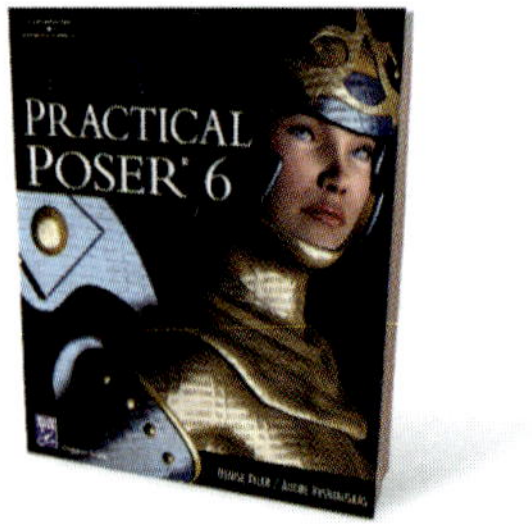

Practical Poser 6
ISBN: 1-58450-443-9 ▪ $49.95

Animating Facial Features & Expressions
ISBN: 1-58450-474-9 ▪ $49.95

Physics-Based Animation
ISBN: 1-58450-380-7 ▪ $69.95

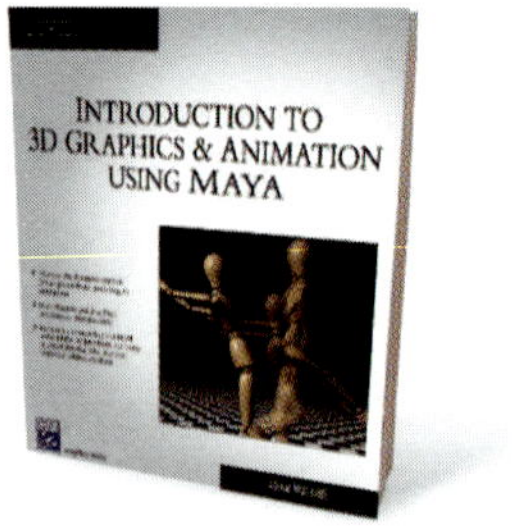

Introduction to 3D Graphics & Animation Using Maya
ISBN: 1-58450-485-4 ▪ $49.95

Check out the entire list of Charles River Media guides at www.courseptr.com

Call 1.800.648.7450 to order
Order online at www.courseptr.com

THOMSON
COURSE TECHNOLOGY
Professional ■ Technical ■ Reference

Digital art...

no canvas, no boundaries, no end to the possibilities

Digital 3D Design
ISBN: 1-59200-391-5 ■ $24.99

Adobe Photoshop for VFX Artists
ISBN: 1-59200-487-3 ■ $39.99

I've Got a Human in My Throat:
Create MORE Optical Delusions with Adobe Photoshop
ISBN: 1-59863-070-9 ■ $34.99

Creating 3D Effects for Film, TV, and Games
ISBN: 1-59200-589-6 ■ $49.99

Hollywood 2D Digital Animation:
The New Flash Production Revolution
ISBN: 1-59200-170-X ■ $39.99

Mastering Digital 2D and 3D Art
ISBN: 1-59200-561-6 ■ $39.99

THOMSON
COURSE TECHNOLOGY
Professional ■ Technical ■ Reference

Call 1.800.648.7450 to order
Order online at www.courseptr.com

THOMSON
COURSE TECHNOLOGY
Professional ■ Technical ■ Reference

CREATE AMAZING GRAPHICS AND COMPELLING STORYLINES FOR YOUR GAMES!

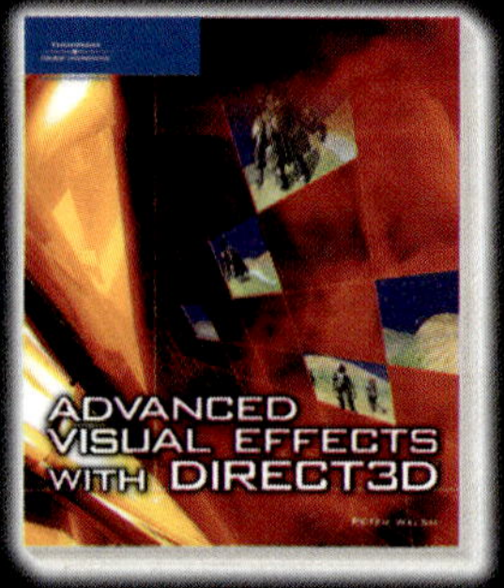

Advanced Visual Effects with Direct3D
ISBN: 1-59200-961-1 ■ $59.99

Basic Drawing for Games
ISBN: 1-59200-951-4 ■ $29.99

Beginning Game Art in 3ds Max 8
ISBN: 1-59200-908-5 ■ $29.99

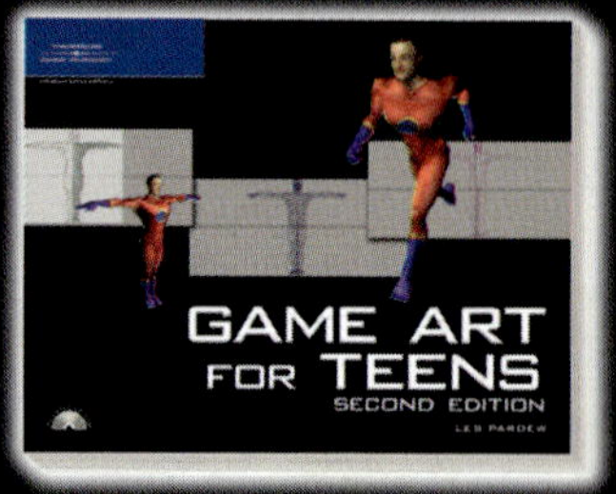

Game Art for Teens, Second Edition
ISBN: 1-59200-959-X ■ $34.99

Beginning Game Graphics
ISBN: 1-59200-430-X ■ $29.99

The Dark Side of Game Texturing
ISBN: 1-59200-350-8 ■ $39.99

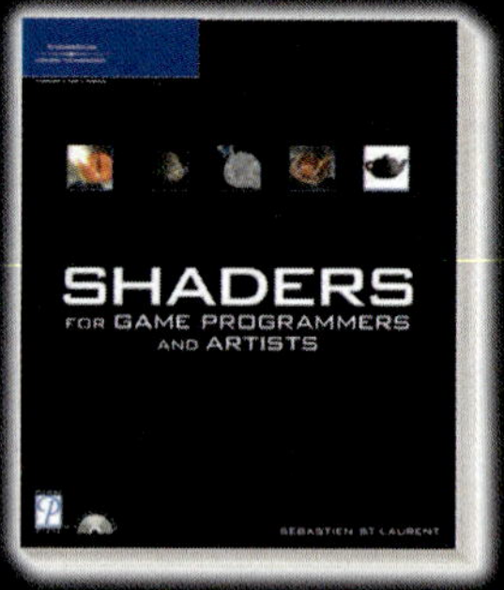

Shaders for Game Programmers and Artists
ISBN: 1-59200-092-4 ■ $39.99

Character Development and Storytelling for Games
ISBN: 1-59200-353-2 ■ $39.99

THOMSON
COURSE TECHNOLOGY
Professional ■ Technical ■ Reference

Call 1.800.648.7450 to order
Order online at www.courseptr.com

THOMSON
COURSE TECHNOLOGY
Professional ■ Technical ■ Reference
GOT GAME?
GAME PROGRAMMING ALL IN ONE 2ND EDITION
GAME DESIGN SECOND EDITION
BEGINNING JAVA 5 GAME PROGRAMMING
3D GAME PROGRAMMING ALL IN ONE
Game Programming All in One, 2nd Edition
1-59200-383-4 ■ $49.99
Game Design, Second Edition
1-59200-493-8 ■ $39.99
Beginning Java 5 Game Programming
1-59863-150-0 ■ $29.99
3D Game Programming All in One
1-59200-136-X ■ $49.99
Call 1.800.648.7450 to order
Order online at www.courseptr.com

License Agreement/Notice of Limited Warranty

By opening the sealed disc container in this book, you agree to the following terms and conditions. If, upon reading the following license agreement and notice of limited warranty, you cannot agree to the terms and conditions set forth, return the unused book with unopened disc to the place where you purchased it for a refund.

License

The enclosed software is copyrighted by the copyright holder(s) indicated on the software disc. You are licensed to copy the software onto a single computer for use by a single user and to a backup disc. You may not reproduce, make copies, or distribute copies or rent or lease the software in whole or in part, except with written permission of the copyright holder(s). You may transfer the enclosed disc only together with this license, and only if you destroy all other copies of the software and the transferee agrees to the terms of the license. You may not decompile, reverse assemble, or reverse engineer the software.

Notice of Limited Warranty

The enclosed disc is warranted by Thomson Course Technology PTR to be free of physical defects in materials and workmanship for a period of sixty (60) days from end user's purchase of the book/disc combination. During the sixty-day term of the limited warranty, Thomson Course Technology PTR will provide a replacement disc upon the return of a defective disc.

Limited Liability

THE SOLE REMEDY FOR BREACH OF THIS LIMITED WARRANTY SHALL CONSIST ENTIRELY OF REPLACEMENT OF THE DEFECTIVE DISC. IN NO EVENT SHALL THOMSON COURSE TECHNOLOGY PTR OR THE AUTHOR BE LIABLE FOR ANY OTHER DAMAGES, INCLUDING LOSS OR CORRUPTION OF DATA, CHANGES IN THE FUNCTIONAL CHARACTERISTICS OF THE HARDWARE OR OPERATING SYSTEM, DELETERIOUS INTERACTION WITH OTHER SOFTWARE, OR ANY OTHER SPECIAL, INCIDENTAL, OR CONSEQUENTIAL DAMAGES THAT MAY ARISE, EVEN IF THOMSON COURSE TECHNOLOGY PTR AND/OR THE AUTHOR HAS PREVIOUSLY BEEN NOTIFIED THAT THE POSSIBILITY OF SUCH DAMAGES EXISTS.

Disclaimer of Warranties

THOMSON COURSE TECHNOLOGY PTR AND THE AUTHOR SPECIFICALLY DISCLAIM ANY AND ALL OTHER WARRANTIES, EITHER EXPRESS OR IMPLIED, INCLUDING WARRANTIES OF MERCHANTABILITY, SUITABILITY TO A PARTICULAR TASK OR PURPOSE, OR FREEDOM FROM ERRORS. SOME STATES DO NOT ALLOW FOR EXCLUSION OF IMPLIED WARRANTIES OR LIMITATION OF INCIDENTAL OR CONSEQUENTIAL DAMAGES, SO THESE LIMITATIONS MIGHT NOT APPLY TO YOU.

Other

This Agreement is governed by the laws of the State of Massachusetts without regard to choice of law principles. The United Convention of Contracts for the International Sale of Goods is specifically disclaimed. This Agreement constitutes the entire agreement between you and Thomson Course Technology PTR regarding use of the software.